Discovery!

Discovery!

Unearthing the New Treasures of Archaeology

Edited by Brian M. Fagan

with 320 illustrations, 312 in color

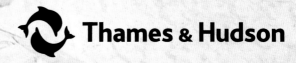

Thames & Hudson

Half-title: Maya wall-painting found at San Bartolo, Guatemala.

Title-page: The shaft leading to KV 63, Valley of the Kings, Egypt.

*p. 5 above: A skull from Atapuerca; below: statuette of an acrobat
from the Tomb of the First Emperor of China.*

*p. 6 above: Pottery vessel from the tombs of Dos Cabezas, Peru;
centre: statue of a Celtic warrior prince from Glauberg, Germany;
below: Saxon coin with an inscription mentioning London.*

*p. 7 top to bottom: The Nebra Sky Disc;
stela recovered from Aboukir Bay, Egypt;
facial reconstruction of the Egyptian pharaoh Tutankhamun;
inscription found at Tel Dan, Israel.*

© 2007 Thames & Hudson Ltd, London

First published in 2007 in hardcover in the United States of America by
Thames & Hudson Inc., 500 Fifth Avenue, New York, New York 10110

thamesandhudsonusa.com

Library of Congress Catalog Card Number 2006940560

ISBN 978-0-500-05149-8

Designed by Maggi Smith

Printed and bound in China by Toppan

Contents

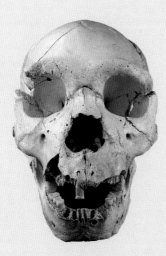

Contributors

Brian M. Fagan is Emeritus Professor of Anthropology at the University of California and the author of many widely read books on archaeology, including *The Rape of the Nile* (1977), *The Little Ice Age* (2000) and *Fish on Friday* (2005). He is the editor of *The Seventy Great Mysteries of the Ancient World* (2001) and *The Seventy Great Inventions of the Ancient World* (2004).

Matthew Douglas Adams is associate director of the Abydos Early Dynastic project and research scholar at the Institute of Fine Arts, New York University.

Peter Andrews is Curator of Blandford Museum and was formerly head of Human Origins at the Natural History Museum, London. He has authored or edited 10 books, including *The Complete World of Human Evolution* with Chris Stringer (2005), and over 200 articles.

Holger Baitinger is correspondent member of the German Archaeological Institute. He was involved in the preparation of the exhibition on the Glauberg statue in Frankfurt in 2002. Since 2002 he has worked at the Römisch-Germanische Kommission at Frankfurt.

Ian Blair is a Senior Archaeologist at the Museum of London Archaeology Service (MoLAS). He has written on a range of subjects including the water supply of Roman Londinium.

Charles Bonnet is a member of the Institut de France and Emeritus Professor. He has excavated in Europe, Egypt, Sudan and the Middle East for 42 years, and directed excavations at Kerma (Sudan).

Steve Bourget is associate professor in the department of Art and Art History at the University of Texas at Austin. His most recent book is *Sex, Death and Sacrifice in Moche Religion and Visual Culture* (2006).

Stefano Bruni lectures on the Etruscans and ancient Italy at the University of Ferrara and directed excavations at the port of Pisa. He is the editor of the journal *Science and Technology for Cultural Heritage* and the author of numerous articles.

Dan Carlsson is an archaeologist and historical geographer at Gotland University, Sweden, with interests in historical landscape studies and the Vikings.

Jan Chochorowski is Professor of Archaeology and head of the Institute of Archaeology of Jagiellonian University (Krakow, Poland); he is the author of 7 books and almost 300 articles.

Jean Clottes, Conservateur Général du Patrimoine, was Scientific Adviser for prehistoric art to the French Ministry of Culture. He is the former Chairman of the International Committee for Rock Art and President of the International Federation of Rock Art Organizations.

Michael D. Coe is Professor Emeritus of Anthropology and Curator Emeritus in the Peabody Museum of Natural History at Yale University. He is a member of the National Academy of Sciences. His numerous books include *Breaking the Maya Code* (1992) and *Reading the Maya Glyphs* (with Mark Van Stone, 2001).

Robert Cowie is a Senior Archaeologist with the Museum of London Archaeology Service and has undertaken numerous excavations, including several on the site of Lundenwic. He is co-author of *Lundenwic: Excavations in Middle Saxon London, 1987–2000*.

Christopher B. Donnan is a Professor of Anthropology at the University of California, Los Angeles, and a Fellow of the American Academy of Arts and Sciences. He has written numerous books on Moche civilization and is currently completing one on the Moche tombs at Dos Cabezas.

Robert Early is Head of International Business for Oxford Archaeology. He is currently involved in research exploring the practical relationships between archaeology, heritage, tourism and sustainable development.

Andrew P. Fitzpatrick is Head of Communications at Wessex Archaeology and a Fellow of the Society of Antiquaries. He has undertaken numerous excavations and has published on the prehistory of western Europe, especially the Celts. In 2004 the Amesbury Archer project was awarded a British Archaeological Award.

Peter Gesner directed stage 2 of the Pandora Project, 1993–2000, as the Queensland Museum's Curator of Maritime Archaeology. He is now Senior Curator Maritime Heritage in the Queensland Museum's Cultures & Histories programme.

Franck Goddio is one of the leading pioneers of modern maritime archaeology. In 1985 he founded the Institut Européen d'Archéologie Sous-Marine (IEASM), of which he is currently president. His publications include *Underwater Archaeology in the Canopic Region in Egypt – The Topography and Excavation of Heracleion-Thonis and East Canopus (1996–2006)* (2007).

Adriana von Hagen writes on the archaeology of Peru, where she is currently studying the Chachapoya and their interaction with the Incas. She is the author, with Craig Morris, of *Cities of the Ancient Andes* (1998).

Roberta L. Harris has lectured on the archaeology of the ancient Near East for over three decades, specializing in the biblical period. She is the author of *Exploring the World of the Bible Lands* (1995).

Zahi Hawass is Secretary General of the Supreme Council of Antiquities (SCA) in Egypt. He has excavated

around the pyramids of Giza and Saqqara, as well as in the Bahariya Oasis. He has lectured all over the world and has published numerous articles and books, including his memoirs *Secrets from the Sand* (2003).

Fritz-Rudolf Herrmann is correspondent member of the German Archaeological Institute. From 1973 to 2001 he was Landesarchäologe of the federal state of Hesse and for many years he was the leader of the archaeological excavations at the Glauberg site.

Jeremy D. Hill is an archaeologist and curator at the British Museum, London, where he co-ordinates research activities. His many publications include *Ritual and Rubbish* (1995) and *Prehistoric Britain: The Ceramic Basis* (with A. Woodward, 2002).

Catherine Johns was curator of the Romano-British collections at the British Museum. She continues to research on aspects of Romano-British studies and provincial Roman art, and is the author of several scholarly books on Roman art, jewelry and silver plate.

Eamonn P. Kelly is Keeper of Irish Antiquities at the National Museum of Ireland. He has developed a radical new theory to explain the phenomenon of Irish Iron Age bog bodies, which has inspired a major exhibition in the museum entitled 'Kingship and Sacrifice'.

William M. Kelso is a historical archaeologist at Jamestown, Virginia, and is a Fellow of the Society of Antiquaries of London. His publications include *Jamestown, The Buried Truth* (2006).

Antti Korpisaari is an archaeologist and post-doctoral researcher at the University of Helsinki, Finland. He has carried out fieldwork in the Bolivian Andes since 1998. His publications include *Death in the Bolivian High Plateau* (2006) and articles on Bolivian archaeology.

Mark Lehner is a Research Associate at the Oriental Institute of the University of Chicago and at the Harvard Semitic Museum. He is president of the non-profit research organization AERA, Inc., which sponsors the Giza Plateau Mapping Project. He is author of *The Complete Pyramids* (1997).

Patrick E. McGovern is a Senior Research Scientist in the Museum Applied Science Center for Archaeology (MASCA) at the University of Pennsylvania. His publications include *Ancient Wine: The Search for the Origins of Viniculture* (2003).

Christophe Maniquet is an archaeologist at the French Institut national recherches archéologique préventives and has overseen numerous excavations in the Limousin region. Since 2001, he has led the research project at the Tintignac sanctuary.

Harald Meller is Director of the State Office for Heritage Management and Archaeology, Saxony-Anhalt, and Director of the State Museum of Prehistory, Halle (Saale), State Archaeologist.

Mark Merrony is Editor of *Minerva (The International Review of Ancient Art and Archaeology)*. His publications include *The Vikings: Conquerors, Traders and Pirates* (2004) and many articles on Roman and Early Byzantine art and archaeology.

Robert S. Neyland is the Head of Underwater Archaeology at the US Navy's Naval Historical Center, Washington Navy Yard, Washington, DC. His publications include numerous articles and monographs on underwater archaeology.

Joan Oates is an archaeologist who, with her late husband, has excavated at many sites in the Near East, including Nimrud. She is Project Director at Tell Brak (Syria). Among her books are *Babylon* (1986) and *Nimrud, an Assyrian City Revealed* (2001).

David O'Connor is the Lila Acheson Wallace Professor of Egyptian Art and Archaeology at the Institute of Fine Arts, New York University. He has excavated in Egypt and Nubia for many years, especially at Abydos. His recent publications include *Ancient Egypt in Africa* (2003) and *Tuthmosis III: A New Biography* (2006).

Martti Pärssinen is Director of the Ibero-American Centre and Professor of Latin American Studies at the University of Helsinki, Finland. His publications include *Tawantinsuyu: The Inca State and its Political Organization* (1992).

Peter Pfälzner is Professor for Near Eastern Archaeology at the University of Tübingen in Germany. He has conducted excavations at various Bronze Age sites in Syria, including ancient Qatna, since 1999. He has published on ancient Syrian pottery, the ancestor cult and Mesopotamian houses and households.

Mike Pitts was formerly curator of Avebury Museum and is now a freelance writer and broadcaster, with interests in the history of archaeological practice and ideas, and the archaeology of prehistoric Britain and beyond. He is editor of *British Archaeology*.

Johan Reinhard is an archaeologist and Explorer-in-Residence at the National Geographic Society, Washington, DC. He is a Fellow of the American Anthropological Association and the Royal Geographical Society. His latest book is *The Ice Maiden: Inca Mummies, Mountain Gods, and Sacred Sites in the Andes* (2005).

Charlotte Roberts is a Professor of Archaeology at the University of Durham. Senior author of *The Archaeology of Disease* (1995) and *Health and Disease in Britain: Prehistory to the Present Day* (2003), she has also authored over 100 papers and is currently working on a book on leprosy.

William A. Saturno is an Assistant Professor of Anthropology at the University of New Hampshire and a Research Associate at Harvard University's Peabody Museum. His publications include *The Murals of San Bartolo, El Petén, Guatemala Part 1: The North Wall* (with Karl Taube and David Stuart).

Chris Scarre is Professor of Archaeology at the University of Durham and a specialist in the prehistory of Western Europe. He is editor of the leading textbook on world prehistory *The Human Past* (2005).

Klaus Schmidt is based at the German Archaeological Institute in Berlin and lectures at Erlangen-Nürnberg University. He began excavations at Göbekli Tepe in 1995. Recently he published a record of the first decade of work at the site, *Sie bauten die ersten Tempel* (2006).

Ruth Shady is organizer and head of the Caral Archaeological Project, working at Caral-Supe and other contemporary settlements. Among her publications are *Caral, the City of the Sacred Fire* (2004).

Izumi Shimada is a Professor of Anthropology at Southern Illinois University. Since 1978, he has directed the Sicán Archaeological Project. His many books include *Craft Production in Complex Societies* (2007), *Cultura Sicán* (1995) and *Pampa Grande and the Mochica Culture* (1994).

Sergey Skory is Professor of Archaeology and head of the Department of Archaeology of the Early Iron Age at the Institute of Archaeology of the National Academy of Sciences of Ukraine, Kiev. His main research areas are the Cimmerians and Scythians and the tribes of the Early Iron Age at the Ukrainian Forrest-Steppe, on which he has written numerous articles and 7 books.

Chris Stringer is a Research Leader in Human Origins at the Natural History Museum, London. He is leader of the Ancient Human Occupation of Britain project (AHOB) and its successor AHOB2. His recent books include *The Complete World of Human Evolution* (2005, with Peter Andrews) and *Homo Britannicus* (2006).

David Stuart is the Linda and David Schele Professor of Mesoamerican Art and Writing at the University of Texas at Austin and the Director of The Mesoamerica Center there. His primary research focuses on the archaeology and epigraphy of ancient Maya civilization.

George Stuart is President of the Center for Maya Research. He worked for 38 years at the National Geographic Society and was Vice President for Research and Exploration and Senior Assistant Editor for the magazine. He has written many articles on the Maya and the book *Lost Kingdoms of the Maya* (1993).

Jan Stuart, a China specialist, is Keeper of Asia at the British Museum, London. Previously, at the Freer and Sackler Galleries, Washington, DC, she was curator for 'Return of the Buddha: the Qingzhou Discoveries'. Her most recent book, with Evelyn Rawski, is *Worshiping the Ancestors* (2001).

Saburo Sugiyama is a professor at Aichi Prefectural University, Japan, and an Associate Research Professor of the School of Human Evolution and Social Change at Arizona State University. He is co-director of the Moon Pyramid Project and is preparing a series of publications about the extensive explorations there.

Wang Tao studied in Kunming, Beijing and London. He is now a Senior Lecturer in Chinese archaeology at the Institute of Archaeology, University College London, and the School of Oriental and African Studies, University of London.

Christopher Thomas is a Project Manager for the Museum of London Archaeology Service. His publications include *The Archaeology of Medieval London* (2002) and is he editor of *London's Archaeological Secrets: A World City Revealed* (2003).

Gary Urton is Dumbarton Oaks Professor of Pre-Columbian Studies and Director of the Khipu Database project, Harvard University. His books include *The Social Life of Numbers: A Quechua Ontology of Numbers and Philosophy of Arithmetic* (1997) and *Signs of the Inka Khipu: Binary Coding in the Andean Knotted-String Records* (2003).

Dominique Valbelle is Professor of Egyptology at the University of Paris IV-Sorbonne. She is the author of various books and publications on ancient Egypt and is President of the French Society of Egyptology.

Kent R. Weeks is Professor Emeritus of Egyptology at the American University in Cairo and Director of the Theban Mapping Project. His many publications include numerous works on the Valley of the Kings, including *The Lost Tomb* (1998), about his excavations of KV5.

Toby Wilkinson is a Fellow of Clare College, University of Cambridge. He lectures widely on ancient Egypt and has extensive experience of the archaeological sites in the Nile Valley and Egyptian deserts. His publications include *The Thames & Hudson Dictionary of Ancient Egypt* (2005) and *Lives of the Ancient Egyptians* (2007)

Jay Xu is the Pritzker Chairman of the Department of Asian and Ancient Art in the Art Institute of Chicago. He was guest editor for the special section on archaeology of the Sichuan Basin in *Journal of East Asian Archaeology*, Vol. 5 (2003) and his other publications include contributions to *Ancient Sichuan: Treasures from a Lost Civilization* (2001) and *Art of the Houma Foundry* (1996).

Zhang Yinglan is Associate Professor of Archaeology and Assistant Director at the Terracotta Army Museum of Warriors and Horses of Emperor Qin Shihuang, Xi'an, China. One of his recent publications is *Archaeological Report of Emperor Qin Shihuang's Mausoleum, 2000* (2006).

Alain Zivie is Director of Research at the French National Centre of Scientific Research (CNRS) and the Director-Founder of the French Archaeological Mission of the Bubasteion (MAFB), working with the Egyptian Supreme Council of Antiquities and supported by Hypogées, of which he is President-Founder. He is Vice-President of the French Society of Egyptology.

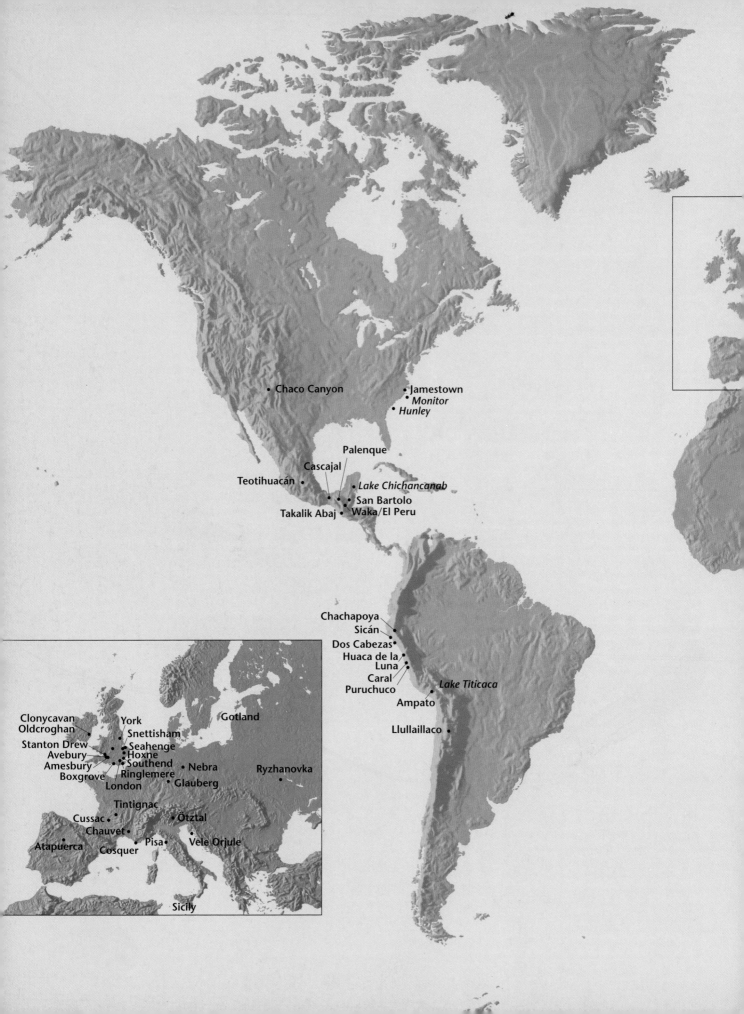

Chaco Canyon

Jamestown
Monitor
Hunley

Palenque

Cascajal

Teotihuacán

Lake Chichancanab

San Bartolo

Takalik Abaj
Waka/El Peru

Chachapoya
Sicán
Dos Cabezas
Huaca de la
Luna
Caral
Puruchuco
Ampato
Lake Titicaca

Llullaillaco

Clonycavan
Oldcroghan
York
Snettisham
Stanton Drew
Seahenge
Avebury
Hoxne
Amesbury
Southend
Boxgrove
Ringlemere
London
Gotland
Nebra
Ryzhanovka
Glauberg
Tintignac
Cussac
Otztal
Chauvet
Pisa
Vele Orjule
Atapuerca
Cosquer
Sicily

Dmanisi

Zeugma
Göbekli Tepe
Nimrud
Qatna
Dan
Palmyra
Alexandria
Jerusalem
ebda
Giza
Ekron
Saqqara
Abydos
hariya Oasis
Valley of the Kings

Kerma

Asa Koma • Dikika
Aramis

Kanapoi • Lake Turkana

Qingzhou •

Jiahu
Xi'an
Jinsha

Flores

Pandora

Sterkfontein

Archaeology Now: New Finds and Fresh Perspectives

Brian M. Fagan

Lost civilizations, unsolved mysteries, gold-laden royal tombs: archaeology has always been the stuff of legend, romance and astonishing finds. Here we reveal the most remarkable discoveries made during the past 15 years, from every corner of the world. The discoverers themselves are the authors of most of the articles – they speak directly to the reader, giving vivid first-hand accounts of the painstaking processes involved and the excitement of the moment of discovery, as well as assessing the significance of their finds. Today's archaeology has become a truly international science, operating from the high peaks of mountains to the depths of the oceans, from deserts to peat bogs. And the excavators and scientists represented here are likewise from all round the globe – from China and Germany, France and Italy, the United States, Britain, Egypt, Australia and elsewhere.

opposite
Today, many archaeological discoveries are made in the laboratory. Here the Nebra Sky Disc, the earliest known representation of the heavens, undergoes detailed scientific examination and conservation under a microscope.

above
At altitudes of over 6,000 m (19,700 ft) in the Andes conditions are very difficult, but Johan Reinhard and his team have successfully excavated several frozen mummies of Inca children sacrificed to the gods.

Discovery! is a journey through a science transformed by more refined excavation and survey, and by collaboration with experts from a variety of disciplines. Many recent fascinating discoveries come from the laboratory rather than the trench, through work on hominin fossils, artifacts or human bone or tissue, and from cutting-edge research on ancient DNA. We can 'excavate' a person's ancestry through their genes, trace their life history from their bone strontium and analyze the traces of their last meals from pottery buried with them in their tombs. We can thus reconstruct ancient royal banquets and study pharaoh's vintage wines.

More archaeological discoveries have been made in the past 15 years than since Victorian times. This is hardly surprising, since the handful of archaeologists active in 1900 has now become a global army. At the same time, industrial activity and looting are disturbing the world's archaeological sites as never before, in an era of unbridled urban population growth. We can only be thankful that so much has survived. As the recent devastation of the Iraq Museum in Baghdad has shown, there are no grounds for complacency when the global illegal antiquities trade is a growth industry on a par with arms trafficking and drug dealing.

The discoveries in these pages are dazzling in their range and complexity, so we've grouped them into seven broad sections. The first part surveys developments in the study of human origins and Ice Age societies. New fossil hominins from tropical Africa date human ancestry to before 4 million years ago; recently unearthed archaic humans in Georgia and western Europe have redefined what we know about the very first settlement of temperate latitudes. The discovery in 2004 of the 'Hobbit', a diminutive human from Flores in Southeast Asia, made international headlines, but it still defies accurate classification.

In the second part we look at tombs, graves and mummies. Joan Oates describes how Iraqi archaeologists explored the sepulchres of three Assyrian queens at Nimrud, with their rich accompanying grave goods. The untouched tombs of kings at Qatna in Syria are described by their discoverer, Peter Pfälzner. And just when it was thought Egypt's Valley of the Kings was thoroughly excavated, an unknown chamber came to light and proved everyone wrong. The discovery caused great excitement, being the first undisturbed chamber opened there since Tutankhamun's tomb in 1922. Also in Egypt, Kent Weeks describes the vast and complex tomb of Ramesses II's many sons, and Zahi Hawass recounts how he explored the Valley of the Golden Mummies, with its lavishly decorated coffins. Some of the most fascinating discoveries come from less conspicuous burials, like that of the Amesbury Archer in England, dating from the time of Stonehenge, whose bone strontium links him to a childhood in Central Europe. There are bog bodies from Ireland, a freshly excavated Scythian mound from Central Asia and newly discovered Maya tombs described by George Stuart.

The third section pushes back the origins of art to well before 30,000 years ago. Jean Clottes reveals the superb paintings at Chauvet and Cosquer caves in France. 'Treasures of Ancient Art' also describes new finds of Roman sculpture and mosaics, and exquisite statues of the Buddha from China which still preserve much of their ancient colouring and gilding. William Saturno tells of his discovery of stunning early Maya paintings at San Bartolo, Guatemala, in 2001.

Lost cities are described in part four. For instance, Ruth Shady recounts how she found a 4,600-year-old city at Caral, Peru. Mark Lehner explains how he unearthed the pyramid-builders' community at Giza, Egypt. William Kelso tells of his long search for James Fort in Virginia, the first permanent British settlement in North America.

The fifth part focuses on the supernatural world. Klaus Schmidt has uncovered some of the world's earliest shrines at Göbekli Tepe in Turkey. Saburo Sugiyama gives us a privileged view of his excavations within the giant Pyramid of the Moon at Teotihuacán, Mexico. We learn of Steve Bourget's discoveries of Moche ritual sacrifice at Huaca de la Luna in northern Peru. In 'Discoveries from the Deep', the sixth section, David O'Connor and Matthew Douglas Adams describe some of the earliest boats in the world, unearthed in the desert at Abydos, Egypt. Franck Goddio tells how he dived in the harbour of Alexandria and in Aboukir Bay to map the cities of Canopus and Heracleion. We join archaeologists working on HMS *Pandora*, the ship sent to capture the mutineers of *Bounty* fame, and on the

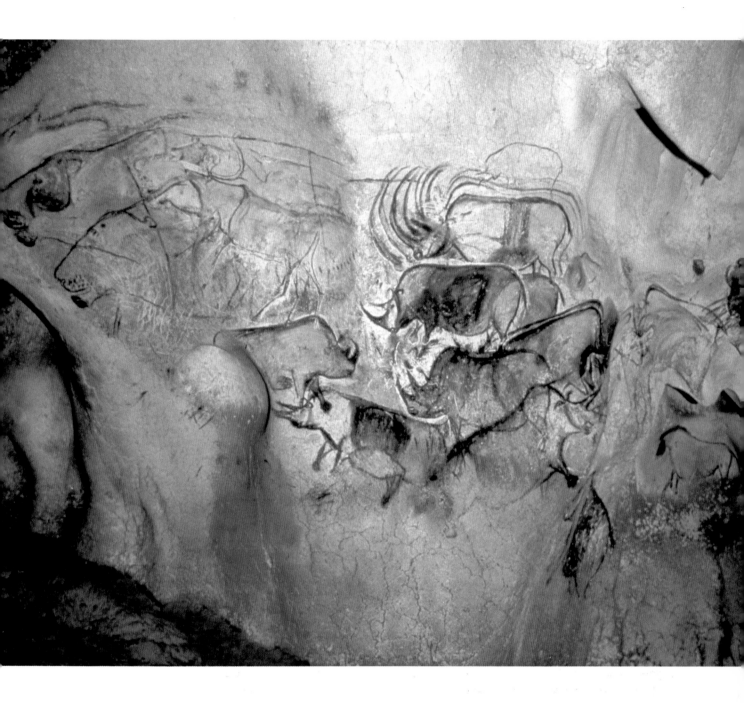

American Civil War wrecks of the submarine *Hunley* and the ironclad *Monitor.*

Finally, we cover some of the scientific methods that are revolutionizing archaeological discovery – from DNA and climate change research to medical science, including the reconstruction of ancient faces from their skulls. Epigraphy too has seen spectacular advances. Roberta Harris details the 9th-century BC Tel Dan stela from Israel, which bears an Aramaic inscription that refers to the 'House of David'. Wang Tao analyzes philosophical manuscripts of the 4th century BC,

written on bamboo slips, from a tomb in Hubei Province, China, known as the Chinese 'Dead Sea Scrolls'. David Stuart, the leading decipherer of Maya script, outlines some of the staggering recent advances in knowledge.

The pace of dramatic archaeological discovery shows no signs of abating in the 21st century, even as archaeologists become increasingly concerned about conserving humankind's priceless cultural heritage. And whatever we find today, we can be sure that many more exciting surprises and revelations await the archaeologists of tomorrow.

Discoveries from the Ice Age

previous pages
The huge cave of Liang Bua, on Flores, Indonesia, where remains of Homo floresiensis *have been found. Excavations are continuing, so more discoveries may await archaeologists.*

right
David Lordkipanidze of the Georgian Academy of Sciences holds a skull and jawbone excavated at Dmanisi.

right
Excavations – 11 m (36 ft) below the surface – inside Liang Bua cave, Flores, in June 2004. The team of archaeologists from Australia and Indonesia, led by Mike Morwood, made the astonishing discovery of the remains of an adult 'human' just 1 m (3¼ ft) tall and dating to around 18,000 years ago.

opposite
Reconstruction of a male individual from Boxgrove, based on the strongly built tibia (leg bone) found at the site, as well as other evidence of Homo heidelbergensis. *He is shown holding a wooden javelin.*

THE SEARCH FOR HUMAN ANCESTORS continues unabated. Peter Andrews describes how the discovery of *Sahelanthropus tchadensis* (over 6 million years old) in Chad and the slightly younger *Orrorin tugenensis* in northern Kenya are opening new and controversial chapters in human evolution. Ethiopia has also proved to be a fertile source of early hominins. In 1994, Tim White and his colleagues unearthed *Ardipithecus ramidus*, a 4.5-million-year-old small, somewhat ape-like hominin, now also known from an even earlier ancestor, *Ardipithecus kadabba*, dating to 5.8 to 5.2 million years.

Meave Leakey discovered *Australopithecus anamensis* (over 4 million years old) in 1995, now also known from Ethiopia. It may be an intermediate form between *Ardipithecus* and *Australopithecus afarensis*, the famous 'Lucy' found by Don Johanson in 1974. Zeresenay Alemseged announced results of his study of a juvenile skull and partial skeleton of a three-year-old child from Dikika, also in Ethiopia, in 2006. This fascinating discovery tells us that *A. afarensis* walked upright over 3 million years ago, but also had gorilla-like characters, and was at home in the trees.

Chris Stringer moves on to discuss successor species, such as the very primitive *Homo erectus* fossils found by a German and Georgian team at Dmanisi, Georgia, that date to about 1.8 million years ago. He theorizes that an increasing switch to meat-eating after 2 million years ago may have helped trigger these very first human population movements out of Africa.

When did humans settle in Europe? José Bermúdez de Castro and his colleagues have made the exciting discovery of about 80 human fossil fragments, many of them children, from Gran Dolina in the Sierra de Atapuerca, northern Spain, dating to about 780,000 years ago. They have classified them as a new species, *Homo antecessor* ('Pioneer Man'), an ancestor of the Neanderthals. Remarkably, they also believe them to have been the first victims of cannibalism in the world. Nearby, a deep pit has yielded remains of some 30 individuals dating to about 400,000 years ago, people intermediate between the archaic *Homo heidelbergensis*, the primordial European, and the later Neanderthals.

Stringer also describes the Boxgrove site, where Mark Roberts unearthed a strongly built leg bone from the oldest known human in Britain. Far more controversial is the newly found, diminutive human excavated on the island of Flores, Indonesia, dating to 18,000 years ago. Does it represent an entirely new species of dwarf human, or is it simply medically abnormal? The jury is still out.

New Evidence from Africa: Rewriting the Story of Human Origins

Peter Andrews

Human ancestry can be traced back to around 7–5 million years ago. Both molecular evidence and a recent flood of fossils indicate that the human lineage diverged from that of chimpanzees during this time. These early fossil ancestors are classified as hominins, grouped with chimpanzees and gorillas in the family Hominidae. At this stage they would still have looked very much like apes, and, like them, they still lived in woodlands and forest. So, what is the new evidence for human origins?

The story of human evolution for much of the 20th century was a comparatively simple one: three types of hominin, one robust, the other gracile, with the emergence of *Homo* from some part of this spectrum. The story became slightly more complex with the discoveries made by Mary Leakey in the 1970s at Laetoli, Tanzania, where both fossil hominins and their footprints were found in deposits much earlier than previously known. This species was named *Australopithecus afarensis* and it dated to over 3.7 million years ago.

The presence of footprints was important and dramatic because they showed that this early hominin walked bipedally, one of the key characters for identifying human ancestors, for it distinguishes us from the apes. A few years later, some fossil leg bones were found by Don Johanson at Hadar in Ethiopia from deposits dated to between 2.8 and 3.3 million years ago. These specimens were identified as the same species as the one from Laetoli, and this was enough to confirm that this early hominin was a bipedal human ancestor.

In the five years following this first discovery, many additional fossils were recovered in Ethiopia, including the famous skeleton named Lucy and a collection of 13 individuals from another site, both described by Don Johanson and his colleague Tim White. But it was another 10 years after that, in 1994, that the first skull of *Australopithecus afarensis* was found. Even more recent is the announcement in 2006 of a juvenile skull and a partial skeleton – more complete than Lucy – again from Ethiopia, from Dikika. This three-year-old child walked upright, but it also had gorilla-like characters and was undoubtedly at home in the trees. The environment *Australopithecus afarensis* lived in was a mixture of woodland and forest, with marshy areas and rivers in some places.

Also in 1994, the first of a string of sensational discoveries was made by Tim White and his team, yet again in Ethiopia. The first of these is *Ardipithecus ramidus*, from 4.5-million-year-old deposits in Aramis. This was a small hominin whose lightly built jaws had small, thin-enamelled teeth. One fragment of the base of a skull suggests that the head was held upright on the spinal column, rather than projecting forwards as it does on all four-footed animals, including apes. So far, however, no direct evidence has been published showing that this hominin stood and walked upright. Ten years later, a second species of *Ardipithecus*, from much earlier deposits, was found by Tim

opposite
Reconstruction of Australopithecus afarensis *in its preferred environment. This species was at home in mixed woodland and forest, where it foraged for food on the ground and in the trees.*

right
Two sets of footprints in Pliocene sediments at Laetoli (Tanzania) show clearly that hominin ancestors were walking upright on two legs 3.7 million years ago.

White's team in Ethiopia. This is *A. kadabba*, from Asa Koma, dated to 5.8–5.2 million years ago. It has small molar teeth and projecting canines and premolars, as in living apes.

In the meantime, several other early hominins had been found. In 2001, *Orrorin tugenensis* was unearthed by Martin Pickford and Brigitte Senut in northern Kenya. This came from the Lukeino Formation – from which I described a single tooth back in the late 1970s. It has been dated to about 6 million years ago, which is even older than *Ardipithecus kadabba*, but where comparisons are possible it appears to have been similar to *Ardipithecus*, sharing, for example, the relatively small teeth. No skull has yet been found, but it is controversially claimed by Senut that *Orrorin* had a straight-legged form of bipedalism different from that of the australopithecines and from *Ardipithecus*, which Senut and Pickford put on the line leading to the apes.

An unexpected twist to the tale came with the discovery in 1995 of a hominin fossil in Chad, at least 2,500 km (1,550 miles) away from East Africa, where the earlier discoveries had been made. Found by Michel Brunet, it is similar both in age and appearance to *Australopithecus afarensis*. Seven years later Brunet found an even earlier fossil hominin in the same place. This is named *Sahelanthropus tchadensis*, and the fossil, dated to between 7 and 6 million years ago, is a complete skull that has a mixture of characters, combining small molars with apparently thick-enamelled teeth, small canines but a relatively robust skull.

Also in 1995, a fine piece of detective work by Ron Clarke in South Africa identified some hominin toe bones from Sterkfontein Member 2 as *Australopithecus africanus*, dating to around 3.5 million years ago (but dated to 2.2 million years ago in late 2006). They include the base of the big toe, which appears to show that it was divergent, as in apes. These specimens were linked with a nearly complete skeleton that is still only partly excavated in the Sterkfontein deposits. Enough has come out, however, to show that it also had short arms and short fingers, rather like modern humans – it therefore did not knuckle walk like African apes and was not specialized for hanging from branches. It must have combined both bipedal walking on the ground with abilities to climb trees perhaps almost as great as those of living apes.

Meanwhile, discoveries in East Africa were continuing unabated through the efforts of Meave Leakey in Kenya. In 1995 she had described a 4.3–4.1-million-year-old hominin named *Australopithecus anamensis* from Kanapoi in northern Kenya. A single fossil had been discovered there many years previously, and it is proposed as a possible ancestor for *Australopithecus afarensis*. This has been taken still further by Tim White, who in 2005 identified *A. anamensis* in Ethiopia, suggesting that it is an intermediate form between *Ardipithecus ramidus* and *Australopithecus afarensis*. A single leg bone indicates that *A. anamensis* was bipedal, though its jaws are remarkably ape-like.

left
Michel Brunet, with the skull of Sahelanthropus tchadensis, dated to 7–6 million years ago, and a chimpanzee skull for comparison. Brunet found this complete skull in Chad, rather than East Africa, where most earlier finds of hominin fossils had been made.

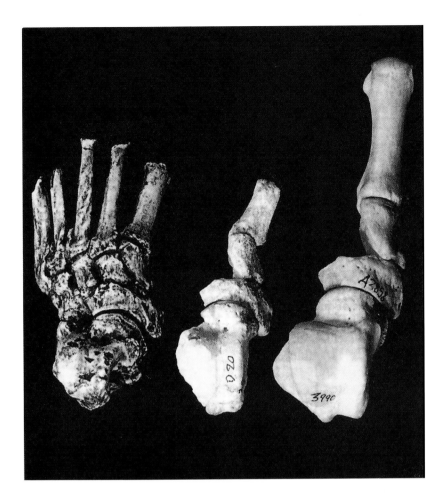

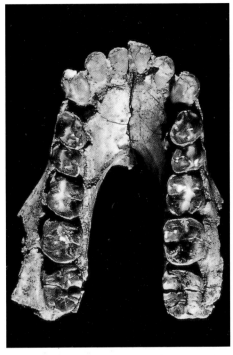

above

The ankle and big toe of 'Little Foot' from Sterkfontein, South Africa (centre), are compared with the corresponding bones from a modern human foot (right) and the foot of Homo habilis *(left).*

above right

The lower jaw of Australopithecus anamensis *illustrating its ape-like parallel tooth rows and large teeth.*

Meave Leakey also found a later hominin in 2001, which she assigned to a new genus and species, *Kenyanthropus platyops*. This comes from the west side of Lake Turkana in northern Kenya, from deposits dated to 3.5–3.3 million years ago. A skull and numerous teeth and pieces of jaw were recovered, but nothing has been found of the rest of the skeleton, so it is far from clear that it was bipedal.

The hominin status of many of these fossils still remains in doubt, for they are all fragmentary. Many retain ape-like characters, and it is interesting that there appear to be two groups of early hominins, one with small teeth and lightly built jaws, such as *Ardipithecus*, and the other with more robust jaws and large and thick-enamelled teeth. This dichotomy parallels the distinction made between the two groups of fossil apes known from the period immediately preceding the hominins, 12 to 9 million years ago. But one things seems clear at least, that Africa is where evidence for our earliest ancestors is still to be found.

The Mystery of the Skulls from Dmanisi, Georgia

Chris Stringer

Archaeologists excavating the cellars of a ruined medieval village at Dmanisi in Georgia made a very surprising discovery – the fossilized jawbone of a long-extinct rhinoceros. This find showed that, by chance, the medieval village had been built on top of very ancient deposits that may contain the oldest fossil humans yet found outside the African continent.

The first remains of the species *Homo erectus* ('Erect Man') were discovered by the Dutchman Eugène Dubois at Trinil on the island of Java, in Indonesia, around 1890. These fossils included a very flat and small-brained skullcap with enormous brow ridges, and a thighbone indicating a human body size and gait. Subsequent remains of this species have been found not only in Java but also in China, at sites such as Zhoukoudian and Hexian, and African sites dating from at least 1.3 million years ago, such as Olduvai Gorge (Tanzania), and East Turkana and Nariokotome (Kenya). *Homo erectus* is thus the earliest widespread human species, and is thought to be the first to have emerged from our African homeland. Although the evolutionary origins of *Homo erectus* are still not clear, it is generally assumed that the species developed in Africa around 2 million years ago from ancestors similar to the more primitive form *Homo habilis*. These early humans were thought to have dispersed from Africa eastwards into China and Indonesia about 1.5 million years ago,

keeping to the subtropical and tropical environments that were familiar to them.

In 1991, this picture changed when a chinless *H. erectus* lower jaw with teeth was discovered in western Asia at the site of Dmanisi in Georgia during excavations by a joint Georgian-German team. The team had been working at the site for several months, finding fossils of species such as scimitar-toothed cats, rhinos and large ostriches, as well as simple stone tools. It was on the very last day of the excavation that Antje Justus, a German graduate student, uncovered the jawbone, lying underneath the skeleton of a scimitar-toothed cat. The jawbone seemed to represent a quite advanced form of *H. erectus*, but the associated animal bones suggested an earlier age, close to 1.5 million years, and this was subsequently supported by argon-argon dating of underlying volcanic rocks, giving an age of about 1.8 million years.

Dmanisi has now yielded three more jawbones, five human skulls and many other elements of skeletons. The brain capacity

left
The Georgian palaeontologist David Lordkipanidze and colleagues examine a find at Dmanisi. Fossils of creatures such as giraffe, ostrich, scimitar-tooth cat and gazelle have been found there, along with stone tools and human fossils, all dating from around 1.75 million years ago.

opposite
This skull and lower jaw from Dmanisi are remarkable because of the complete absence of teeth. These had not fallen out after death, as bone had grown over the sockets, which means the individual had survived for months or years without teeth. This has raised the possibility that at this very early date, others had helped to find food for a potentially disabled individual.

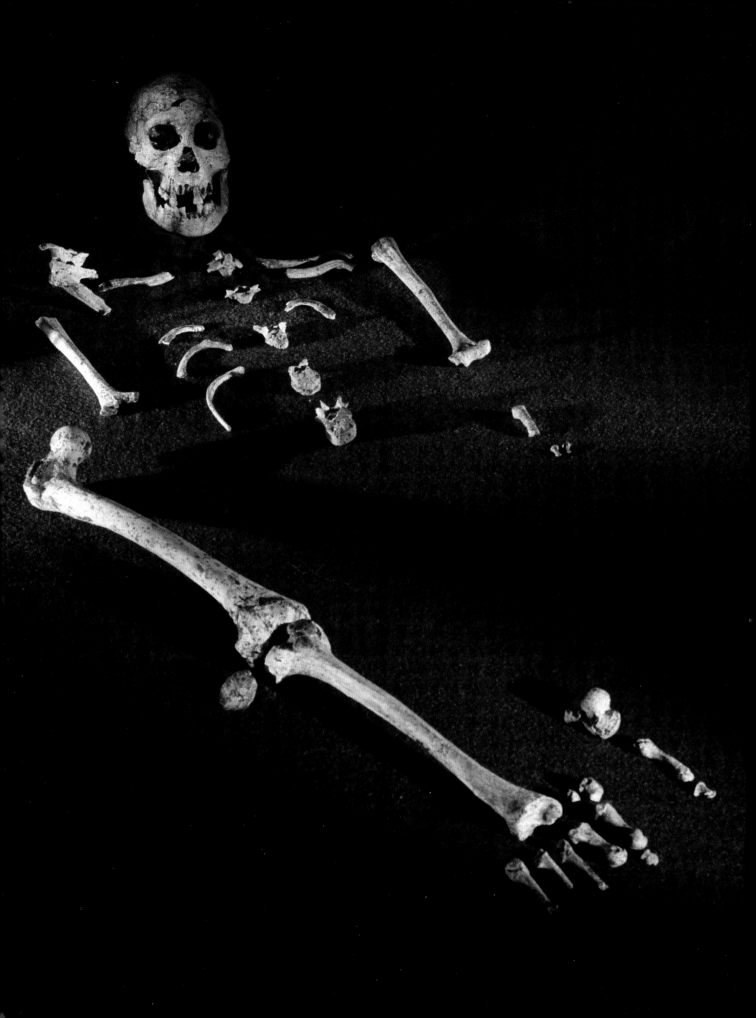

of the skulls overlaps with that known for *Homo habilis* and the lower end of the range of *Homo erectus*, and overall the Dmanisi finds appear to be very primitive fossils of *H. erectus*, being similar to the earliest African examples yet also showing some of the features found in the later Asian specimens. The bones of the rest of the skeleton, while not yet described in detail, appear to be small, yet quite human in form. The excavators also discovered a large number of stone tools manufactured from volcanic rocks at Dmanisi, and these closely resemble those made by their presumed African ancestors from 2 million years ago – sharp but simple pebble and flake tools, made with one or two blows of a hammer stone.

Out of Africa

The discoveries at Dmanisi have challenged a number of previous assumptions about the first dispersals of humans from Africa. It used to be thought that the first migrations out of Africa ('Out of Africa 1') must have been facilitated by enhancements in human behaviour, brains or tools, but it is difficult to discern such developments in the evidence preserved at Dmanisi, which in each of these respects in fact seems so similar to the earliest African examples of the species. Some of the animals at Dmanisi, including the large carnivores and ostrich, do appear to have originated in Africa and spread from there, so perhaps western Asian environments were not that different from those of the rift valleys of northeast Africa from where they migrated. In which case the early humans may have spread in the same way, following familiar environments.

Yet there are other indications that the climate at Dmanisi was somewhat cooler than that of Africa at the time.

Interestingly, two of the large carnivores of African origin at Dmanisi were specialized scimitar-tooth cats, and these animals lacked the appropriate back teeth needed to strip a carcass clean of its meat, or to break the thicker bones of their prey. Their inability to scavenge may well have presented opportunities for early *erectus* individuals who also lacked the right teeth, but could extract meat, offal and marrow from such carcasses by the use of their stone tools. By vigilance and mobility across the landscape they could have competed with hyenas and jackals and fended off vultures to acquire a good supply of meat, whether the carcass was a natural death or the victim of a predator.

Archaeological evidence suggests that human ancestors in Africa increasingly switched to meat-eating about 2 million years ago, and this would have required much wider feeding ranges. Perhaps this alone was enough to push the expansion of early humans out of Africa and would have released them from a narrower dependence on particular plant resources. The switch to meat-eating probably also affected early human physiology, since meat is a much more concentrated food and energy source than plant materials. Some experts believe that an increasing reliance on meat freed up energy previously needed by the gut to process large quantities of plant foods, which could then be used to grow and operate an equally expensive larger brain. The remarkable Dmanisi fossils perhaps show us humans still in the early stages of that process.

right
It was the discovery of a fossil jawbone in 1991 that really put Dmanisi on the early human map, followed by two skulls in 1999. Then in 2001, this skull resembling Homo habilis *from Africa was discovered. Dmanisi is now one of the richest sites for human fossils anywhere in the world.*

opposite
The Dmanisi human fossils include other bones from the human body apart from skulls. In one case enough matching bones have been found together to suggest that they represent the skeleton of a single person. The height of this individual was only about 1.5 m (5 ft), but the bones indicate a very human-shaped body.

The First Europeans and the Pit of the Bones at Atapuerca, Spain

Chris Stringer

Until recently many archaeologists believed that when humans first began to emerge from their African homeland they would have found Europe's very different environments a great challenge to survival, and for this reason Europe might only have been settled about 500,000 years ago. There were claims that a few sites perhaps had stone tools much older than this, but it was only with the discoveries at Gran Dolina, in the hilly limestone country of the Sierra de Atapuerca, near Burgos in northern Spain, that views really began to change.

The site, in a railway cutting through the hills, is filled with earthy sediments containing bones and stone tools. One layer containing human fossils and associated stone tools lies immediately under a level that can be dated by a reversal of the Earth's magnetic poles to about 780,000 years ago – much older than some previous estimates for the appearance of humans in Europe.

A Spanish-led team of palaeontologists and archaeologists has now excavated around 80 fossils belonging to several individuals – strangely most are from children. They include the bones of a forehead, a face, lower jaws, teeth, arm and foot bones, and a kneecap. In addition to their unexpectedly early age, one other feature of these fossils is remarkable. Many are covered in marks that suggest they were cut by stone tools, and while this could have resulted from burial practices if the remains belonged to modern people, such behaviour seems unlikely for humans of this antiquity. What, then, could have caused such damage? The excavators suggest that it is evidence of cannibalism, making these individuals not only the oldest European fossils, but also some of the earliest victims of cannibals, whether of their own or another group.

So who were these people? While some of the Gran Dolina teeth show features found in African fossils that are over 1.5 million years old, the frontal (forehead) bone suggests a rather

right

Many human trunk and limb bones, representing at least four individuals, have been recovered from the Gran Dolina site, in the Sierra de Atapuerca, Spain. In some respects they more closely resemble the bones of modern humans than those of species such as Homo heidelbergensis *and Neanderthals.*

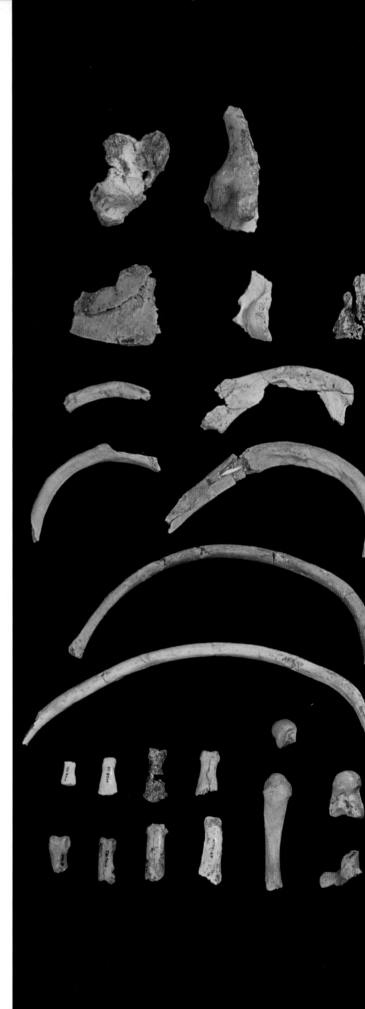

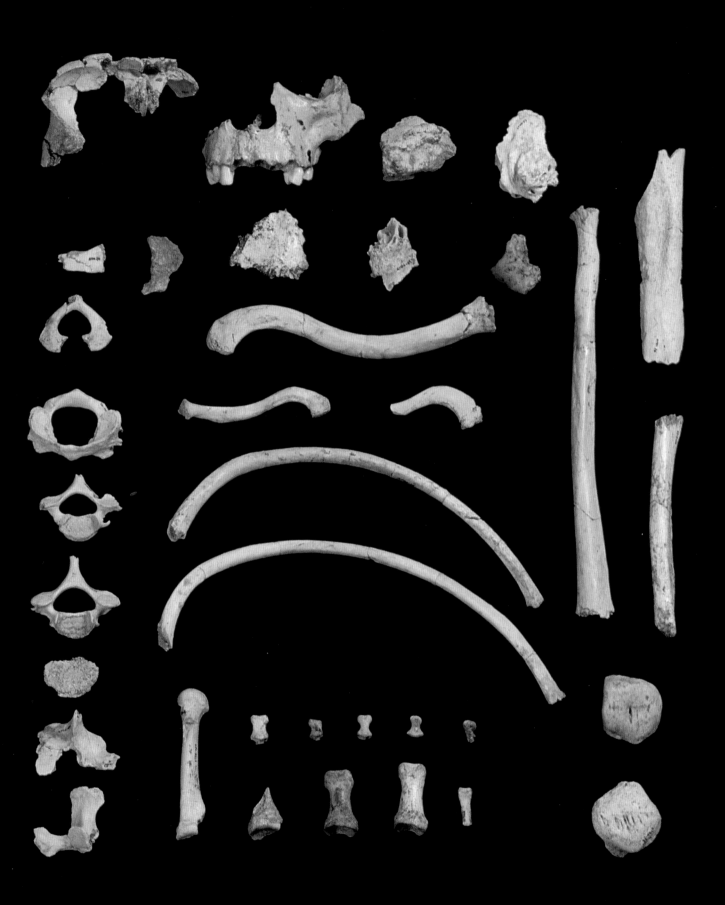

large brain size, and the face looks quite modern in the shape of the nose and cheekbones. This has led Spanish scientists who have studied the bones to propose that they represent a new species of human which they have called *Homo antecessor* ('Pioneer Man'). They argue that this species originated in Africa, where it eventually gave rise to our own species (*Homo sapiens* – 'Wise Man'), while in Europe it gave rise to the Neanderthals, implying a very ancient split for the two lineages. A fossil human braincase of a similar date and with large brow ridges that resembles both *H. erectus* and the later species *H. heidelbergensis* ('Heidelberg Man') has been discovered on a hillside in central Italy at Ceprano and perhaps represents an adult example of *Homo antecessor*.

The Pit of the Bones

The Sierra de Atapuerca has also yielded a much larger group of human fossils – in fact the densest accumulation of fossil human bones ever found – from a later period. These finds are more definitely on the evolutionary line leading to the Neanderthals, the early humans who inhabited Europe during the Ice Age.

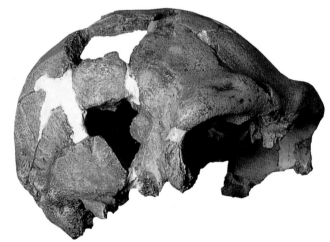

top
Here the rich level TD6 of the Gran Dolina site, dated to about 800,000 years ago, is under excavation. It has produced most remains of Homo antecessor.

above
The Ceprano skull from Italy may be about 900,000–800,000 years old. It is possible that it is an adult equivalent of a partial child's skull from Gran Dolina, of a similar date.

The site lies deep within a cave system at the bottom of a pit called the Sima de los Huesos – the Pit of the Bones. To reach it now requires a long caving expedition using ropes and metal ladders. At the bottom of a 13-m (43-ft) deep vertical shaft is a muddy and unprepossessing chamber that has so far yielded the staggering number of some 4,000 fossils of about 30 individuals – men, women and children. From the maturity of the bones and teeth the great majority were in their teens or twenties when they died. The material is dominated by teeth but includes numerous examples of every part of the skeleton, down to the smallest hand and foot bones, generally jumbled up in the sediment. Some of the bones can be fitted together to show that they belong to the same person – for example, a lower jaw that can be fitted to a skull – but in other cases, such as individual hand bones, it is much more difficult to join them. Nevertheless, several composite skeletons have been built up, showing the large and strong bodies of these early Europeans, with brain sizes ranging from a volume of only about 1,100 ml (typical of *H. erectus*) to 1,400 ml (matching large-brained examples of Neanderthals and modern humans).

How did the bones end up in this small chamber deep within the cave system? One theory is that these individuals died in a disaster or an epidemic and their bodies were thrown down the pit by their fellows, who at that time could access the area through a nearby entrance, now blocked. Another idea is that the bones were naturally deposited there from somewhere else in the cave in a mudflow.

However the bones got there, they provide a wonderful, unparalleled sample of a population showing features of the older species, *Homo heidelbergensis* (see Boxgrove, p. 33), and of the later Neanderthals (*H. neanderthalensis*). The Atapuerca Sima de los Huesos fossils date from about 400,000 years ago and may document an evolutionary transition between the two species. Combinations of ancestral and derived features occur throughout the Atapuerca collection in an almost random fashion, so that it is difficult to decide how best to classify the sample as a whole. Some Spanish researchers favour assigning the material to a late form of *heidelbergensis*, while others refer to them as early Neanderthals – but the significance of the fossils remains the same. They show that an evolutionary transition was taking place in European populations about 400,000 years ago that would lead on to the late Neanderthals, and that in Europe it is their evolution rather than that of *H. sapiens* that is recorded.

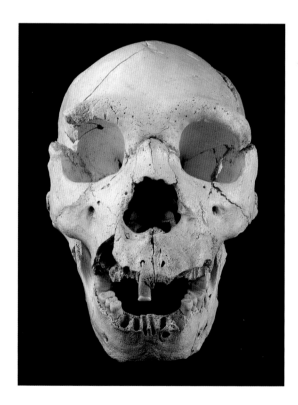

above
The most complete skull and jaw from the Sima de los Huesos is from an elderly individual, possibly a woman, with heavily worn teeth.

right
The huge collection of bones and teeth from the Sima de los Huesos now numbers over 4,000, from men, women, youths and children.

Boxgrove: The Oldest Human Fossils in Britain

Chris Stringer

About half a million years ago, the sea reached some 10 km (6 miles) further north than it does today in southern Britain, in what is now Sussex, and was cutting huge cliffs of chalk. As sea level gradually fell, salt marshes and coastal grasslands took over from sandy beaches, and herds of animals such as horse, bison, red deer and even elephant and rhinoceros grazed on the newly created coastal plain. Not surprisingly, predators were also there, including lion, hyena, wolf and early humans. Some 500,000 years later, the sediments laid down by slow-running water on this coastal plain were exposed by commercial quarrying near the village of Boxgrove.

The presence of fossil bones and handaxe tools was noted by archaeologists, and a team led by Mark Roberts of University College London had been digging at Boxgrove for eight years, recovering wonderful ancient land surfaces with associated stone tools and animal bones – but no human fossils. Funding for the excavations was running out, but in the winter of 1993, Roberts took a chance: he hired a mechanical excavator to sample a new part of the site. Just before Christmas, a human leg bone was found, and a whole new phase began. Roberts's finds represent the oldest human remains known from the British Isles, and the site has also yielded a wealth of data on the behaviour of these people, representing the species *Homo heidelbergensis*. From the species of mammals present, Boxgrove can be dated to a warm stage, or interglacial, in the Middle Pleistocene. This interglacial can in turn be placed immediately prior to a major cold stage that dates from about 450,000 years ago.

Conditions at Boxgrove mean that much of the material has been preserved virtually undisturbed for half a million years. We can see how people selected large chunks of flint from the chalk cliff and worked them down to smaller cores, using a stone hammer. With stone or bone hammers they then created characteristic almond-shaped handaxes – the knapping debris can be excavated and we can reconstruct the precise sequence of manufacture. These tools were then used skilfully to skin, disarticulate and butcher carcasses of horse, deer and even rhinoceros, and the bones, covered in cut marks, are scattered across the ancient landscape, alongside the tools used on them.

But how did the Boxgrove humans acquire the carcasses? Were they actively hunting game, even as large as rhinos, or were they scavenging already dead animals? They were certainly spending a considerable time on butchery in a potentially dangerous open landscape, which meant they were organized enough to secure the carcasses from competing animals such as lions or hyenas. Wherever bones have both cut marks and signs of carnivore chewing, the cut marks were always made first – so humans had primary access. More direct evidence of hunting may come from an apparent spear-point hole in the shoulder blade of a horse. Although no spears are known from Boxgrove, wooden spears of yew and spruce have been discovered at Clacton in Essex and Schöningen in Germany, dating from about 400,000 years ago. The German spears are some 2 m (6½ ft) long and beautifully made; that they were used for hunting seems established by the fact that they were found among about 20 horse skeletons.

Boxgrove Man

The Boxgrove tibia is one of the most strongly built ancient human leg bones ever found. The individual it came from must have been about 1.8 m (5 ft 11 in) tall, and the thickness of the bone walls suggest that he (he was probably male) was heavy and muscular – likely over 90 kg (200 lb) in weight. The strength of the bone no doubt also reflects the physically demanding lifestyle that these people had to endure.

Two teeth found at Boxgrove – incisors from the front of a lower jaw – are not so remarkable in size, although heavily worn. They were found in a different part of the site and in a slightly lower level than the leg bone, and so are not thought to be from the same individual. Under a microscope, they reveal a mass of scratches and pits on their surfaces – many probably made as their owner held meat or vegetable materials clenched in their teeth and sliced them with flint tools. The direction of the slices can even be determined, and indicates that the tools were held in the right hand. Such a level of detail in reconstructing the activities of someone living so long ago is extraordinary.

right
One of several hundred handaxe tools discovered at Boxgrove. These were made from flint blocks extracted from nearby chalk cliffs and were often found in direct association with butchered bones of horse, deer and rhinos.

opposite
Excavations at Boxgrove in 1995: these yielded a rich collection of stone tools and fossil bones, including teeth around 500,000 years old. A human shinbone was found earlier, in 1993.

The 'Hobbit': An Unknown Human Relative?

Chris Stringer

Until recently archaeologists thought that only one species of early human lived in Southeast Asia before **Homo sapiens** *arrived there –* **Homo erectus,** *best known from the island of Java. Moreover, according to this view, Java represented the furthest limit of human colonization in the region before modern humans used boats to disperse towards Australia and New Guinea, perhaps 60,000 years ago. But that all changed in 2004, when archaeologists led by Mike Morwood published remarkable evidence of a new human-like species from the island of Flores, about 500 km (310 miles) east of Java. What they found in a cave called Liang Bua continues to challenge scientific thinking and stir up fierce debate.*

Morwood and his colleagues from Australia and Indonesia had already found tools on Flores dating from about 800,000 years ago, but when they began working in much more recent deposits in Liang Bua cave, they could not have known that they were going to make even more astonishing discoveries. They uncovered the remains of a skeleton of an adult 'human' estimated to be only about 1 m (3¼ ft) tall, the size of an average modern 3-year-old child, and with a brain volume of about 400 ml (about the same as that of a chimpanzee). What made it even more extraordinary was its date – only about 18,000 years ago, when no other forms of humans apart from

us, *Homo sapiens*, were thought to exist. The skeleton was assigned to a species completely new to science, called *Homo floresiensis* ('Flores Man'). Other, more fragmentary material in Liang Bua was associated with stone tools and the remains of a pygmy form of the extinct elephant-like creature called *Stegodon*.

Controversy immediately surrounded this discovery and many questions were asked about the nature of the finds and their interpretation. Some scientists argued that they were wrongly dated and might represent small-bodied modern humans; others argued that the unusual features were signs of abnormality, perhaps due to a condition called microcephaly.

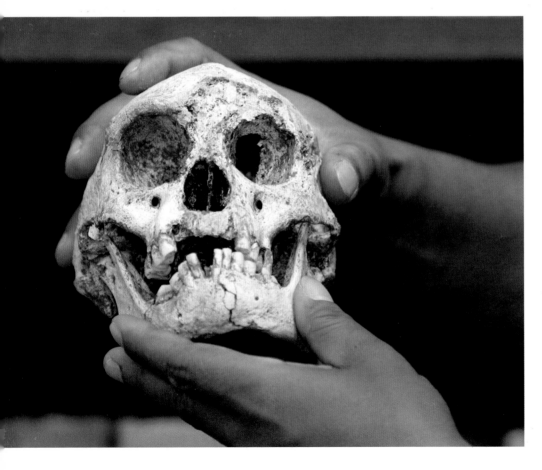

left and above
While the general pattern of human evolution is becoming clearer, discoveries such as this skull of a new human-like species, named Homo floresiensis, *can still surprise the experts. Above is a reconstruction of what this species may have looked like.*

The authors of the original studies suggested that *H. floresiensis* might be a descendant of *H. erectus* that had arrived early on Flores, perhaps using boats. They argued that the species then evolved its very small size under isolated conditions – a phenomenon known to occur in island populations where food resources are limited, and called island dwarfing. If the ancestors of *H. floresiensis* made watercraft to reach the island, this would be surprising, because such behaviour is thought to have been exclusive to modern humans. The alternative of accidental rafting on mats of vegetation must also be considered – the recent Asian tsunami dispersed people on rafts of vegetation for over 150 km (90 miles).

Further studies of the original skeleton and other individuals found since have provided more detailed information on *H. floresiensis*. The team confirmed that a second individual was even shorter than the first one described. Puzzlingly for a supposed member of the human genus, the body proportions and other features of *H. floresiensis* are in some ways more similar to fossils of prehuman African species like *Australopithecus afarensis* (the most famous example of which is 'Lucy') than to later humans. Other unusual features, as well as the fact that *H. floresiensis* seems to have had relatively large feet, have fuelled speculation that the remains are abnormal, while other workers argue that this is evidence for an unusual evolutionary trajectory.

Fossils of *H. floresiensis* have been found in different layers of the cave covering the period from about 80,000 to 12,000 years ago and appear to show consistently distinct features. Most experts consider that *H. erectus* was the first human-like creature to emerge from the ancestral African homeland, nearly 2 million years ago. But for some researchers, the Flores material raises the possibility that more primitive forms had previously spread from Africa across southern Asia, where the remoteness of Flores allowed them to survive and evolve along their own peculiar path in isolation. There is further uncertainty about the evidence for the behaviour of the individuals excavated in Liang Bua. Some of the stone tools are delicately shaped, and there is evidence of the use of fire as well as possible hunting of young *Stegodon*. It is still unclear whether *H. floresiensis*, with its ape-sized brain, was capable of such behaviour, and more excavation and analyses will be required to exclude the possibility that early modern humans were also using caves on Flores. Nevertheless, stone tools are known from other sites on Flores stretching back to 800,000 years ago, thus providing a plausible ancestral population for *H. floresiensis* and its technology.

If the species is indeed genuine and distinct, rather than abnormal – and this is far from being finally accepted, with partisans on both sides – a final intriguing question remains: what happened to *H. floresiensis*? Perhaps climatic changes at the end of the Pleistocene affected its habitat, or modern humans killed it off directly or indirectly by consuming the resources on which it lived. But there is also evidence of a massive volcanic eruption that devastated Flores about 12,000 years ago, leading to the extinction of species such as *Stegodon*, and this may also have been the fate of *H. floresiensis*. Wherever it came from, and whatever happened to it, its very existence shows how little we still know about human evolution in Asia.

Tombs, Graves and Mummies

One of the seven coffins found in the newly discovered tomb in Egypt's Valley of the Kings awaits detailed examination by archaeologists.

right
Pottery vessels stand in neat rows against the walls of the main chamber of the royal tombs at Qatna, Syria, just as they were left over 3,000 years ago.

right
The stone sarcophagus of the governor of Bahariya, discovered in his previously unopened tomb in a maze of underground corridors beneath the modern town of El Bawiti, in Egypt.

right
Beautifully made flint arrowheads from the burial of the Boscombe Bowmen, excavated near Stonehenge – the men in the grave were perhaps involved in the transport of stones to the monument.

FEW DISCOVERIES GENERATE as much excitement as a richly adorned royal burial. We feature many in this section from all round the globe. We follow Zahi Hawass as he describes the extraordinary media event surrounding the opening of a new tomb in the Valley of the Kings, Egypt, possibly of Tutankhamun's mother. Likewise in the Valley, Kent Weeks gives the inside story of his painstaking excavation of the gigantic sepulchre of Ramesses II's sons.

In nearby Syria lies the newly revealed tomb of the kings of Qatna, whose discoverer, Peter Pfälzner, describes the unique statues and other remarkable finds unearthed there that belonged to this little-known civilization. Equally spectacular are the royal treasures from Assyrian queens' tombs at the great city of Nimrud, Iraq; Chinese emperor Qin Shihuangdi's mausoleum; the Maya Red Queen's grave in Mexico; and the burial of an Anglo-Saxon prince at Prittlewell, England. All these finds give us special insight into the lives of privileged elites.

Almost as privileged as royalty were those slightly lower down the social scale. Alain Zivie describes the impressive tombs of Egyptian nobles and generals he has unearthed at Saqqara, while Sergey Skory and Jan Chochorowski recount how they excavated the intact burial mound of a Scythian aristocrat. On the other side of the world, in Peru, Christopher Donnan and Izumi Shimada have been digging elite tombs of the Moche and Sicán civilizations respectively, and they give us first-hand accounts of their triumphs. In Britain, Andrew Fitzpatrick has been equally fortunate: he has uncovered, as he describes, the first burials thought to be linked in some way to the builders of Stonehenge.

Yet it is the remains of actual people that literally bring us face-to-face with the past. The famous Iceman of the Alps is well-known – we reveal here his recently discovered manner of death – but much less familiar are the extraordinary Iron Age bodies in the bog from Ireland. Mummies and mummification also continue to fascinate. Zahi Hawass reports how he has been excavating the spectacular golden mummies from Bahariya Oasis, west of the Nile, while Adriana von Hagen and Johan Reinhard describe their respective discoveries of Chachapoya and Inca mummies in the cloud forests and mountain peaks of Peru.

As the dramatic accounts in this section show, new discoveries of burials are casting the distant past in a new light. That is part of the continuing fascination of archaeology.

The Iceman: A 5,000-Year-Old Murder Victim?

Chris Scarre

On 19 September 1991, two experienced mountaineers, Erika and Helmut Simon, discovered the oldest-known preserved human body while crossing the Similaun glacier near the crest of the Alps. First thoughts were that it might be the remains of a recent mountaineer – several people have died or disappeared in this treacherous terrain of glaciers and crevasses during the past 100 years. It was the copper axe and flint dagger recovered from beside the corpse that first alerted archaeologists to the true importance of the find: the body of a 45-year-old man who died in the high Alps some 5,300 years ago. The discovery of the 'Iceman' caught the imagination of the world.

The body had been preserved by a process of natural freeze-drying. A thin layer of snow must have fallen soon after death, covering the dead man and protecting the corpse from fly larvae and scavengers. Cold dry winds then set to work to desiccate and preserve the body. Konrad Spindler, Professor of Prehistory at Innsbruck University, assembled a team of international specialists to undertake a thorough investigation of the Iceman and his equipment.

The excellent and unusual conditions of preservation allowed them to ask questions that usually lie well beyond the reach of prehistoric archaeology. Examination of the colon contents, for example, revealed intestinal parasites which would have given the Iceman chronic diarrhoea. He had tattoos on his lower back, his left calf, behind his right knee and on both his ankles; these may have been intended to alleviate pain.

Along with the body were the remains of clothing and other equipment that had also been well preserved by the freeze-drying process: the stave of a wooden bow, a quiver containing 2 finished and 12 unfinished arrows; 2 birchbark containers and a back pannier; and the copper axe and flint knife that first alerted archaeologists to the antiquity of the find. The Iceman wore fur leggings and a coat beneath a grass cape, a fur cap and leather shoes packed with grass to protect his feet from the cold.

How had this prehistoric man come to die in such a remote location? The body was released from the Similaun glacier a short distance below the Hauslabjoch, a saddle across the main ridge of the Alps that connects the Ötztal, where the body was found, to the Val Senales. So remote was it that it was several days before the exact course of the Austrian/Italian frontier in this area was determined, and the Iceman could be shown to have died on what is today Italian territory.

First theories suggested that the Iceman had met his end through misadventure. His clothing (the grass cape and grass-lined shoes) shows that he was equipped for life in the high mountains, and the bow and arrow might have been used for hunting. Alternatively, he may have been a shepherd, tending his flocks on the upland pastures of the Ötztal during the summer months, bringing them down for winter in the Val Venosta to the south. Perhaps, it was suggested, he had been overcome by an unseasonably early snowstorm.

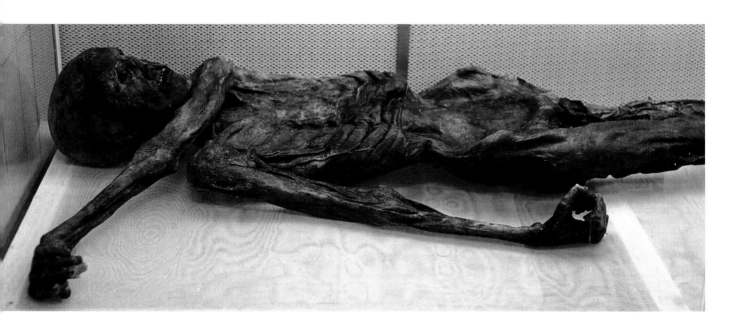

opposite and bottom

Among the equipment found with the body of the Iceman (opposite) were a knife with a flint blade in an ash handle, kept in a plaited scabbard attached to a leather strap (bottom left) and a copper axe (bottom right), the blade hafted in a forked branch of yew trimmed to an L-shape and fixed in place by leather binding.

below

A CT scan showing the flint arrowhead in the left shoulder of the Iceman. This unexpected discovery indicated that he had been a victim of violence rather than just an unlucky traveller overwhelmed by the weather.

The theory of death by misadventure had to be radically revised following the discovery in 2001 of a flint arrowhead in the Iceman's left shoulder. It was found during an X-ray, then confirmed by CT scan, and subsequent study of the body revealed an entry wound in the back, pointing upwards from left to right. Hence the Iceman had been shot from behind but had escaped and fled. Other studies confirm this picture of a violent end. Examination of the Iceman's right hand showed a deep cut across the palm, perhaps sustained in close-quarters fighting. DNA analysis suggested blood on his leather jacket and knife came from four separate individuals, and that there was blood from two different people on a broken arrow in his quiver, though many people have handled the body since its discovery and whether the DNA is ancient has yet to be confirmed. Had the Iceman broken the arrow while pulling it from the body of one of his victims? He may have been trying to mend the arrow when he was shot in the back. He could have struggled on after the encounter for some time – perhaps even a day or two – before succumbing to pain and exhaustion in this hostile terrain, leaving a puzzle for people 150 lifetimes away to try to unravel.

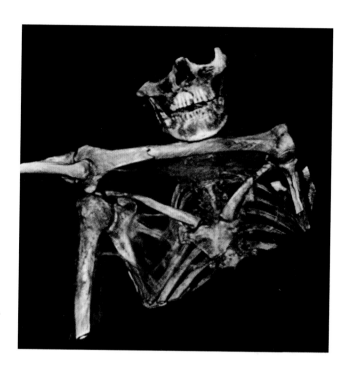

The Amesbury Archer and the Boscombe Bowmen: Men of Stonehenge

Andrew P. Fitzpatrick

The Amesbury Archer, found in a grave just 5 km (3 miles) from Stonehenge along with another man, perhaps a relative, is the richest Early Bronze Age burial excavated in Europe. Thanks to state-of-the-art scientific analyses, this burial and that of the Boscombe Bowmen discovered close by reveal startling new facts about the builders of the ancient stone circle.

'They've found something shiny.' It was 3 May 2002. I put paperwork to one side and set off immediately for the excavations at Amesbury. On site, the small muddy object looked unremarkable, but it appeared to be a type of gold ornament that is usually found in pairs.

For security reasons, I decided that we had to complete the excavation of the burial that day. As the light faded we had passed the point of no return. We had to finish. Working by car headlights and under the scrutiny of the TV crew we had called out, the sense of quiet excitement was palpable. I was the person last off site at 1.42 a.m. By then we had completed the excavation of the burial of the Amesbury Archer, a man who lived at the time when the first metals arrived in Britain and the great stone elements of Stonehenge were being erected.

In many ways the Archer's burial was typical of his time, the beginning of the Bronze Age in Britain, about 2500 BC. His mourners laid him out as if he were asleep and around him they placed the accoutrements of an archer or warrior. But in significant ways his burial is unique and is the richest known from his time, not just in Britain but in Europe. He was accompanied by lavish offerings, including what proved to be the earliest pair of gold ornaments in Britain. With his body were copper knives, boar's tusks, beautifully made flint tools and arrowheads, and Beaker pots – more than have been found in any other Bronze Age grave – and also a strange, deliberately shaped black stone. Stone wristguards, one black, one red, would have protected his left forearm from the lash of the bowstring and were also status symbols.

He had lived to be 35 to 45 years old, a good age then, but not without suffering. A traumatic injury had destroyed his left knee. He survived, but the wound caused an infection of the bone that must have left him in constant pain. His left thigh withered and he must have walked with a pronounced limp.

Few burials of this date lie close to Stonehenge. For the first time, we had evidence for people of wealth and status from the period when the great stones were hauled to the site. Whatever his rank, it was certainly no coincidence that the richest known Bronze Age burial lay just a few kilometres from the great monument.

above
The grave of the Amesbury Archer, in a photograph taken as the excavation drew to a late night finish. The black stone behind his back is the key to unlocking why he was considered so important – it is a cushion stone, a metalworker's tool.

Nearby we then found the Companion, a 20–25-year-old man. He had died after the Archer, but had a pair of identical gold ornaments. From the shape of the two men's skulls and a rare genetic trait in their feet bones we know that they were related. However, we cannot say whether they were father and son, brothers or cousins.

We noticed at once that a number of the objects in the Archer's grave could be matched in continental Europe, notably the copper knives. To our astonishment, we discovered that the Archer grew up overseas. We tested both men's teeth, as the isotopes in the enamel of our teeth store a chemical fingerprint of the environment where we grew up. Oxygen isotopes showed that the Companion was raised in the region, but the Archer had lived in a much colder climate, somewhere overseas. Judging

from the artifacts, he probably grew up in Central Europe. This sensational revelation provided us with irrefutable proof that people had travelled long distances during the Early Bronze Age.

The Archer was clearly no ordinary individual, but who was he? Suddenly the significance of the black stone became apparent. It was a 'cushion stone' – a metalworker's tool. If the Archer used it, he is the earliest metalworker yet found in Britain, one of the few people able to work exotic, scarce materials like gold and copper. His metallurgical skills may explain why he travelled so far and the great respect shown him in death.

The Boscombe Bowmen

It was May 2003, and archaeologists were watching construction work at the nearby Boscombe Down airbase.

Suddenly fragments of human bone and Beaker pots appeared in the soil brought up by the digging machine. I immediately set off for the site and when I arrived, I realized at once that the pottery and flint arrowheads were almost identical to those from the Archer's grave and also dated to the time of Stonehenge. But this was a collective rather than an individual burial.

Slowly we recorded the remains of as many as nine people, mostly men. There was only one complete adult skeleton, a man of 30 to 40 years old, whose left thigh had been badly broken. When it healed the bones were not aligned and, like the Archer, this Bowman would have limped. Only parts of the other men were present, mainly skulls and limb bones, many of which had already been buried elsewhere, then reinterred here. Again the similarities between their skulls and the pattern of bones in them showed that they came from a close-knit community. Very different from other burials found near Stonehenge, this multiple burial was reminiscent of graves in the Alps or Armorica (Brittany). Yet the strontium and oxygen isotopes pointed to the west. These men had spent their early years in Wales. And of course, the first stones erected at Stonehenge, the bluestones, came from the Preseli Hills, over 240 km (150 miles) away, in Wales. Could the Bowmen have been involved in the transport of the bluestones? This may possibly be the grave of some of the builders of Stonehenge.

For centuries Stonehenge has stood as a solitary and enigmatic icon of a distant prehistoric past. Now, thanks to these discoveries and modern science, we are learning something of the people who built it.

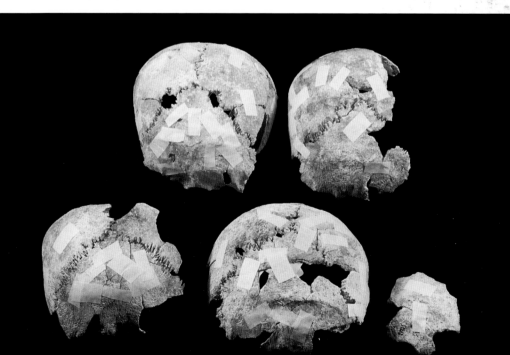

above
The complete skeleton of the disabled man can be discerned in the grave of the Bowmen. Below his feet are the skulls and jaws of some of the other men. The area to the left of the scale rod was dug away by mechanical excavator.

right
Parts of the skulls of some of the Bowmen and youngsters. The shape of the top of their heads is very similar and the zip-like pattern of tiny bones between the individual pieces of the skulls confirms that the Bowmen came from a close-knit community.

New Revelations from the Pyramids of Giza

Zahi Hawass

Visible and familiar for thousands of years, the pyramids of Giza can even now produce fresh surprises. During the last 20 years, many significant discoveries that enrich our knowledge of these monuments and their construction have been made, and I have been fortunate to be directly involved in many of them, including excavating the tombs of the workmen who built the pyramids and investigating secret doors inside the Great Pyramid.

The tombs of the pyramid builders

By 1989, Mark Lehner and I had already been looking for traces of the builders of the pyramids for over 10 years, and thought the most likely place was southeast of the Great Sphinx, south of a large wall called the Wall of the Crow. Some excavations had been carried out here, but nothing conclusive had been found. Then one day an American tourist was riding her horse near the pyramids when the horse stumbled and exposed a mud-brick wall that on investigation turned out to be the tomb of an overseer of the pyramid builders. I have been supervising excavations here since, and we are uncovering a large cemetery for the workmen involved in the construction of the pyramids. This discovery is significant in many ways, and provides proof that the pyramid builders were free Egyptians and not slaves.

The necropolis is divided into two main cemeteries. On the lower slopes of the plateau are the tombs of the workmen who actually dragged the stones, and those of their families and their supervisors. Built of mud brick mixed with rubble, most are mastabas (tombs with low rectangular superstructures), but a number of architectural styles unique in the repertoire of the early Old Kingdom (mid-3rd millennium BC) are also found: one tomb has a vaulted roof, another has a *serdab* (an enclosed statue chamber) outside, several are in the form of mini-pyramids (one a step pyramid), and another is a beehive-shape.

Among the fascinating details revealed by forensic study of the skeletons found in the tombs is evidence for spinal stress, presumably due to the heavy labour of pyramid building. There were indications that medical treatment was available: for example, one skull showed evidence that a brain tumour had been removed through surgery; its owner lived for another 14 years. We found few inscriptions, but several of the tombs' occupants were able to afford small statues or offering tables. Clearly, these were not slaves, but free Egyptians proud to labour for their kings.

The upper cemetery, high up on the ridge, was reserved for higher-ranking officials, including draftsmen and overseers. The titles found here tell us a great deal about pyramid building: for example, 'overseer of the workmen who dragged the stones', 'overseer of the harbour' and 'overseer of the side of the pyramid'. Most tombs here are in the mastaba style, built of limestone or sun-dried brick, and decoration is much more extensive than in the lower cemetery. One tomb, belonging to a minor official named Petety and his wife, was decorated with reliefs, including two curse inscriptions to protect the tomb against any violators. We also found a number of statues, including four of an overseer of the boats of the goddess Neith named Intyshedu.

Study of these tombs, along with evidence from Mark Lehner's excavations of a town for the pyramid builders (p. 161), leads to the conclusion that there were probably not more than 10,000 workmen at any one time – a far cry from the 100,000 or more of legend. The presence of regional variation among the workers' tombs also tells us that the building of the pyramids was a national project worked on by households from all over Egypt.

The secret doors in the Great Pyramid

In 1992, we closed the Great Pyramid of Khufu in order to install a ventilation system to reduce the humidity inside its chambers, which had risen to dangerously high levels. We had decided to

opposite
This seated statue of the overseer Intyshedu is one of five statues discovered in his tomb in the upper cemetery of the pyramid builders.

above
The lower cemetery of the pyramid builders' necropolis contains the burials of the families of the workmen who moved the stones, grouped around the larger tombs of their overseers

place the equipment in the small tunnels, nicknamed airshafts by Egyptologists, which lead from the north and south walls of the middle (Queen's) and upper (King's) of the pyramid's three interior chambers. No one knows what these shafts – just 20 cm (8 in) in cross-section – were for, and although the tunnels from the King's Chamber reach to the outside of the pyramid, those from the Queen's Chamber do not. Many Egyptologists believe that the shafts from the King's Chamber were to allow the soul of the pyramid's owner, Khufu, to travel to join his ancestors and other gods, thought to live in the skies. But these 'airshafts' have always been one of the Great Pyramid's unsolved mysteries.

Working with the German Archaeological Institute in Cairo, we hired Rudolf Gantenbrink to design a robot to study and clean the shafts before installing the ventilation equipment. In March and May of 1992, the shafts from the King's Chamber were cleared and videotaped by a robot named Upuaut I, and the upper ventilation system was successfully installed.

We then turned to the shafts from the Queen's Chamber. In 1993, we sent a new robot, Upuaut II, into the southern shaft. After travelling 62 m (203 ft), the robot stopped in front of a stone slab into which two copper handles were set. This was an extraordinary discovery, and one we could never have anticipated. The investigation of the northern shaft was less successful, because it bends at several points and the robot was unable to negotiate the first turn.

But what lay behind the secret door in the southern shaft? In association with the National Geographic Society, we built a new robot, the Pyramid Rover, and sent it into the shaft in September 2002. Reaching the slab, it drilled a hole just over 1 cm (0.4 in) in diameter and 6 cm (2.4 in) deep, and inserted a camera. About 21 cm (8 in) beyond was an even more surprising discovery – a second limestone door. The Rover also investigated the northern shaft, finding that it bent after 18 m (60 ft), then zigzagged left and right before running straight. This pattern of turns was apparently made to avoid the Grand Gallery, the large corridor from the Queen's Chamber to the King's Chamber. After 62 m (203 ft), the robot was stopped again by another door with two copper handles. These doors are still shrouded in mystery, and we are studying various proposals to see how we can reveal what lies behind them. Most Egyptologists agree that the King's Chamber was Khufu's burial chamber; I cannot help but wonder if the 'airshafts' from the Queen's Chamber hide a secret tomb. Soon, I hope, we will find out.

top
Dr Hawass looks inside the southern 'airshaft' in the Queen's Chamber. A limestone slab with two copper handles was discovered partway up this shaft by Upuaut II, the robot designed by Rudolph Gantenbrink.

above and right
In 2002, a new robot, the Pyramid Rover, was sent inside the southern 'airshaft' of the Queen's Chamber to discover what was beyond the limestone slab. It drilled a small hole and inserted a camera: beyond the first slab was a second, which has yet to be investigated.

opposite
Intyshedu's four painted limestone statues, as discovered inside his serdab (statue chamber) in his tomb in the upper cemetery of the pyramid builders. The fifth was of wood, and had completely disintegrated.

The Tomb of Tutankhamun's Mother?
An 18th Dynasty Chamber in the Valley of the Kings

Zahi Hawass

After over eight decades of quiet, uneventful work in the Valley of the Kings, almost 100 years after Howard Carter found the tomb of the golden boy-pharaoh, 'King Tut', a major discovery was recently made. In 2005, an unknown shaft, which turned out to lead to an underground chamber containing seven coffins and a variety of pottery and alabaster vessels, was found near the tomb of Tutankhamun. This is indeed an amazing find – no one believed that anything more could be discovered in the Valley of the Kings.

The story began when Otto Schaden from the University of Memphis was working in the tomb of Amenmesse, one of the kings of the 19th Dynasty (around 1200 BC). Normally, Schaden would not have worked outside this tomb, since it is the only place he had permission to excavate. However, when I became Secretary General of the Supreme Council of Antiquities, I initiated site management programmes to protect the monuments in the Valley. We wanted to make sure that the area around the tomb of Amenmesse had been cleared down to bedrock in order to re-route floodwater, and asked Schaden to carry this out. Thus the discovery of the shaft came about, as so often, through a mixture of planning and accident.

What is especially remarkable is that this area had been excavated before. Howard Carter and Theodore Davis (a wealthy American who sponsored excavations in the Valley of the Kings in the early 20th century) had found workmen's huts, but neither had stumbled across the shaft of KV 63. When Schaden discovered the top of this unrecorded shaft, he wrote a letter explaining it to me, including pictures. But as it did not look very impressive, just a shaft covered with stones, I did not think it worth making an announcement at that stage.

Schaden began excavating the shaft in January 2006. Every day, he would email me about the progress of the excavation, step by step, until he was at a depth of 5.24 m (17 ft) below the surface. Finally, I visited the work and told Schaden that I could only smile at his discovery, because I still believed that the shaft was not intact. When the excavators reached a chamber, they sent another email asking me to the official opening. On Friday, 10 February, I woke at 4.00 a.m. and flew to Luxor. When I arrived in the Valley, I discovered hundreds of film crews and journalists – an indescribable scene! The atmosphere was full of mystery and anticipation. I slowly climbed down the ladder and found myself in front of a niche closed by stone rubble with no seals. Schaden followed, and we began to remove the stones until we had opened a small hole. Now came the incredible moment when I took a flashlight and looked inside. I can still see

the scene in front of me – a chamber hidden for more than 3,000 years, but soon to be known around the entire world.

So far the excavators have found seven coffins and 28 large pottery jars (most of them sealed). Of the coffins, five were for adults, one was for a child and one was for an infant. Most are in bad shape, as they were covered with resin and have been eaten away by termites, but we can tell that they were once very beautiful. The biggest surprise was to find that there were no mummies inside. Instead, they were used as containers for miscellaneous objects – sherds from small and large vessels, miniature vessels, two alabaster vessels, natron (a salt-like material used in mummification), the bones of small animals, linen, small sealings and bits of wood. The youth-sized coffin held six down pillows, some inscribed with hieroglyphs saying such things as 'life, health, stability', and an exquisite miniature coffinette (about 42 cm/16.5 in long) of gilded wood. Twelve of the jars have been opened and their contents examined: they also contained various objects, including smaller vessels or fragments, resined bandages, natron, chaff, pieces of twine or rope, clay 'trays' used in embalming, and mud seal impressions.

The style of the coffins and the jars, as well as the seal impressions, date the tomb to the late 18th Dynasty: specifically, close to the time of Tutankhamun (about 1320 BC). There are many impressions of the official necropolis seal – a jackal over nine captives; this seal is also found in Tutankhamun's tomb. The excavators hope that at least one will include a royal name. Other sealing motifs also have links with Tutankhamun, and the pots are similar to ones from the tomb of Yuya and Tjuya, probably Tutankhamun's grandparents. The excavators have also found a number of inscriptions, most of them fragmentary: Dr Schaden's favourite is a label on a wine jar reading 'Year 5, wine from Tjaru' (a site at the edge of the Eastern Delta). A wine jar from Tutankhamun's tomb is also from Year 5, and contains 'wine from the estate of the Aten in Tjaru'. Could these two jars hold the same vintage?

The period to which this tomb belongs was a fascinating era of Egyptian history. The man who was probably Tutankhamun's father, Akhenaten (c. 1353–1336 BC), had turned the country's religion upside down, rejecting the main state gods and instead worshipping the sun disc, the Aten. After Tutankhamun, who

had been born Tutankhaten, came to the throne, he changed his name and restored the old faith, bringing Amun-Re back into favour. KV 63 contains the names of both gods: that of Amun-Re is found on an alabaster jar and a seal impression, and the Aten's on another sealing. So far, no king's name has been found.

The last coffin was opened in June 2006. It is inscribed, although we have not yet been able to read what it says because of its delicate condition. The face is beautiful, and very much in the style of the period. Everyone hoped that it might contain a mummy, but instead it held more fascinating artifacts associated with embalming, including, most surprisingly, numerous collars, made of cloth with flowers at the edges, that would have been placed across the chest of the mummy or worn by mourners at a funerary feast. Eleven large jars are still sealed; they will also be full of embalming materials, but we all hope at least one of the seals that is sure to be inside is inscribed with a royal name.

It seems, then, that this tomb was a place where embalming materials, possibly left over from an important royal funeral, were stored. One such cache (KV 54), discovered in 1907, contained materials from Tutankhamun's mummification and funerary feast. But who was the original tomb cut for? I do not think it was for Ankhsenamun, Tutankhamun's wife, or the beautiful Nefertiti, his stepmother, because both of these important queens would have had larger, more elaborate tombs. I like to imagine that it was built for Kiya, a secondary wife of Akhenaten's, whom many believe was Tutankhamun's mother. She disappears from the historical record at around the time he was born, and might even have died in childbirth. I believe that the Valley of the Kings still hides important secrets. Who knows what we will find next?

pages 52–53
The coffins in KV 63's chamber were piled on top of each other. However, no mummies were found inside. Instead, they were full of a variety of objects connected with mummification and funerals: cloth, natron, broken pottery, and even pillows.

opposite below
Dr Schaden, director of the excavations in KV 63, and Dr Hawass examine one of the coffins.

below
View into the burial chamber just after the discovery. The coffins and storage jars all sit on a bed of rubble, much of which has yet to be cleared.

Pharaoh's Children: The Tomb of the Sons of Ramesses II in the Valley of the Kings

Kent R. Weeks

What began as a routine excavation of a rediscovered tomb in Egypt's Valley of the Kings soon became something very different, as we learned that it belonged to several sons of Ramesses II and unearthed chamber after chamber. It is already the largest tomb in the Valley – and we still haven't reached the end.

In 1825, the English adventurer James Burton visited the Valley of the Kings and cursorily explored the 20 tombs known there at the time. He found the entrance of one of these, KV 5 (King's Valley tomb number 5), filled with debris and he hired local workmen to dig a narrow channel at ceiling level. With effort, he crawled into the tomb's first seven rooms before further progress was blocked. In his notes, Burton wrote that the tomb had an unusual plan, no decoration, no objects and no particular historical interest. It lay ignored for the next 163 years.

Since 1979 the Theban Mapping Project (TMP) has been preparing a detailed map of the Valley of the Kings. It has also gathered information on the Valley's tombs, especially those seen previously but which have since become lost. One of these was KV 5 and, based on Burton's notes, the TMP relocated its entrance in 1988. At first, we were inclined to agree with Burton: KV 5 was unimportant. But in 1989 we found a wall carved with hieroglyphs with the name and titles of Amenherkhepeshef, the first-born son of the great New Kingdom pharaoh Ramesses II who reigned in the 13th century BC; a few weeks later, elsewhere, we found the name of another son, Ramesses.

With these discoveries, KV 5 became a tomb of considerable interest, and we decided to explore it. Work proceeded slowly, but by 1995 we had cleared a pathway through Chamber 3, a large pillared hall. In its rear wall we found a blocked doorway. Clearing away the debris and crawling through, we found ourselves in a 30-m (100-ft) long corridor lined with doorways that led to still more corridors and rooms. Suddenly, KV 5 had become the largest tomb ever found in the Valley, with over 67 rooms. Today, 11 years later, KV 5 continues to grow: we have now found over 128 chambers, and more are sure to come.

Not only is KV 5 much larger than typical royal tombs in the Valley, but its plan is also completely different. Instead of a few corridors cut along a single axis, KV 5's plan radiates off a pillared hall in many directions and on several different levels. From inscriptions on the tomb walls and on objects lying on its floor, we now know that Ramesses II buried at least six, and perhaps as many as 22, of his numerous sons in KV 5.

KV 5 is unique in plan, unique in size and unique in function as a family mausoleum. But it is hard to explain why – because there is so little to compare it with we have to depend on evidence from KV 5 itself for interpretation. And this means we must be especially meticulous in its excavation: even tiny pieces of evidence may offer meaningful clues. Every one of the 900,000 fragments of pottery we have found in the tomb has been described and studied; from them we are learning about the functions of the individual chambers. Every square centimetre of exposed wall surface has been examined for traces of inscriptions, and we are now reconstructing the tomb's complex programme of decoration. Four skeletons were found tossed by thieves into a pit in the floor of Chamber 2: measurements suggest they are genetically related, and could be sons of Ramesses II.

As this meticulous work continues we are learning more about the reign of one of Egypt's most powerful kings and about the royal family. Perhaps KV 5 was dug because Ramesses II made several of his sons his heirs, elevating them to positions of great authority and sharing with them some of his regal powers. When his sons predeceased him (he lived to be nearly 90) they were buried in a tomb indicative of their exalted position – not as elaborate as pharaoh's perhaps, but far more impressive than for most royal children. It is thus an architectural reflection of a significant change in the structure of Egyptian kingship.

New Kingdom Tombs at Saqqara

Alain Zivie

Overshadowed by the presence of the famous cemetery of cat mummies of the Bubasteion – the sacred precinct dedicated to the goddess Bastet – the New Kingdom rock-cut tombs at Saqqara, the burial ground of the great royal capital of Memphis, had been ignored and were scientifically virgin territory when the French Archaeological Mission began investigating them. Our discoveries have now shown that these remarkable tombs of major figures of the 18th and 19th dynasties are worthy of comparison with Egypt's greatest sites.

The Mission Archéologique Française du Bubasteion (MAFB) has been working in the escarpment of the Bubasteion for 25 years, concentrating on one zone of the necropolis of Saqqara which corresponded, at least in part, to what the Egyptians called the *dehenet* (cliff) of Ankhtaouy. Our aim is to restore this site to its rightful place in the archaeology of Egypt's New Kingdom period, and demonstrate that it forms an ensemble far greater and more important than is usually thought. Along with the programme of study and excavation, we are also working on the conservation, restoration and presentation of the tombs.

In the New Kingdom period, the royal court of ancient Egypt resided more often in Memphis than Thebes (modern Luxor) and briefly also at Amarna, but if the kings were buried in Thebes, a majority of nobles and officials continued to have their tombs in Memphis (mainly at Saqqara). While in some respects the hypogeums of the Bubasteion are comparable to the tombs of the nobles at Thebes of the same period, there are also significant differences. On the whole, the tombs are carved completely from the rock, and are therefore underground chambers, on several levels, although some also had a section built from white limestone blocks. Their ground plans vary, according to the importance of their owner or date of construction. The method of decoration also varies, sometimes within the same tomb, between largely painted relief (engraved or 'sunken'), and simple painting. In general the reliefs and paintings are very good, and sometimes even of exceptional quality.

Since the full extent of the Bubasteion tombs had been ignored or was unknown in modern times, when we began work we knew that exciting discoveries might await us – as was shown by the tomb of the Vizier and Father of the god, 'Aper-El. First visited by me in 1976, excavation of the vast tomb, with its four levels, began in 1980. Its funerary chamber, only plundered in antiquity, was discovered in 1987, and a large part of its chapel, blocked up by later masonry, in 1993. The mummified remains of the Vizier, his wife and son, the general Houy, were scattered with the remains of their coffins inside the room, accompanied by canopic jars, as well as numerous objects and gold jewelry, comparable both in quality and quantity to discoveries made in Thebes in the early 20th century. This is the first, and till now only, time that such a New Kingdom funerary ensemble has

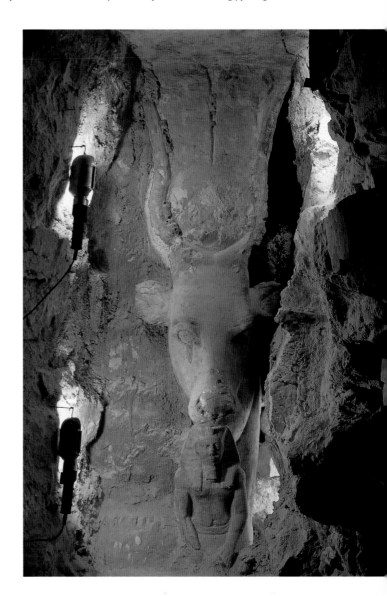

opposite
The rear of the chapel of 'Aper-El's tomb (Bubasteion I.1), discovered in 1993–94.

above
The discovery in progress of a rock-cut statue of the goddess Hathor in the form of a cow and a king, certainly Ramesses II, in the tomb of Pirikhnawa or Netjerouymes (Bubasteion I.16).

been revealed in the context of an archaeological excavation at Saqqara – indeed in the entire Memphite necropolis. The tomb also contained paintings, including ones of 'Aper-El receiving garlands of flowers.

What is especially remarkable about our researches in this small area of the Saqqara necropolis is the social status of the tombs' owners and the fact that several of them were unknown before we excavated their burials. And even in cases where some were mentioned in scant references in a text or an inscription, we did not suspect that they were buried at Memphis.

As excavations continued it was clear that the necropolis became most important during and after the reign of Amenhotep III (c. 1390–1353), though some tombs date to earlier times, such as that of the chancellor Nehesy, who organized the famous expedition to the land of Punt in the reign of queen Hatshepsut, in the early 15th century BC. And far from marking a break in the use of the cemetery as might be expected, in accordance with the traditional view of Egyptian history, the Amarna period – the reign of Akhenaten and his immediate successors, when the royal capital became Tell El-Amarna – is in fact particularly well represented at the site.

In addition to the tomb of 'Aper-El, in 1997 we discovered that belonging to Maïa, Tutankhamun's wet-nurse and certainly a key-figure for the transition after Akhenaten. A relief in the tomb shows Maïa with Tutankhamun as a child on her lap and a dog beneath the king's chair. We subsequently made a most

unexpected discovery in this tomb, dating from a much later period: the mummified remains of a lion – the first one found in Egypt. More recently, in 2002, we discovered and examined the tomb of the scribe of the treasury of the temples of Aten at Memphis (and perhaps Amarna), named Raïay or Hatiay, again decorated with carved reliefs of high quality in the Amarna style. The Bubasteion cliff is thus providing exciting – and unexpected – new information about this fascinating period of Egyptian history, when Akhenaten abandoned the worship of some of the traditional gods of Egypt, in particular Amun, and replaced it with the cult of the sun-disc, the Aten.

When the new royal residence of Pi-Ramses was founded during the Ramesside dynasty (1293 BC on), Memphis remained at the heart of the country, as royal city and an economic, strategic, military and artistic centre. Its necropolis, in particular the *dehenet* (cliff) of Ankhtaouy, was now more than ever the place where high-ranking officials wished to spend eternity. It is here, among the tombs of the Bubasteion, that we can hope to discover more new information about the reign of Ramesses II. As just one instance, we have recently investigated the beautiful funerary chapel of Netjerouymes, or Pirikhnawa, director of the treasury and high steward of Memphis, and a diplomat in the reign of Ramesses II. We have yet to explore the funerary levels of the tomb of this prominent official, who is mentioned in Hittite sources and who was the main craftsman of the peace negotiated with the Hittites – who knows what we may find?

right
The middle coffin of Lady Taouret, wife of the Vizier 'Aper-El, found in his tomb (Bubasteion I.1). It is made of gilded wood with coloured inlays.

opposite left
The fine profile of the ambassador, director of the treasury and high steward of Memphis, Pirikhnawa, or Netjerouymes, on a limestone pillar in his tomb (Bubasteion I.16).

opposite right
Lady Maïa, Tutankhamun's wet nurse, as represented on a rock-cut pillar in her tomb (Bubasteion I.20).

Where the Living Feasted with the Dead: The Royal Tombs of Qatna, Syria

Peter Pfälzner

Qatna was one of the most powerful and splendid kingdoms of ancient Syria – between 1900 and 1350 BC it was a dominant political, economic and cultural centre of the eastern Mediterranean. Yet it was virtually forgotten until an international archaeological team, of which I was part, rediscovered the tombs of the kings of Qatna beneath the royal palace. Remarkable not just for their gold and jewelry – though there were many objects of great splendour – the tombs were even more exciting because they had been completely untouched since the day they were abandoned.

The ancient city lies in the fertile plains of Syria, about 200 km (125 miles) north of Damascus on a strategic crossroads from Mesopotamia to the Mediterranean, and from Egypt through Palestine into Anatolia. Qatna was first explored in the 1920s, but it was not until 1994 that Michel Maqdissi of the Syrian Directorate of Antiquities and Museums began a new, long-term excavation. Since 1999, three international teams have worked here: one from Syria directed by Maqdissi, an Italian group directed by Daniele Morandi Bonacossi and a German one led by myself. We have concentrated on the Royal Palace in the centre of Qatna. Built around 1700 BC, it was the royal residence and a symbol of the kingdom's power for more than 350 years.

The Royal Palace

The palace complex measures some 150 m (490 ft) from east to west and stands on a 15-m (50-ft) high natural cliff, dominating the site. The interior must originally have been decorated with fabulous wall-paintings – one room alone has yielded over 4,000 fragments of paintings, which proved to resemble closely Minoan frescoes from Crete. The largest room, the audience hall, was once covered by a wooden roof supported by four massive wooden columns and is the largest known covered room in the Near Eastern Bronze Age. Beyond, reached through a monumental gateway, were two further spacious halls: the throne room, where the king held his receptions, and another one devoted to cult and ceremonial. Only the foundations of the spectacular palace survived, but in 2002 we made a discovery that surprised us all: north of the huge ceremonial hall was a long, mysterious corridor leading down beneath the palace.

The corridor was entered from a staircase, at the foot of which was a secure doorway – it could thus be firmly blocked off. We found numerous cuneiform tablets that had fallen into the corridor during the destruction of the palace. These yielded

important historical information about Qatna in the 14th century BC, at the time when Akhenaten ruled Egypt, and included letters from other Syrian kings and from the Hittites to King Idanda of Qatna.

We followed the corridor down, finding traces of a second and a third door. Where would it lead? The passage stopped before it reached the outer wall of the palace. Could it be the entrance to a tomb? It soon became clear that this was the case. At the end of the 40-m (130-ft) long passage, we discovered an entry to the right, which opened into a 5-m (16-ft) deep shaft, accessible only by ladder. At the bottom of the shaft, 12 m (nearly 40 ft) below the surface, was a doorway in a side wall, cut into the bedrock. Two identical basalt statues stood one on each side, probably idealized representations of kingship. Offering bowls and animal bones lay beside them and we believe that the kings of Qatna would have stood here to address the ancestors and supply them with food offerings.

The entrance to the tomb was not solidly blocked but was filled with debris and we could peer inside – was it safe to enter? Remembering rumours of the 'mummy's curse' after Tutankhamun's tomb had been opened, we first arranged for a fungal analysis of the interior, which showed no dangerous concentrations. What would we find within? The suspense was almost unbearable. We were stunned to find it completely undisturbed, just as it had been left when the palace was finally captured and abandoned. We had to work extremely carefully, lying on planks above the floor, since many of the objects, including fragile bones, were scattered around. We recorded over 2,000 objects in their original positions before anything was removed.

The tomb chambers

The tomb consisted of a central chamber and three side rooms, jointly explored by the German and Syrian teams at the end of 2002. The central chamber contained a basalt sarcophagus with no lid. Inside were the remains of three individuals, none complete. Their bones had been laid elsewhere first and then redeposited here. Other burials lay on four wooden biers – the wood had rotted away but they were outlined on the floor. The bodies had originally been covered in purple cloth, as shown by

opposite
The two statues of basalt are among the most outstanding examples of ancient Syrian sculpture. They served to receive offerings to the ancestors in the antechamber of the Royal Tombs.

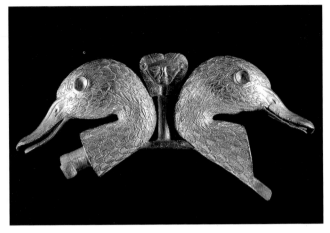

above left and right
A golden hand (left) was mounted on a wooden stick and was perhaps used as an arm-like instrument for presenting offerings. These two golden ducks (right) are a brilliant example of the high standard of Syrian craftmanship in the 2nd millennium BC.

below
A gold disc decorated with griffins in repoussé technique. It was once sewn on to a piece of textile or leather.

opposite
The main chamber of the Royal Tombs of Qatna, with benches for feasting and storage jars for food offerings.

chemical analysis. Hundreds of gold and stone beads lay on the biers, as well as spearheads, a golden hand and a lion head made of Baltic amber, presumably a cosmetic box.

Stone benches lined two walls and numerous jars and bowls stood under and on them, with an Egyptian calcite vessel dating to the early 18th Dynasty (16th century BC). Animal bones lay beneath the benches. We are convinced that these are the remains of communal meals of the living and the dead – ritual feasts known from ancient literature as *kispu*-offerings.

No human bones were found in the southern chamber. Vessels had been deposited at the foot of a wooden bench, together with symbolic food offerings, probably for the dead king, and this may have been his banqueting room. The western chamber was the most exciting of the side rooms. On the right stood a stone bench with a complete skeleton – the only one in the whole tomb in its proper anatomical arrangement. Presumably this was the most recent burial, and still in its original resting place. What is most remarkable – although not yet finally proven – is that the body had probably been heated to around 200–250° C (392–482° F) for at least an hour. Was this for preservation, sterilization or to

reduce odours? The skeleton had then been placed in a wooden box, of which only the bronze clamps at the four corners survived. Textiles had been placed over it, which we studied with a microscope before they crumbled away, identifying different layers dyed in various colours.

Around the waist of the body was a girdle of gold, carnelian, amethyst and amber beads strung on gold thread. On the left side of this chamber stood a second basalt sarcophagus containing the remains of two bodies, several pottery and stone vessels and a gold bowl.

The fourth, eastern chamber was clearly the ossuary, for in it we found a thick layer of animal and human bones, deposited over a long period as bodies were cleared from the other chambers and brought here. We were surprised to find numerous offering bowls, as if these older human ancestors were still supplied with food offerings.

Our discoveries of these undisturbed kingly burials are providing fascinating insights into both the royal burial practices and rituals of ancient Syria, and a major cultural and artistic centre of the ancient world.

The Royal Tombs of Nimrud, Iraq:
The Treasures of Assyrian Queens

Joan Oates

The Assyrian capital Nimrud (ancient Kalhu) in modern Iraq is one of the greatest cities of the ancient world. It is known especially for the magnificent stone reliefs found in the 19th century, now decorating many of the world's great museums, and for the beautiful carved ivories recovered in more recent British and Iraqi excavations. The discovery of tombs of Assyrian queens, containing over 40 kg (88 lb) of gold vessels and jewelry, together with hundreds of other beautiful objects, must rate not only as the most extraordinary discovery made at the site itself, but as one of the greatest archaeological finds of recent years.

In 1988 Iraqi archaeologists led by Muzahim Mahmud Hussein were continuing their extensive programme of excavation and restoration at Nimrud. A major part of the project involved clearing and restoring rooms in the great palace built by King Assurnasirpal II (883–859 BC), the walls of which had been decorated with the massive stone sculptures found by the British archaeologist Austen Henry Layard a century and a half ago. While cleaning the floor of one room in the harem (the queen's residence), the archaeologists noticed an uneven area of floor which they removed, intending to replace it. Much to their surprise, the crown of a brick vault lay just beneath. Further investigation revealed something even more astonishing – the presence of a tomb, within which was a well-preserved terracotta sarcophagus. This contained not only the body of an elderly woman with a silver bowl beneath her skull, but also extraordinary grave goods including large numbers of gold

objects: elaborate earrings of exquisite workmanship, heavy gold armlets, rings (five on her left forefinger alone) and very large numbers of beads of gold and semiprecious stones.

The second tomb

Not surprisingly, this discovery caused great excitement and also alerted the Iraqi archaeologists to the possibility of further tombs. In April 1989, a second vault was identified beneath a room not far to the west of the first. Here a stone funerary tablet provided the first historical information, including the name of the tomb's occupant, an 8th-century BC queen called Yaba, identified on inscriptions on a gold bowl as wife of King Tiglath-Pileser III (744–727 BC). Among numerous other threats, the funerary inscription imposed a curse of 'thirst and restlessness for all eternity' on anyone disturbing the tomb – despite which the sarcophagus contained not only the original body, but also a second, apparently hastily added skeleton.

In the chamber itself were a number of gold, bronze and alabaster vessels. Grave goods within the sarcophagus were truly spectacular – a total of 157 different objects, plus thousands of

opposite
Gold earrings from Tomb II, remarkable not only for their delicate, granulated decoration, but also for their size, over 6 cm (2.4 in) in length; their total weight is 52.3 g (1.8 oz).

right
Gold flask found with 11 smaller examples in Tomb II. This one is 13.5 cm (5.3 in) high and weighs over 221 g (7.8 oz).

below
Two of the many gold armlets from Tomb II, inlaid with coloured glass and semiprecious stones. The total weight of gold objects from Tomb II was 14 kg (31 lb); these armlets weigh over 800 g (28 oz) each.

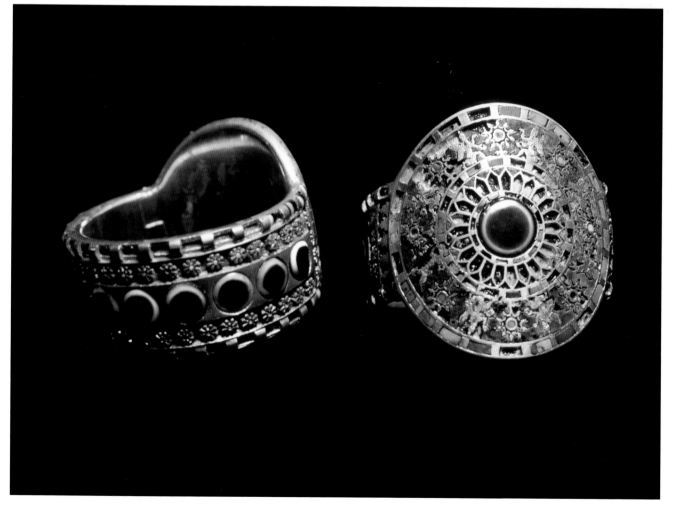

left

Gold bowls from Tomb II, inscribed with the names of three late 8th-century BC queens. The largest, 20 cm (8 in) in diameter and weighing 980 g (34.5 oz), belonged to Atalia, the wife of Sargon.

below left

Ornate gold ewer from Tomb III, Coffin 2. It is 13 cm (5 in) high and weighs 263 g (9.3 oz).

below right

One of a number of decorative centre-pieces from gold diadems; this one weighs 33.4 g (1.2 oz).

opposite

A gold crown found lying on a child's head in Tomb III, Coffin 2, ornamented with clusters of lapis lazuli grapes which hang inside the crown. It is 24 cm (9.5 in) in diameter and weighs over 1 kg (2.2 lb).

beads, making this one of the most remarkable tombs ever found in the Near East. Among the objects were a gold crown, a gold mesh diadem with tasselled gold fringe and tiger-eye rosettes, 79 gold earrings, 6 gold necklaces, 30 finger rings, 14 gold armlets, 15 gold vessels, 4 massive gold anklets, one pair weighing over 1.5 kg (3 lb) each, a gold chain and perhaps 90 separate necklaces of semiprecious stones. A mass of badly decayed but clearly very fine, delicately embroidered linen was also present. Among the bones lay some 700 tiny gold rosettes, stars, triangles etc, which had obviously been sown on to these linen garments, within which were also found large numbers of gold and carnelian beads, presumably representing further clothing ornament.

The two bodies lay one above the other and above both was one of the most splendid objects: a copper/bronze mirror with a beautiful palmette handle made of ivory, gold, carnelian and other semiprecious stones. On the chest of the upper body was a gold bowl, in which were 11 tiny gold flasks and a larger flask on a gold chain. The bowl bore an inscription identifying it as property of 'Atalia, queen of Sargon, king of Assyria' (721–705 BC). The identification of the bodies is further complicated, however, by the presence in the sarcophagus of a gold bowl and an electron cosmetics container bearing yet another royal name, 'Banitu, queen of Shalmaneser V' (726–722 BC), though the mirror-lid of the same container bore the name of Atalia.

Herewith a mystery: two bodies, despite the curse, and inscriptions of three Assyrian queens – a mystery compounded by the fact that the two queens in Yaba's sarcophagus had died at approximately the same age (30–35), and that the upper body had not only been buried a number of years after the first but had also been exposed for several hours to a temperature of 150–250° C (302–482° F), perhaps an attempt at preservation. The second burial had been hasty, perhaps even surreptitious. The simplest solution is that the lower body is Yaba, whose tomb it was according to the inscription, and that the second was that of Sargon's wife, Atalia, perhaps a daughter of Yaba, who had acquired valuables belonging to her predecessor, Banitu. The fact that this upper body had been rather hurriedly buried and may have been transported some distance may be related to the death of her husband, Sargon, who was killed in battle far from home and whose body was never recovered, a serious matter in Assyria, where a king's body required proper burial in the ancient capital, Assur. Indeed, both king and queen would seem to have been cursed by the circumstances of their deaths.

The third tomb

Yet another tomb was found in August 1989, in a room just south of Tomb II. The tomb chamber was virtually empty except for the sarcophagus, the lid of which bore an inscription of the wife of Assurnasirpal II, the king who rebuilt Nimrud and Assyrian power in the 9th century BC. Although the tomb

chamber had clearly been robbed, the antechamber, separated by a double stone door, was found to contain yet another spectacular collection of royal treasure, surpassing that even of Tomb II. Here three bronze coffins contained the reburied bones of at least 13 individuals. In one coffin was the greatest treasure yet recovered, some 450 separate items, with the gold and silver alone weighing 23 kg (50 lb). Among the gold items were a crown of extraordinarily delicate workmanship and a gold ewer, as well as gold plates and jewelry. Traces of clothing included small, beautifully made tassels like those in Tomb II. Unique inlaid glass and frit vessels were also recovered.

Surprisingly, among the inscribed objects were a seal and a gold bowl belonging to eunuch courtiers – perhaps of royal lineage, they would have been the only other men allowed in the women's quarters. The bowl belonged to a famous eunuch who had served as commander-in-chief under at least three early 8th-century Assyrian kings, and whose corpse may have been the powerfully built male among the five adults in Coffin 3.

Inscribed objects in this treasure hoard suggest a date later than Assurnasirpal's reign, and it would seem that his wife's tomb had been robbed and then, at a later time, though earlier than Tomb II, both bodies and grave goods had been hastily reburied, perhaps a reflection of power struggles.

In terms of sheer spectacle there has been no comparable discovery in Mesopotamian archaeology since the 'royal tombs' at Ur found by Leonard Woolley over 80 years ago. Many of the Nimrud objects are without parallel, and it is not only the gold and the sheer excitement of the discoveries themselves, but the fact that our knowledge of contemporary craft skills has been increased to an extraordinary degree that makes the discovery of the Nimrud tombs such a unique event.

The Great Ryzhanovka Barrow:
An Intact Burial of a Scythian Nobleman

Sergey Skory and Jan Chochorowski

Almost all the great tombs of the Scythians – nomads who roamed the Steppes of Ukraine and southeastern Europe in the 1st millennium BC – were robbed, either in antiquity or later. Only a very few avoided this fate and survived undamaged. One of them is the Great Ryzhanovka Barrow, on the right bank of the Dnepr River, near Ryzhanovka village in Ukraine, which we excavated in the late 1990s, discovering the intact burial of a Scythian nobleman.

Tombs of the Scythian elite, covered by massive kurgans or burial mounds, are outstanding due to their magnitude and profusion of grave goods; the so-called royal tombs especially capture the imagination. Some of these high-status burials – for example Alexandropol, Chertomlyk or Oguz, up to 20 m (66 ft) high and with a diameter of more than 100 m (328 ft) – represent true Steppe 'pyramids'. Buried in them, the noble dead were accompanied by human and horse offerings. The ancient Greek historian Herodotus colourfully narrates the

bloody ceremony of the entombing of Scythian kings. Greek wares – evidence of close contacts between Scythians and the Hellenic colonies of the northern Black Sea area – are quite frequent among the various, and often highly valuable, objects recovered in such graves.

The Great Ryzhanovka Barrow lies approximately 150 km (93 miles) to the south of Kiev, almost on the border with the Steppe, and measures 7.56 m (25 ft) high with a diameter of 30 m (98 ft). The first excavations were conducted here by

Polish and Russian scholars in the 19th century, during which the intact Side Grave was found, but it was not until 1995–98 that we undertook a complete investigation of the burial mound, at the head of an international expedition. We had the amazing good fortune to reveal the still intact Central Grave, containing the remains of a high-status Scythian noble and his grave goods.

The Central Grave consisted of a wide entrance shaft and underground chamber measuring 30 sq. m (323 sq. ft). On the floor of the entrance shaft we found the remains of an armed guard, apparently sacrificed, as well as a horse with harness. The main chamber, 2 m (6.5 ft) high, was designed as an imitation of a dwelling room. Its floor was covered by mats made of reeds, while the walls and ceiling were draped with cloth. In the centre was a clay partition – probably representing a hearth. The remains of the noble Scythian man (45–50 years old, 180 cm/almost 6ft tall) were discovered laid on a wooden platform, originally partitioned from the main space of the chamber by a cloth screen. The dead man was accompanied by a gold neck ring, a known symbol of power. He also had a full set of weaponry including a sword with a gold handle. Wooden and bronze Scythian vessels, as well as ceramic, bronze and silver wares of Greek provenance were discovered next to him. Especially impressive is a beautiful silver vessel with images in the Scythian animal style.

Next to the foot of the dead man we recovered 140 gold ornaments from a woman's headdress, probably symbolizing the burial of his wife. The unusually large dimensions of the Central Grave, along with the rich grave goods, lead us to think that this was the burial of a Scythian 'nomarch' or governor of one of the domains (nomas) of Scythia. Based on the style of the grave goods, together with radiocarbon dating, we can say that the burials date to around 270–260 BC.

We also re-located the Side Grave, which had contained the remains of a female, of small stature and aged around 20 years old, possibly the daughter of the noble Scythian man. Her headdress and clothes were adorned by gold appliqués and she was wearing gold jewelry – her grave goods amounted to more than 460 valuable metal artifacts. Of particular note were three rings set with gold coins from a Greek colony, one depicting the head of a Satyr wearing an ivy wreath, which we discovered in 1995. These rings and the headdress ornaments, which depicted dancing maenads, suggest that the woman had some special, perhaps ritual status.

The importance of the Great Ryzhanovka Barrow cannot be overestimated. It represents a unique example of an intact and very well-preserved aristocrat's tomb dating to the final stage of the history of the Scythians, providing us with new insights into their burial customs and religious beliefs.

The Valley of the Golden Mummies, Egypt

Zahi Hawass

Considered by scholars to be the 'Tutankhamun' of Graeco-Roman Egypt, the Valley of the Golden Mummies can certainly be counted among the most important recent finds in archaeology. One day in 1996, a donkey ridden by a guard at the Temple of Alexander in the Bahariya Oasis, 375 km (233 miles) southwest of Cairo, stumbled into a hole. When the guard looked into the hole, he saw the glint of gold. It was immediately obvious that this was a site of great significance, and so I rushed in my team from Giza and we began the excavation at the site.

opposite
Over 250 mummies have been discovered so far in the Valley of the Golden Mummies. Many, like this female mummy, were covered with painted and gilded cartonnage.

right
The tombs in the Valley come in a number of different styles. Most are family tombs, such as this one. The mummies were placed in rock-cut niches around the walls. The rectangular pedestal here may have been meant for the head of the family.

On the first day at Bahariya, I made a survey of the cemetery and discovered that it is vast – around 6 km (3.7 miles) square. Based on this initial survey, I estimated that the Valley contained about 10,000 mummies, most likely many covered in gold. When we opened the first tomb, the brilliance of gold shone in the sunlight among the piles of desert sand. The ancient people of Bahariya were able to obtain this gold from the mines of Nubia because of the wine they produced and sold all over Egypt.

The tombs in the Valley of the Golden Mummies date to the period of Roman rule in Egypt and differ in their plans and the types of burial they contain. There are multi-chambered tombs, with sections for the burial of different generations of one family; there are also underground tombs cut into the sandstone, supported by pillars carved from the rock. Some mummies are simply placed in niches in the bedrock, while others are interred in anthropoid coffins made of pottery. The jackal-god Anubis, painted on the wall, guards the entrance of one tomb.

The decoration of each mummy is distinctive, primarily because it represents an individual, though the mummies can be divided into two main types: those decorated with gold applied in layers over the face and chest and those without gold. However, there are also mummies with gold on their faces only, while their chests are encased in cartonnage – layers of plastered linen – decorated with scenes that appear in other cases in gold. These painted scenes depict gods and goddesses of ancient Egypt, including Anubis, Thoth and the four sons of Horus. Royal

symbols once used exclusively by the pharaoh, such as a cobra on the forehead and the falcon god Horus, are now assimilated by the upper class people of Bahariya. The second type of mummy, without gold, is unique in its own way, being entirely wrapped in linen. One mummy of a woman, with her son buried above her, was found with a wooden panel at her feet painted with a Roman-style scene set inside an Egyptian temple showing a woman dressed for the journey to the other world.

The lives of the people buried in the Valley of the Golden Mummies can be understood from the objects buried with them, including wine jars, coins and amulets, and above all by studying their mummies. X-rays were conducted on 15 mummies, which showed that the average age at death was 35 to 40, although the people seemed healthy. This made us wonder what caused their early deaths. It was then discovered that the water in Bahariya contains iron, which affects the bones.

The tombs of the family of the governor of Bahariya
While I was working in the Valley of the Golden Mummies, I also became aware of several tombs hidden around 6–7.6 m (20–25 ft) underneath houses in the town of El Bawiti. After studying the inscriptions on a large limestone sarcophagus in one tomb, I realized that they had previously been excavated by Ahmed Fakhry. I was fortunate, however, to discover a new tomb, although its first chamber did not provide any conclusive name. The burial chamber was closed by a door in the shape of

opposite above, left and right
The sarcophagus of the governor of Baharia, Djedkhonsuefankh, was decorated with an image of Osiris, god of the underworld, and an inscription giving the governor's name and titles. His tomb lies not in the Valley of the Golden Mummies, but in a maze of underground chambers beneath the modern houses of nearby El Bawiti.

opposite below
The tombs in the Valley of the Golden Mummies were usually undecorated. Here, Dr Hawass examines the mummies of various family members laid side by side within niches in a burial chamber.

right
The mummies in the Valley also wore plaster masks. Their features, including the wide-open eyes and lips, were often painted in black and red.

below
This beautifully painted wooden foot panel from a coffin found in the Valley of the Golden Mummies shows the deceased emerging from the gates of the underworld, protected by winged sun discs and snakes.

a temple's pylon-gate, with a depiction of a mummy above and an *ankh* (life) sign. Inside, the lid of the sarcophagus was inscribed with the name of the tomb owner, Djedkhonsuefankh, and his titles, priest of Isis and Osiris and mayor of Baharia. He was the governor of Baharia during the reign of King Wahibre (664–610 BC), and the genealogy of his family, who ruled Baharia in the 26th Dynasty, is written in the temple of Ain El-Muftella. A second room was discovered, decorated with scenes from the Book of the Dead; they were probably drawn from memory since they were not accurately copied and contain numerous mistakes. We found the tomb of the governor's father, Badi Isis, containing a sarcophagus and *shabtis*, small figurines that act as servants for the deceased in the afterlife. And the tomb of the governor's wife was also located, north of her husband's, consisting of two rooms: one for the canopic jars and the other for the sarcophagus. Inside the sarcophagus were the remains of a mummy covered with 104 pieces of gold, one with the name of King Wahibre. There were also 200 *shabtis* with the lady's name, Naesa.

In 2005, we discovered a second shaft, its entrance sealed with mud, containing Roman pottery. At the end of this shaft was a large inscribed sarcophagus with the name of the tomb owner, Badi Her-ib, the brother of the governor of Baharia and a priest, although his name is not written in the family tree. Many sealed sarcophagi were excavated in this passage, inside which were intact mummies, including a woman with a smaller sarcophagus beside her containing a baby, and a priest.

Currently, we are excavating more houses to uncover the remaining tombs of this family. In particular, we hope to find the tomb of Shebenkhonsu, another important figure who ruled Baharia in the 26th Dynasty.

Bodies from the Bog:
New Insights into Life and Death in Pagan Celtic Ireland

Eamonn P. Kelly

Bog bodies are rare survivals of human remains from earlier times – the properties of bogs are such that, occasionally, bodies are preserved to an exceptional degree, with hair, skin, hands, internal organs and other soft tissue intact. Uncovered by accident in Ireland in 2003, two such discoveries have provided important new insights into pagan Celtic times.

left and below left
So well preserved were Oldcroghan Man's hands that it was possible to take his fingerprints. The carefully manicured fingernails and uncalloused hands indicate that he was a person of high social standing.

below
Despite mutilation, the body of Oldcroghan Man continues to convey the impression of a powerfully built young man in the prime of life. On his left arm he wore an armlet made from plaited leather, with decorated bronze clasps bearing inscribed La Tène designs.

At a peat extraction works in Ballivor, Co. Meath, workers discovered the preserved body of a young man in a peat-screening machine. Investigation indicated that he had lain originally in a deep bog at Clonycavan on the county border between Meath and Westmeath. Although damaged from the waist down due to the action of a peat-harvesting machine, the man's internal organs were partially preserved and his head was intact, with a clearly distinguishable face and a very distinctive hairstyle. The hair on the back of his head was cut short while the rest of it, about 30 cm (1 ft) long, was gathered into a bundle on the top of his head. Clonycavan Man was of slight build and diminutive stature, estimated at about 157 cm (5 ft 2 in) tall.

By contrast, a second body found shortly afterwards at Oldcroghan, Co. Offaly, was a veritable giant, estimated at about 190 cm (6 ft 3 in) tall, and powerfully built. Uncovered during the digging of a bog drain along the parish boundary, the remains consist only of a severed torso that had been decapitated. However, the surviving part of the body was in remarkable condition, with superbly preserved hands and intact internal organs. On the man's upper left arm was a plaited leather armband with metal mounts bearing Celtic ornament. Both bodies were radiocarbon dated to the Early Iron Age, between 400 BC and 200 BC.

A large team of international specialists assisted in analyzing and interpreting the remains of the two men, yielding a wealth

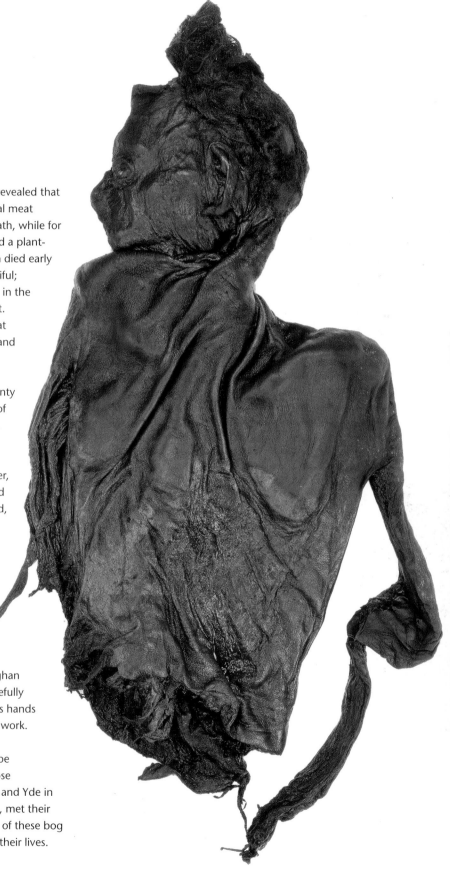

of information about their lives and deaths. It was revealed that Oldcroghan Man had eaten a diet with a substantial meat component during the four months prior to his death, while for four months prior to his death Clonycavan Man had a plant-based diet. This may suggest that Oldcroghan Man died early in the year, before plant-based foods became plentiful; Clonycavan Man on the other hand may have died in the autumn, before the onset of a meat-rich winter diet. Analysis of the contents of his stomach revealed that Oldcroghan Man had eaten a final meal of cereals and buttermilk.

The two men had been ritually killed and may represent fertility offerings associated with sovereignty rites. Clonycavan Man met his death from a series of blows to his head and chest, probably from an axe. He also suffered a 40-cm (16-in) long cut to his abdomen, suggesting disembowelment. A stab wound to his chest killed Oldcroghan Man; however, a defence-wound on one arm indicates that he tried to fend off the fatal assault. He was then decapitated, had his nipples cut and his thorax severed from his abdomen. Withies tied through cuts made in the upper arms may have been used to fasten down the body to the bottom of a bog pool.

The extraordinary hairstyle of Clonycavan man was held in place by a sort of hair gel made from resin imported from France or Spain. This suggests that he was a person of high status who commanded the resources necessary to obtain exotic foreign imports. Oldcroghan Man was also a person of high social rank, with carefully manicured fingernails and an absence of wear to his hands indicating that he did not engage in heavy manual work.

These Irish bog bodies form part of a broader, northwestern European cultural tradition and may be compared with earlier well-known finds such as those from Tollund in Denmark, Lindow Moss in England and Yde in Holland. It is still not certain why men, and women, met their deaths in this way, but the remarkable preservation of these bog bodies means that we can learn a great deal about their lives.

Warriors, Musicians and Acrobats
at the Tomb of the First Emperor of China

Zhang Yinglan

A short description by Sima Qian in his Records of the Historian (Shi Ji) is almost all the information we have about the mysterious tomb of the First Emperor of China, Qin Shihuangdi, as it has never been excavated. Writing some 100 years after the emperor's death in 210 BC, Sima Qian mentions treasures and rarities, as well as a map of the sky on the ceiling with pearls representing stars and one of the earth on the floor, with rivers and oceans flowing with mercury. But Sima Qian did not describe other elements of the vast mausoleum, which remained completely secret for over 2,000 years, until archaeologists recently began to uncover them.

First to be investigated, after their accidental discovery in 1974, were the thousands of terracotta warriors and horses in three burial pits 1.5 km (1 mile) east of the tomb mound. This was one of the most exciting archaeological discoveries of the 20th century, and, more importantly, it was the beginning of modern archaeological research at the site. The unearthing of the terracotta army inspired archaeologists to explore the area around the tomb using survey and excavation to see if anything else lay hidden, buried deep in the earth. As a result of this work, new discoveries made in recent years equal the terracotta army, both in scale and importance.

In 1998, some 200 m (650 ft) southeast of tomb mound, archaeologists found a burial pit measuring 13,000 sq. m (140,000 sq.ft), almost as big as the Terracotta Army Pit 1. In just 200 sq. m (2,150 sq. ft) of experimental excavation, they unearthed hundreds of pieces of armour, as well as helmets, all made of stone. The armour and helmets were made up of numerous individual limestone flakes, each with a different shape, rectangular, square, trapezoid or round, according to their position. Tiny holes in the flakes allowed them to be strung together using copper wire. These are life-size replicas of actual armour and helmets: one restored suit of armour consists of 612 stone flakes, and measures 1.25 m (4 ft) tall and weighs 18 kg (40 lb); and a stone helmet was made up of 74 stone flakes and weighs 3.1 kg (7 lb). This is the first time helmets and horse

above right
It is estimated that about 6,000 terracotta warriors and horses are buried in Terracotta Army Pit 1, seen here.

right
Emperor Qin Shihuangdi's mausoleum: the tomb, which took 38 years to build, is situated at the northern foot of Mount Li, 35 km (22 miles) east of modern Xi'an city. About 180 burial pits and 500 associated tombs have so far been found within an area of 56.25 sq. km (22 sq. miles).

opposite
One of the sets of restored stone armour: it consists of 612 stone flakes, each one connected by thin copper wires. Measuring 1.25 m (4 ft) tall and weighing 18 kg (40 lb), it was made purely for burial, not for actual fighting.

armour dating to the Qin dynasty have ever been found, even though they were made for funerary purposes rather than practical use in battle. Archaeologists believe that this pit is perhaps an underground model of an armaments storeroom of the Qin dynasty.

In 1999, Chinese archaeologists found another pit, 40 m (130 ft) south of that containing the armour. In an excavation area of only 9 sq. m (97 sq. ft) they unearthed 11 pottery figures and a large bronze tripod cauldron. Around life-size, the figures were clothed only in a short skirt or kilt. Exquisitely made and varying in build – some are tall and strong, while others are short and slim – the figures are shown in different postures. One extends a finger as if spinning a plate, another may have held a weight (perhaps a bronze tripod, according to Chinese tradition). These pottery figures were identified by the archaeologists as acrobatic performers of the Qin dynasty, created to amuse the emperor's spirit in his afterlife. Even more exciting, these are the earliest life-size statues found in China that are shown with realistic bodies, representing a major artistic

breakthrough in a culture whose art traditionally never emphasized the anatomy of the human body.

Then, in 2001, yet another burial pit was found in the environs of the mausoleum. In two years of excavation, archaeologists have uncovered the entire pit, unearthing 46 bronze birds, including cranes, swans and geese. All are life-size and painted to imitate real birds. Modelled in lifelike postures – some lower their heads to search for food while others turn to look at them – they were positioned on a platform 50 cm (20 in) high along a water channel as if searching for food by the river in the imperial garden of Emperor Qin Shihuangdi. One fascinating detail was revealed when archaeologists cleaned a bronze crane and found a small bronze worm in its mouth.

In another part of the pit, archaeologists found 15 life-sized pottery figures which can be divided into two types according to their posture – kneeling and sitting. The kneeling figures raise their right arm, as if holding a short stick to beat something with, while the sitting figures extend their arms forwards, grasping something in their hands. Unfortunately the objects

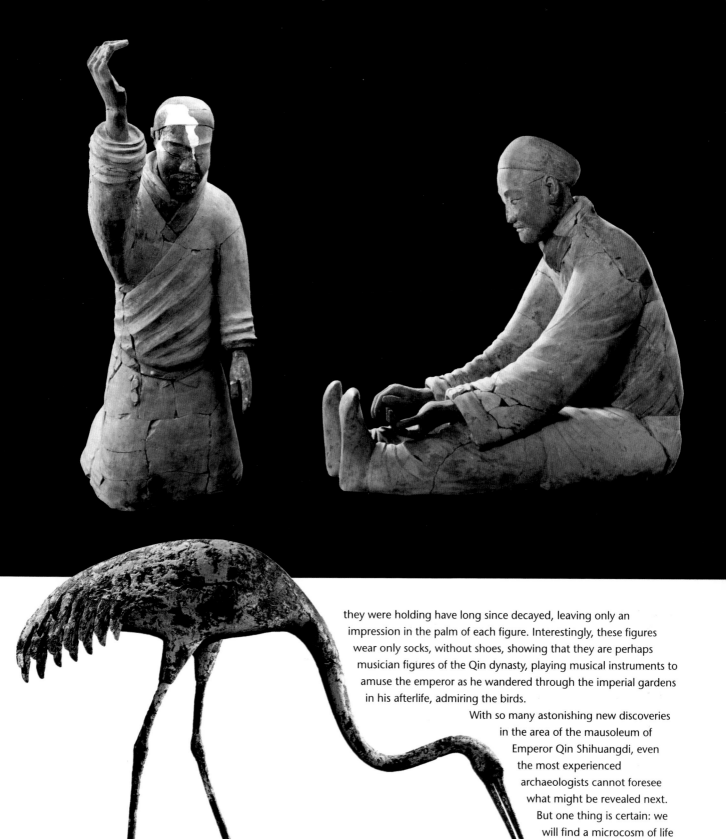

they were holding have long since decayed, leaving only an impression in the palm of each figure. Interestingly, these figures wear only socks, without shoes, showing that they are perhaps musician figures of the Qin dynasty, playing musical instruments to amuse the emperor as he wandered through the imperial gardens in his afterlife, admiring the birds.

With so many astonishing new discoveries in the area of the mausoleum of Emperor Qin Shihuangdi, even the most experienced archaeologists cannot foresee what might be revealed next. But one thing is certain: we will find a microcosm of life in the Qin dynasty in the emperor's underground palace. And that will be a constant inspiration for future generations of archaeologists.

The Spitalfields Lady:
The Finest Roman Grave Ever Found in London

Christopher Thomas

Roman law forbade the burial of the dead within a city's walls, so areas alongside the roads leading out of cities were commonly lined with graves. Spitalfields, just northeast of the historic Roman and medieval City of London and close to Roman Ermine Street, has been known to be the site of a Roman cemetery since at least the end of the 16th century. Even so, during archaeological work there we were still surprised to find the finest Roman grave ever excavated in London.

Since 1991, the Museum of London Archaeology Service has carried out a major series of excavations in advance of redevelopment of the site of the former Spitalfields Market, covering an area of approximately 4 ha (10 acres). These investigations have focused not only on the Roman cemetery, but also on a medieval hospital and the 16th- to 19th-century suburb. The main phase of work lasted from October 1998 to November 1999 and in total formed London's largest single archaeological investigation.

During the early part of 1999 a large section of the Roman cemetery was uncovered in an area where the later medieval cemetery had not disturbed it. The graves were well laid out and many dated to the late Roman period – the 3rd and 4th centuries AD. At the southern end of the excavation area, the most extraordinary discovery was made. Two spectacular graves were found: a timber-lined grave containing the burial of a child, some magnificent glass vessels and fragments of a robbed-out stone sarcophagus, and next to it a complete stone sarcophagus.

This was the first stone sarcophagus to be found in London since the early 1970s and caused a great deal of excitement: the press and public descended on the site once news got out.

Archaeologist Kieron Heard and a team from the Museum of London carefully excavated the grave, and at the foot of the sarcophagus he found a long glass phial. Although it is unique in form, its design suggests a date of the late 4th century AD. Next to it lay three other artifacts made from jet: a long rod, a hairpin and a small cosmetics jar.

When we removed the stone lid of the sarcophagus, we found that inside it was a lead coffin. Two lead coffins were found in the east London cemetery in the 1980s, but the last stone sarcophagus with a lead coffin was found in London in the 1870s and none had been excavated by archaeologists.

Since preservation within the coffin might prove to be exceptional, we decided to lift the sarcophagus and transfer it to the Museum of London where it could be excavated more carefully. The lead coffin lid was then removed in the full glare

left
Archaeologist Kieron Heard begins excavating the large stone sarcophagus on site. The glass phial shown opposite was found at the foot of the sarcophagus, on the right of this picture.

of publicity and inside we found the well-preserved bones of a woman who had died in her late 20s. As we carefully excavated the coffin, we found that her head had been laid on a pillow made of bay leaves, probably contained within a woollen pillow case.

Fragments of gold and silk threads found on the body are very rare examples of Roman clothing in Britain. The weave of the silk indicates that it was made in the Near East and there are indications that the woman may have been buried in a silk garment with gold edging. Finally, as the space between the lead and stone coffins was excavated, conservator Liz Barham discovered a complete glass phial, which perhaps once contained the oils that were used during the burial ritual before the coffin lids were put in place.

Another surprise came when DNA analysis of the woman's teeth was compared to modern populations and the closest match was found to be with someone from the Basque region of Spain. Analysis of the oxygen isotopes in her teeth, produced from drinking water, also suggested that she was brought up in southern Europe. The condition of both teeth and bones showed that the woman had enjoyed a good diet during her life, and there was no evidence for cause of death.

During the excavation of the coffin, tens of thousands of visitors queued to see the remarkable remains as they were being revealed in the Museum of London. These visitors had a fascinating insight into the life and death of this unnamed, wealthy woman, and had the chance to see the uncovering of one of the most remarkable archaeological finds from London.

right above
Museum of London conservators cleaning the delicate scallop-shell pattern of the lead coffin.

above
The late 4th-century AD glass phial found at the foot of the sarcophagus. The phial is unique, but its trail decoration is of a Frankish style.

right below
The skeleton of the young woman buried in the lead coffin: the suits and masks were worn to prevent contamination of the woman's DNA and to protect staff from lead dust.

Moche Tombs at Dos Cabezas, Peru

Christopher B. Donnan

Moche civilization flourished on the north coast of Peru between AD 200 and 800, and although the Moche had no writing system, they left a vivid artistic record of their beliefs and activities in the form of beautifully modelled and painted ceramic vessels, elaborately woven textiles, colourful wall murals and extraordinary objects of gold, silver and copper. The site of Dos Cabezas, which I and my team have been excavating since 1994, revealed three remarkably rich Moche tombs – each containing the remains of an unusually tall man accompanied by a young female and a wealth of offerings. Outside each tomb was a small compartment containing a miniature male figure of sheet copper and additional associated objects, a feature never seen before.

opposite
The gold and copper burial mask that was found over the face of the individual buried in Tomb 2.

We found the three tombs, dating to approximately AD 550, in 1997–99, high up in an enormous mud-brick pyramid; they were in a line along a north–south axis. Inside each, an adult male was lying on his back, fully extended, his head to the south. All three were wrapped in multiple layers of textiles forming a large funerary bundle. Although most of the textiles had decomposed to a powdery residue, they originally enfolded numerous metal objects, including gold and silver jewelry, gilded copper headdresses, war clubs and shields. There were also copper spear-points, chisels and ceremonial knives. The individuals were buried wearing exquisite gold and silver nose ornaments, quartz crystal necklaces and beaded pectorals. One had a gold and copper burial mask over his face. Surrounding the funerary bundles were fine Moche ceramic vessels.

The adjacent compartments were located at either the north or south end of the tomb chambers. On the floor of each compartment was a copper figure that had been wrapped in textiles to create a miniature mummy bundle. They too were lying on their backs with their heads to the south – precisely the same position as the principal individuals in the adjacent tombs.

The quantity and quality of objects found in the full-size burial chambers closely mimicked the selection of objects in the adjacent miniature chambers. For example, Tomb 2 had more objects in its burial chamber than either of the other two tombs, and Compartment 2 also had more objects than either of its equivalents. Furthermore, the mummy bundle of the copper figure in Compartment 2 contained small shields, spear throwers and spears, war clubs, nose ornaments and even a tiny burial mask – miniature versions of the full-size objects that were in the mummy bundle in Tomb 2. This indicates that each of the small compartments was meant to be a miniature version of its adjacent tomb, and the copper figures in the compartments were miniatures of the principal individuals in the tombs.

top
The north side of the pyramid of Dos Cabezas. The tombs were located on its southwest corner, approximately 20 m (66 ft) above the surrounding plain.

above
The excavation of Tomb 3, showing the relationship between the individual in the tomb and the copper figure in the adjacent compartment.

Restoring the balance

To date, more than 500 Moche burials have been excavated archaeologically, yet these at Dos Cabezas are the only ones that have small compartments adjacent to them. Why were they created? One explanation was suggested by the fact that the main occupant of each tomb was a man of unusually tall stature. All Moche males that had been excavated before ranged in height from 1.48 to 1.69 m (4 ft 9 in to 5 ft 6 in), with an average height of 1.58 m (5 ft 2 in). All three men in these tombs were taller. They ranged from approximately 1.75 to 1.79 m (5 ft 7 in to 5 ft 9 in), and are among the tallest individuals ever recorded from Pre-Columbian Peru. Perhaps there was a connection between the height of the men in the tombs and the copper figures that represented them in the adjacent compartments.

In the past four decades of working with Moche art and archaeology, I have become convinced that two basic tenets of the Moche worldview were duality and balance. The Moche frequently juxtaposed gold and silver, light and dark, male and female, young and old, life and death, etc. They appear to have appreciated the balance, or complementarity, of opposites, and to have attempted to maintain a balance between two extremes.

While the three unusually tall men found in the tombs at Dos Cabezas were alive, they probably seemed unnatural, and thus out of balance. When they died, the local people may have attempted to restore the balance by burying them in their tombs, and at the same time burying miniature versions of them in the adjacent small compartments.

Admittedly, suggesting that this was the motivation for creating the small chambers with their copper figures is speculative, and based on a very limited sample. As more archaeological excavations are conducted on the north coast of Peru, it will be interesting to see if small copper figures continue to be found associated with burials of individuals of unusually tall stature.

Meanwhile, the tombs from Dos Cabezas provide a wealth of new information about the nature of Moche funerary practice, and clearly demonstrate the extraordinary artistic and technological sophistication that characterized Moche ceramics and metalworking at the time they were created. They also pose intriguing new questions about the Moche, who developed one of the most remarkable civilizations of the ancient world.

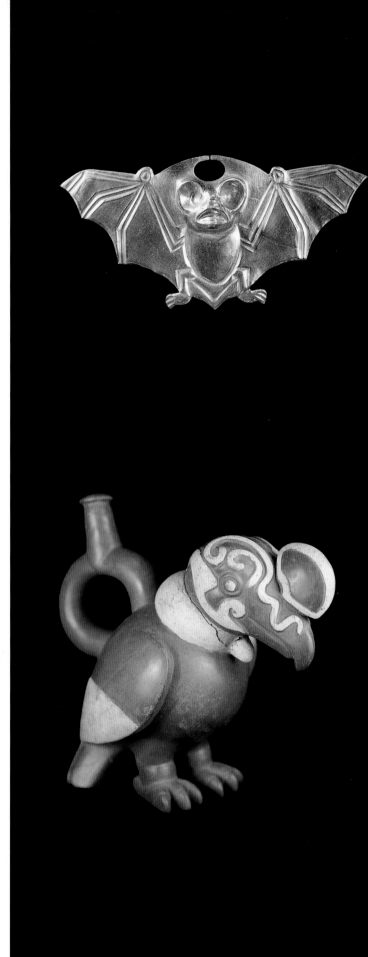

right
Gold and silver nose ornaments (top row) and fine ceramic vessels (lower row) excavated from the three Dos Cabezas tombs (not to scale).

Power and Prestige:
Middle Sicán Elite Tombs of North Coastal Peru

Izumi Shimada

Long before the Inca empire came to dominate western South America, the Middle Sicán culture (AD 900–1100) flourished on the northern coast of Peru. One of its legacies was sophisticated metallurgy, including copper- and gold-alloy objects. Modern looters have plundered thousands of Sicán tombs searching for these sumptuous artifacts and many ancient Peruvian gold objects displayed today in museums around the world came from such tombs, but knowledge of their origins and context have been lost. I was therefore very fortunate to find two largely intact tombs of the Sicán elite.

I began working at the Middle Sicán capital of Sicán in the mid-La Leche river valley (today the Pomac National Historical and Ecological Sanctuary) in 1978, when I founded the Sicán Archaeological Project. It was already widely known as a mecca of grave looting and in my survey that year I documented irreparable damage to numerous tombs and nearby architecture, including the Huaca Loro pyramidal mound. Built of adobe bricks this measures *c.* 100 m (328 ft) to a side and 25 m (82 ft) high.

By 1990, with a good understanding of Sicán chronology, economy, settlement pattern and technology, I began a long-term study of Sicán social organization and religion, based on a comprehensive analysis of tomb construction and contents, as well as associated rituals. Knowledge gained from my earlier examination of looted graves now guided the excavation of burials of individuals who represented a wide range of the social spectrum. A major part of this study was the excavation of two largely intact elite tombs at Huaca Loro.

The East Tomb

Our six-month excavation of the East Tomb represented the first scientifically documented Sicán elite tomb. It proved to be a veritable treasure trove in many ways – because of the numerous sumptuous items it contained, the wealth of information and insights into the Sicán culture it afforded us, and the historical awareness and pride it inspired in the local residents.

At the bottom of the 10-m (33-ft) vertical shaft, we found an intact roofed burial chamber, 3 m (10 ft) square, with seven sealed niches. Inside were the skeletons of five individuals and around 1.2 tons of grave goods, two thirds of which by weight were objects of bronze, *tumbaga* (an alloy of gold, silver and copper) and gold. The entire contents were organized around

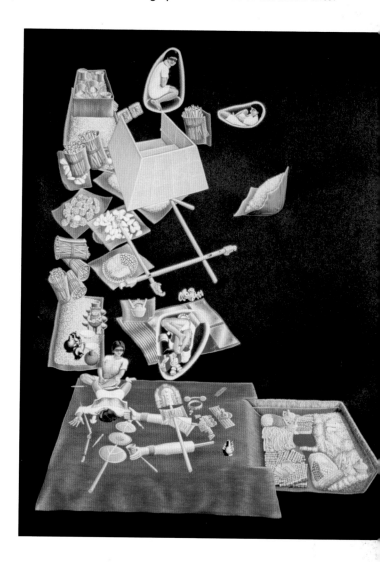

above
An 'exploded' view of the contents of the East Tomb, with grave goods arranged around and above the inverted, bundled body of the principal male at the centre. Brownish objects on the left side are bundles of bronze implements while the piles partly wrapped in mats are tumbaga *scraps.*

opposite
Reconstructed gold mask of the principal person in the East Tomb. It is made of several elements: the mask, with eyes of emerald and amber beads; forehead ornament with a modelled bat head; a cylindrical crown (hidden); and a large head ornament. The entire piece is over 100 cm (39 in) high.

the centrally placed skeleton of a male, 40–50 years old. His body appears first to have been mummified and was then covered with bright red cinnabar paint and dressed in full regalia that included pectorals made with amber, amethyst and other semiprecious stones, a gold *tumi* ceremonial knife, hinged back flap, a pair of gold ear spools (9.2 cm/3.6 in diameter) and a gold mask. His head had been detached from his body and rotated right side up and placed in front of the inverted body looking west. Next to the skeleton were a pair of gold gloves and one of shin covers, together with still more personal ornaments and symbols of status and power. In addition, a nearby chest contained at least 24 superimposed layers of over 60 large ornaments and ritual paraphernalia.

On the floor close by was an adult female skeleton in a prone position, with tightly flexed legs wide open. Another woman sat in front of her, with her hands placed next to the first woman's crotch. I believe the positions of the women and the male were carefully choreographed to symbolize the latter's rebirth.

Although the quantity and quality of gold objects are themselves remarkable, items that are not as sumptuous are far more informative about the power and privileges enjoyed by the Sicán nobility. The preparation of 15 bundles of unfinished cast bronze implements, weighing nearly 200 kg (440 lb), represents the investment of thousands of man-hours in smelting – and without the benefits of bellows and coal. Some 75 kg (165 lb) of perforated semiprecious stone beads and around 500 kg (1,100 lb) of hand-hammered, uniformly thin *tumbaga* sheet scraps tell the same story. Similarly, 179 spondylus and 141 conus shells, imported from the tropical seas of Ecuador or even further north, not only represent the largest caches of

left
This chest from the East Tomb contained numerous rattles, crowns and head bands, and other ornaments and ritual objects that were masterfully formed of gold or tumbaga sheets.

above
The principal personage of the East Tomb under excavation, at the bottom of the 10-m (33-ft) deep shaft. His skull, with a cinnabar-painted gold mask (p. 90), is visible in the foreground.

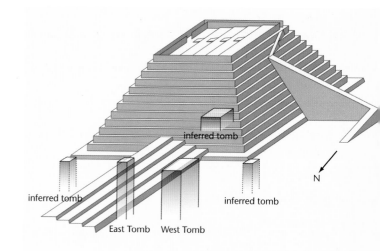

these valuable ritual items ever recorded in the Andes, but also indicate an extensive trade network. Emeralds and amber imported from Colombia also attest to the importance and extent of trade. We believe bronze and produce from large-scale irrigation agriculture were used in exchange.

The West Tomb

The West Tomb, just 25 m (82 ft) west of the first, provided complementary information regarding Sicán social organization and religion. This tomb had a two-tier, 'tomb inside tomb', construction. The principal personage buried there, a man 30–40 years of age, was placed in the central chamber, the same size as that in the East Tomb, surrounded by hundreds of grave goods and flanked by two women. In the large antechamber above, 20 women, mostly 18–22 years of age, were divided equally along the north and south sides of the central chamber.

Analysis of inherited dental traits, health status, ancient DNA and ceramic styles all indicate that this division reflected significant biological, ethnic, lifestyle and perhaps status differences. The women on the south side included two groups of kin, and as a group were biologically close to each other and to the principal personage, and quite healthy. They may have practised endogamy – the custom of marrying within one's community. The north group, in contrast, was biologically quite heterogeneous and not as healthy. I suspect that these women represented various ethnic groups subjugated by the Middle Sicán state. Thus, the tomb organization represents the tremendous social gulf between the principal personage and the two groups of women, as well as the integration of various populations he may have had authority over. Dental analysis also indicates that the principal men of the East and West tombs were closely related, perhaps an uncle (East) and nephew (West).

Ground-penetrating radar surveys and excavations indicate the presence of an extensive elite cemetery around a central tomb under Huaca Loro, including at least three unexcavated shaft tombs at the three undisturbed corners of the huaca. Atop the mound was a temple with polychrome murals depicting images of the principal Sicán deity. These may symbolize the deceased leaders who were buried in the tombs below and their transformation from the living rulers to venerated ancestors. Thus, the mound can be seen as an imposing symbol of the power and lasting legacy of a Middle Sicán ruling lineage.

The Red Queen
and Other New Maya Tombs

George Stuart

Royal tombs and their real or imagined associations with priceless treasure and mysterious curses have always loomed large in the popular image of archaeology – and those of the Maya are no exception. Unfortunately, looters had emptied many tombs of the Maya elite before the arrival of archaeologists – but they missed some major burials that have been discovered in the last decade.

In May 1994 Arnoldo González Cruz, excavating beneath the stairway of Temple XIII at Palenque, found a sealed doorway at the end of an open passageway. Carefully making a small opening to cause minimal disturbance to whatever lay beyond, González recalls 'we were able to glance for the first time in centuries upon one of the richest tombs of Palenque, second only to Pakal's', which was discovered in 1952 by Alberto Ruz.

Enlarging the opening, the archaeologists entered a pristine vaulted chamber 3.8 m long and 2.5 m wide (12.5 x 8.2 ft), occupied by a massive monolithic sarcophagus painted red and sealed with an immense limestone slab. Next to this great stone box the investigators found the remains of a woman and a boy, evidently sacrificed as part of the ritual accompanying the burial.

With the raising of the great lid – which took 14 hours – light illuminated a skeleton that later analysis revealed to belong to a woman 30–35 years old. A treasury of jade ornaments, including 1,140 fragments of a great mosaic mask, beads and

left
These elaborate mosaic masks of jade, along with bivalve shells possibly used in bloodletting rituals, accompanied the burial found in the 'Tomb of the Red Queen' at Palenque, Mexico.

above
Inside the vaulted burial chamber of Palenque's 'Red Queen', archaeologist Arnoldo González Cruz carefully inspects the interior of the great sarcophagus, covered with red cinnabar.

a diadem, lay on and about the skeleton. Both exterior and interior of the sarcophagus were covered with red powdered cinnabar (mercury oxide) – a custom reflected in other Maya burials, perhaps to associate the dead with the colour linked to the direction of the rising sun – and with resurrection. After continuing examination, this 'Tomb of the Red Queen' is yielding new information on late 7th-century AD Palenque. DNA testing of the bones shows that the woman was not genetically related to the great Pakal. Instead, the Red Queen may have been Lady Tz'akabu Ajaw, Pakal's wife, who died in AD 672.

In 2002, at Takalik Abaj, on the Pacific Slope of southwestern Guatemala, Miguel Orrego and Christa Schieber de Lavarreda unearthed a rare royal tomb dating from the Late Preclassic period – the 2nd century AD. The vaulted chamber lay beneath what were apparently the ruins of an astronomical observatory. Although no skeleton was found, the sumptuous funerary offerings included jade and jadeite jewelry and other ornaments, polished pyrite mirrors and even a carved greenstone fish – all again covered with powdered cinnabar. The discoverers believe this tomb held one of the last of the rulers of Takalik Abaj.

Also in Guatemala, the Maya ruins of El Peru, or Waka', according to the hieroglyphic spelling of the city's ancient name, are yielding a series of important burials to an archaeological team led by Hector Escobedo and David Freidel. One, discovered in 2005 by team members Michelle Rich and Jennifer Piehl, contained two women laid on top of each other, one of whom was pregnant. The elaborate painted vases found with the women suggested that they were either members of the royal family or court attendants. Another burial at Waka' proved to be even more spectacular. Discovered by David Lee in a vaulted crypt built into a structure on the summit of the main palace complex, the burial was identified as a queen who ruled the city sometime between AD 650 and 750. Over 2,000 offerings were found with her, including a war helmet made of jade plaques – usually reserved for male rulers – as well as other royal symbols, and 23 complete ceramic vessels.

And El Peru continues to yield surprises – literally for excavation leader Hector Escobedo when in April 2006 he fell through the floor of a tunnel he was excavating in the principal pyramid into a 5-m (16-ft) long chamber. Inside was a single individual, lying on a stone platform with jade objects and the remains of a jaguar skin. This tomb may be of great significance, since excavators believe that it could have belonged to the founder of the ruling dynasty at El Peru. But this was not all. Not long after, another team working at the site discovered yet another possible royal tomb, dating to about 400 years later. Still undergoing investigation, a cache of figurines of ballplayers, women, dwarfs and seated lords has so far been found.

Such discoveries contribute greatly to our knowledge, not only of the trappings of Maya royalty, but also the ever-shifting patterns of power, politics and trade in luxury goods among the Maya city-states. In the end, the true and lasting treasure of royal tombs lies not in their material value, but rather in the information they contain about ancient Maya life and death.

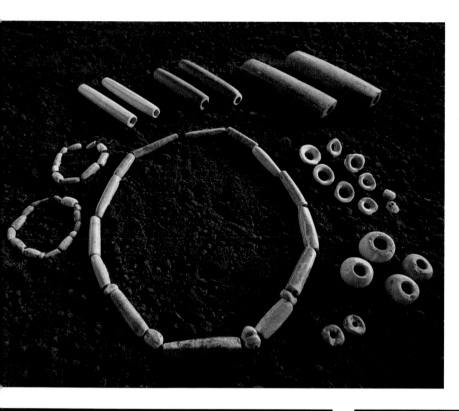

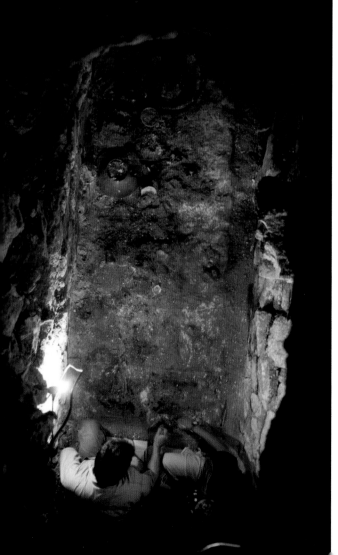

left
*A royal burial from El Peru,
Guatemala, dating from around
AD 700, the height of Classic
Maya civilization. As is typical
of high-status burials, the body
lies in a carefully constructed
stone crypt, surrounded by
special objects.*

above
*Fragments of an elaborately
painted ceramic vessel from
a tomb at El Peru are here
assembled for reconstruction.
By virtue of scenes and hieroglyphic
texts painted on them, pieces such
as these can reveal much about
Maya life and beliefs.*

Chachapoya: Mummies in the Cloud Forest of Peru

Adriana von Hagen

Deep in the cloud forest blanketing the eastern slopes of the northern Andes, looters in November 1996 discovered a Chachapoya-Inca burial site at a remote lake known as Laguna de los Cóndores. Although the looters had ransacked the tombs by the time Peruvian archaeologist Sonia Guillén arrived in 1997, she was able to salvage the extraordinarily well-preserved mummies and burial offerings, including textiles, musical instruments and personal ornaments, and today they are housed in a museum specially built for them.

These extraordinary mummies offer researchers an exceptional opportunity to learn about Chachapoya and Inca burial practices, as well as Inca rule in the region, and provide a tantalizing glimpse of the little-known Chachapoya art style. At the same time, the discovery of well-preserved human remains is also unprecedented for the region, where intense humidity and rainfall promote rapid decay of organic remains.

Who were the Chachapoya? At the cloud forest juncture of the northeastern Peruvian Andes and the upper Amazon basin, the Chachapoya people once held sway over a vast territory, today scattered with the distinctive remains of their trademark cliff tombs and hamlets of circular structures. Feared warriors and famed shamans, the Chachapoya flourished from around AD 800 until their conquest by the Incas in the 15th century. Often labelled as isolated and remote, mounting evidence shows that, far from being inaccessible, Chachapoyas – as the Incas called the province – thrived at a cultural crossroads connecting distant Andean and Amazonian societies, source of valued and vital tropical products. It was this privileged position that allowed the Chachapoya to mediate Andean-Amazonian exchange and made them the target of Inca expansion.

Tucked into a ledge on a limestone cliff 100 m (328 ft) above the Laguna de los Cóndores, the funerary structures – known as *chullpas* – stood untouched by humans for almost 500 years. The *chullpas'* builders took advantage of a natural ledge in the limestone cliff, which forms the back wall of the masonry tombs. Each tomb is about 3 m (10 ft) high and divided into two levels by a platform of small logs. Some of the tombs are painted in shades of white and red and yellow ochre, and are embellished with zigzag friezes – a Chachapoya decorative hallmark – or in one case, a set of deer antlers. The *chullpas* face the lake and the ancient settlement of Llaqtacocha, where excavations and mapping in 1999 uncovered the remains of some 120 circular structures.

Evidence suggests that when the Incas occupied the burial site they removed the earlier Chachapoya burials and relocated them in two undecorated *chullpas*, using the more elaborate tombs for their own people. Offerings of food and evidence that the mummies were covered in new burial wrappings indicate that people frequently visited the tombs, a widespread ancient Andean practice.

One question is why were the mummies so well preserved? The choice by the Chachapoya of dry, cool ledges that receive only a few hours of sun every day was deliberate. The tombs themselves created microclimates that also encouraged preservation, as did the many layers of textiles covering the bodies. Studies indicate also that the Chachapoya were skilled embalmers. They treated the skin with an as yet unidentified substance, lending it a leathery quality. They preserved facial features by placing unspun cotton in the mouth, cheeks and nostrils, and controlled decomposition by emptying the abdominal cavity and inserting a cotton plug in the anus. They reduced the bodies to their minimum volume and

left

A view of the tombs at Laguna de los Cóndores, tucked into a cliffside ledge, before they were cleared and excavated by archaeologists.

below
*Three mummy bundles recovered
from the lakeside tombs arrayed
with embroidered stylized faces
and zigzag patterns.*

right
*Mummy bundles and unwrapped
mummies – their wrappings had
been removed by looters – as
found at the burial site before they
were moved to research facilities
at the nearest town.*

weight: joints are strained to the point that the hyper-flexed,
fetal position of the mummies is almost unnatural.

A research team headed by project director Sonia Guillén
carried out X-rays of 205 mummy bundles and mummies,
determining sex in 147 individuals, identifying 72 males and 75
females. The studies reveal that the lakeside community suffered
from a variety of ailments, including osteoarthritis, dental caries
and abscesses, gum disease and tuberculosis. Only one case of
trauma was uncovered – possibly caused by a carnivorous
animal – suggesting that this lakeside community was not
engaged in warfare and may instead have played a role in
local Inca administration.

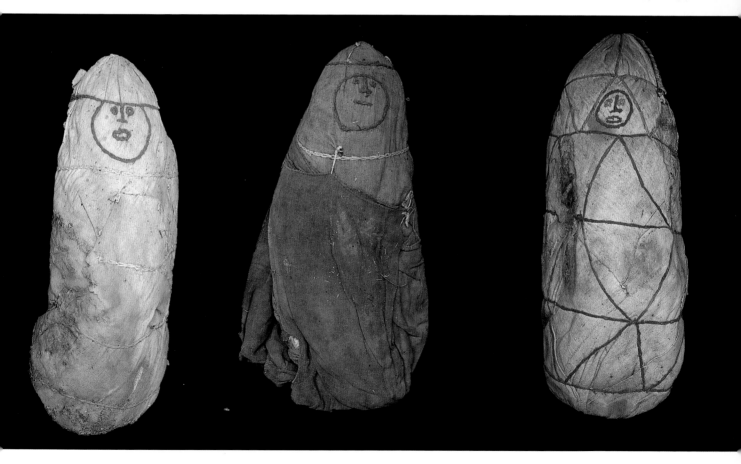

Inca Mummies: Child Sacrifice on Andean Peaks

Johan Reinhard

High up on mountain peaks in the Andes – at some of the highest archaeological sites in the world – I have discovered remarkably well-preserved Inca mummies ceremonially buried in elaborate textiles and accompanied by rich offerings. These naturally frozen bodies provide startling insights into Inca human sacrifice and ritual.

The Incas began expanding their empire from their capital Cuzco, in modern Peru, around 1438, a process that continued until the Spanish Conquest in 1532. During this brief time, they built over 100 ceremonial centres on the summits of many of the highest mountains in the Andes. My interest in these sites was triggered in 1980 when I first visited the Andes and realized that there was no reference to the ruins in standard books on archaeology. No archaeologist had spent more than a few hours at any of them. I wondered about an unanswered question: *why* had people constructed buildings at such incredible heights five centuries ago?

Early Spanish writers were mostly unaware of these sites, but noted the importance of mountain deities throughout the Andes. My research revealed that mountains were worshipped in the belief that they controlled meteorological phenomena, especially the flow of water – and thus the fertility of crops and livestock. As Juan de Ulloa Mogollón wrote in 1586, the Indians worshipped the snow-capped mountains because they 'provided the water that irrigated their fields'. When the Incas conquered

areas where these beliefs already existed, they constructed ritual sites on mountains that local people held in reverence but had never climbed. In this way, the Incas asserted greater economic, political and religious control over the people they had conquered.

The chroniclers described the offerings made to the mountain gods, including food, incense, alcoholic beverages and specially woven textiles and fine ceramics in distinctive Inca styles; intriguingly, they also remarked that offerings could involve human sacrifices. Between 1964 and 1985, a series of mummies had been found by accident, high in the Andes. These finds laid the foundation for my scientific excavations during the

below
View north from Llullaillaco's summit towards the two-roomed 'priests' house' (lower centre) and the ceremonial platform (upper left).

opposite
Male (right) and female (left) gold statues from Llullaillaco dressed in miniature clothing, similar to that worn in ceremonial contexts by Inca nobles.

1990s that resulted in the discovery of exceptionally preserved Inca mummies on the mountains of Ampato and Llullaillaco.

The Ice Maiden

Between 1995 and 1997, José Antonio Chávez and I directed a series of expeditions on the volcano Ampato, 6,312 m (20,708 ft) high, in southwest Peru. These began when my assistant and I first climbed the peak and spotted a mummy bundle lying on the ice. I was momentarily stunned when we lifted up the bundle. The head cloth had been torn open in its fall, and I found myself looking into the face of an Inca girl. Later called the Ice Maiden, this was the first frozen body of an Inca female ever discovered. I carried the mummy bundle off the mountain so that it could be conserved in a freezer for future study.

The Ice Maiden had been ritually sacrificed and buried with female figurines of gold, silver and spondylus shell (a sacred mollusc from the seas off Ecuador), as well as food, woven bags and pottery – all scattered around on the slope. The Inca believed that such a sacrifice brought honour on the parents

and a blissful afterlife for the victim. We later excavated a funerary site at 5,850 m (19,193 ft) on Ampato that contained the intact burials of two girls and a boy. The soft tissue of their bodies had been severely damaged by lightning after they had been interred, but the textiles around the females and other artifacts remained largely undamaged.

Llullaillaco

In 1999 the Argentine archaeologist Constanza Ceruti and I led an expedition to the summit of Llullaillaco, even higher than Ampato, at 6,739 m (22,109 ft). Excavations here of an Inca platform revealed three burials and several groups of offerings. The Incas had placed a 7-year-old boy on a folded tunic, together with a male figurine and one of a llama, and spare clothing, two pairs of sandals and two slings. We next found a feathered headdress on the head of a 15-year-old girl. A male tunic was draped over her right shoulder. Three female figurines made of gold, silver and spondylus shell lay next to her body. But it was the discovery of a third mummy that most affected me.

We excavated a mummy bundle, finding that it too had been hit by lightning while buried in its tomb. I saw the head cloth was loose. As I drew it back, I was astonished to be staring directly into a child's face. None of us had expected to see her face, much less that it would be so well preserved. I felt both deep sadness and a strong realization of her humanity. I was also pleased that she had not been totally destroyed by the lightning. The 6-year-old girl's internal tissues and organs, including her heart and brain, proved to be exceptionally preserved, despite the lightning having burnt a cavity in her chest. The Incas had placed textile and ceramic items around her, and four female figurines made of gold, silver and precious spondylus shell.

The Llullaillaco mummies proved to be a mine of bioanthropological information. Isotopic analysis of the older girl's hair showed that, a year before her death, her diet had changed dramatically to one rich in animal protein and plants such as maize. The other two children showed no such change in diet, suggesting that the older girl had the highest status of the three. Isotopes from the dead children's hair also revealed that they had chewed coca leaves, probably to numb their senses as part of the sacrificial ceremonies. Neutron activation analysis on the fabric of the pottery found with them showed that the classic Inca vessels had come both from Cuzco and from Lake Titicaca, a distance of more than 960 km (600 miles).

The Ampato and Llullaillaco mummies also provided fascinating clues from their DNA. The Ampato Ice Maiden's DNA showed that she had no relationship with modern villagers from Cabanaconde nearby. However, there was a relationship on the maternal side between one of the villagers and the oldest female on Llullaillaco. Eventually, we hope to establish the mummies' places of origin and identify their closest living relatives.

Bringing the past back to life

Unlike most frozen mummies found outside the Andes, very little time elapsed between the sacrifice of the Inca children and their burial. Thus, the bodies were deep frozen before much decomposition had taken place. Such mummies will never stop adding to our knowledge, since the technology for studying them is constantly evolving. The mummies and sumptuous offerings found on Ampato and Llullaillaco significantly increase our knowledge of Inca religious practices and beliefs, thanks to their excellent preservation and the fact that they were documented in their original contexts. These discoveries substantiate descriptions provided by early chroniclers and they also show that the Incas built structures at altitudes that would not even be reached again until nearly 400 years later. This must be considered one of ancient humanity's most awesome achievements.

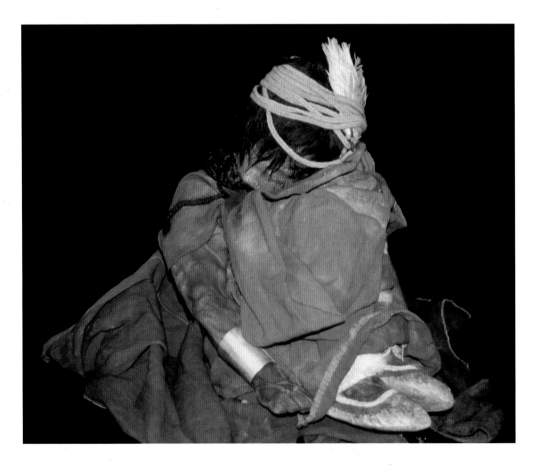

left
The Llullaillaco boy wore a red tunic, leather moccasins, a silver bracelet and a headdress of white feathers.

opposite
The younger female from Llullaillaco was found wearing a silver plaque. Lightning had damaged the upper part of her body.

following pages
The hair of the older girl from Llullaillaco was braided, and she wore a dress and a shawl, with ornaments on her right shoulder. The exceptional conditions of preservation mean that she looks like she is simply asleep.

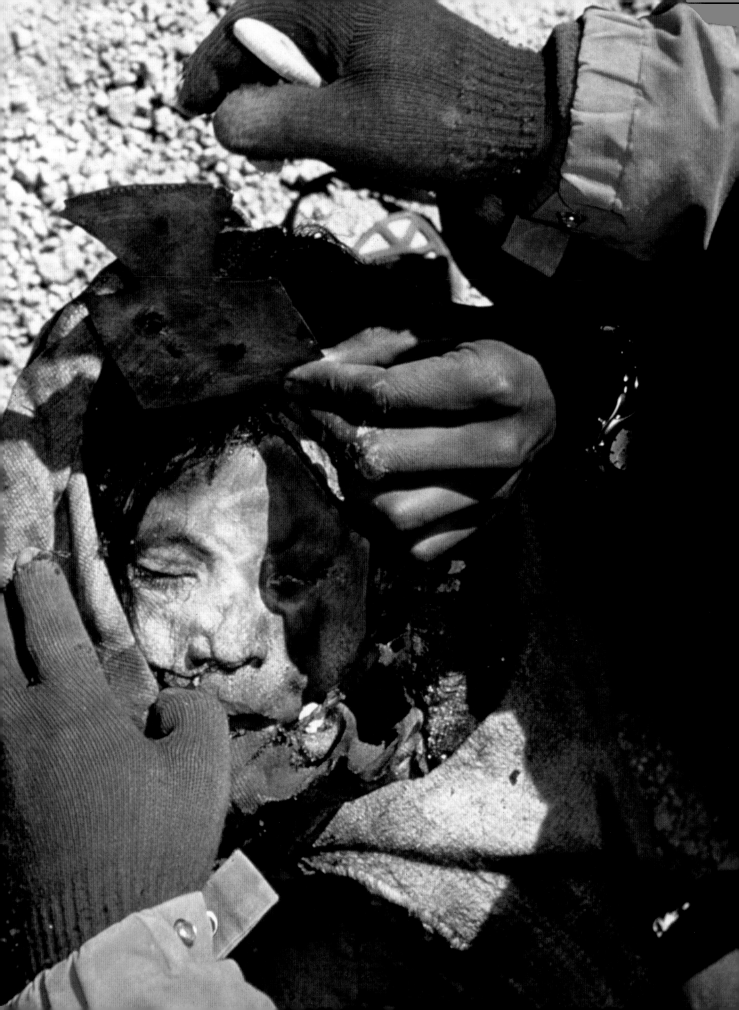

The Prittlewell Prince:
An Anglo-Saxon Royal Burial

Ian Blair

In the cold closing months of 2003 I was the senior archaeologist leading the Museum of London Archaeology Service's investigations at Prittlewell, southeast Essex, in advance of a road-building project. Although the site was a known Anglo-Saxon cemetery and we anticipated that we might find graves of this period, nothing could have prepared us for the moment when, in the very first trench we opened, we found ourselves excavating a burial that was clearly extraordinary. What we went on to uncover at Prittlewell is arguably the most important Anglo-Saxon burial to be found since the 1939 discovery of the great ship burial at Sutton Hoo in Suffolk.

The very first indications that there was a cemetery in the area of the Prittlewell site came in 1889, when a number of Anglo-Saxon spearheads and other grave goods were found during the construction of a railway line. The presence of a multi-period cemetery was later confirmed during road building in 1923, when workmen uncovered the remains of a fragmentary Roman lead coffin and a Roman cremation group. By far the largest assemblages found, however, consisted of grave goods from the 6th- to 7th-century Anglo-Saxon cemetery. Although there were at least three graves containing female jewelry, 19 graves contained weapons, including six swords – a striking dominance of male warrior graves. In this area we have to rely on the types of graves goods found to identify the sex of the person buried because bone preservation in the sandy soil is very poor and only a few traces of human bone survive.

It was on the second day of our excavation that we began to uncover signs of a chamber. As we removed the compacted sand and gravel that formed its upper fill, the first of what would total 140 finds was uncovered. An ornate copper-alloy vessel, decorated with inlaid enamelled mounts and cruciform strips on its underside, lay on its side. On the shoulders were rings indicating that it was a hanging bowl and one of the suspension rings was hooked over a corroded piece of iron. It soon became clear that the bowl was still hanging from an iron hook attached to what was once a wall made of upright wooden planks. We next came across three more vessels, including a 'Coptic' bowl and flagon from the eastern Mediterranean. Miraculously, all were still hanging on hooks fixed in the chamber walls. Organic stains in the soil were the only visible signs of the substantial roof timbers which would originally have spanned the 4-m (13-ft) wide chamber and supported the earth mound above it.

Another exciting moment came when the unmistakable rectangular shape of the coffin was defined off-centre in the north side of the chamber; the iron fittings that once secured its lid had fanned out like the open petals of a flower when its sides had decayed. All that remained of the coffin itself – and indeed of the man it once contained – was a dark organic stain compressed into little more than 25 mm (1 in) of soil. As we removed the soil containing the vestiges of the lid, two tiny gold-foil Latin crosses emerged at the head end of the coffin. These early Christian symbols are a unique find for Britain, but were common in burials in Lombardic Italy and in Alamannia (southwest Germany and northern Switzerland) in the late 6th and 7th centuries AD. In the area where the man's chest would have been we recovered a tiny fragment of gold thread which when X-rayed was found to be a delicate tablet-woven brocade that would have ornamented the edge of a garment, such as the neck of a tunic. Close by was one of two small gold coins, both tremisses from Merovingian France, and at the waist the most stunning and beautiful object of all, a pristine gold belt buckle. Only the third example of a gold buckle from an early Anglo-Saxon burial in England, ours is made in a Continental style that was also copied in Kent.

As the excavation progressed we were astonished at the array of grave goods being revealed on the floor of the chamber. These included an iron folding stool at the head end of the coffin and an enormous copper-alloy cauldron, placed on its side so that it would fit between the foot of the coffin and the chamber wall. Next to this an iron stand – a royal banner or candelabrum –

opposite left
Uncovering the highly ornate gilded rim and neck mounts from a pair of decayed wooden drinking vessels.

opposite right
The copper-alloy hanging bowl being revealed – still suspended on an iron nail that had been driven into the (now decayed) chamber wall.

above
A 'Coptic' flagon found on the north wall of the chamber close to the hanging bowl. The embossed medallions around the neck depict a saint-like figure on horseback.

right
A rare and beautiful belt buckle from the burial – one of only three gold buckles to have been found in Anglo-Saxon graves in England (the others being from Sutton Hoo and Taplow).

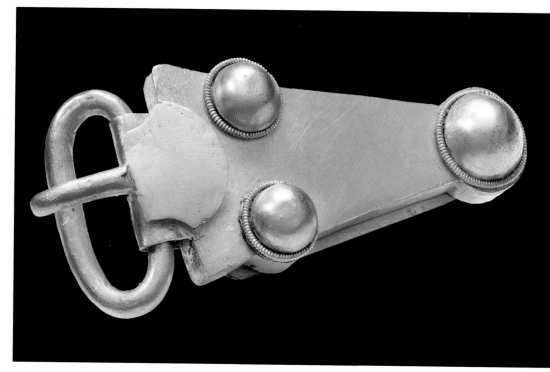

left
Stabilizing one of the decorative drinking horn mounts in the conservation laboratory following its removal from its soil block.

below
One of a pair of blue glass drinking vessels or 'squat jars' decorated with self-coloured trails, thought to have been made in Kent.

was still standing upright on its four feet, measuring around 1.33 m (4 ft 4 in) in height. Placed on the floor along the east wall of the chamber was a row of wooden and horn drinking vessels with highly decorative gilded copper-alloy rim mounts, as well as two matching pairs of blue and green glass squat jars. Another two cups were found on the north side of the chamber, close to 57 bone gaming pieces and two extremely large antler dice that were probably originally in a bag.

And more was to come: on the south side of the chamber we found an iron sword and iron fittings from a wooden shield next to the remains of a small decayed wooden box. The box contained a number of items, including a silver Byzantine spoon, probably made in the 6th century AD, with a two-line Latin inscription reading 'FAB…' and possibly 'RONAM'. Lying on the floor near to the box were the remains of a lyre – by far the most complete example found in an English burial. Although the wooden frame had decayed, leaving only a ghost-like stain, all the external metal fittings had been preserved in their original positions. We know that the lyre had been displaced as it was discovered lying face down beneath an iron object that had fallen on to it. This corroded lump was later found to contain two spearheads and a hook, suggesting that the spears had hung horizontally along the south wall of the chamber.

The manner of the burial – a chamber grave beneath a barrow mound – and the quality and quantity of the grave goods, left us with little doubt that Prittlewell is a rare example of a princely burial in a chamber grave of the early 7th century AD. The fact that it was previously undisturbed made it even more significant, as the only comparable high-status chamber graves of this period are those at Taplow in Buckinghamshire

and Broomfield in Essex, both excavated in the late 19th century. We would usually expect such a burial to be that of a very high-status pagan, but some of the grave goods suggest contact with Christianity. These include the Coptic bowl and flagon which might have been used for the ritual washing of hands or feet, and the silver spoon, perhaps a baptismal gift, used in taking communion. More particularly, the presence of the gold-foil crosses – probably placed on the eyes of the deceased – and the relative simplicity of the man's dress fittings and personal equipment suggest that he was a Christian at his death. If we look to history to identify a Christian king of the East Saxons in the first half of the 7th century, then Sabert, nephew of Ethelbert, king of Kent, who died in AD 616, is the only obvious candidate.

opposite below
The two simple gold foil Latin crosses which were found at the head end of the coffin, suggesting that they had possibly been placed over the eyes of the deceased man.

above
Artist's reconstruction showing the chamber grave and its contents at the time of the burial.

Treasures of Ancient Art

previous pages
As the waters of the Euphrates rise behind a new dam and threaten to submerge the Hellenistic and Roman town of Zeugma in Turkey, archaeologists race to save or record the remains.

right
This statue of Taharqa, a king of ancient Nubia, was found with others, all deliberately broken in antiquity, in a pit in a temple precinct at Kerma, Sudan.

right
Archaeologists in cramped conditions examine the astonishing early Maya wall paintings found at San Bartolo in Guatemala.

right
The figure of an athlete emerges from the sand beneath the sea off Croatia. This almost intact bronze statue may date from the 4th century BC – a very rare survival.

112

THE LAST DECADE has witnessed some extraordinary discoveries of Stone Age sites in France, which have pushed back the date of the earliest known cave art by at least 10,000 years. Jean Clottes, who has been in the thick of these discoveries, here gives his first-hand account of the remarkable caves of Chauvet, Cosquer and Cussac.

A rich portrait gallery of the famous and not-so-famous has come to light in recent years. Charles Bonnet and Dominique Valbelle describe how they unearthed monumental statues of black pharaohs near Kerma in the Sudan. A magnificent life-size statue of a 5th-century BC Celtic warrior prince comes from Glauberg in southwestern Germany. And Antti Korpisaari and Martti Pärssinen reveal their discovery of remarkably naturalistic ceramic portraits of ancient Bolivians of 1,000 years ago.

Spectacular discoveries of Greek and Roman art include a bronze statue of a male athlete of the 4th century BC recovered from the seabed off Croatia. Mark Merrony also describes exquisite mosaics that provide snapshots of Roman life and mythology – gladiators from a villa bath-house at Wadi Lebda, Libya, and Bellerophon on the winged horse Pegasus slaying the Chimaera from a house at Palmyra, Syria. Robert Early takes us to Zeugma, a Hellenistic and Roman city on the Euphrates, where he and other experts raced against time to recover wonderful mosaics including ones of women dining together and of Nereids riding on a sea monster.

In remote and densely forested northeastern Guatemala, William Saturno was searching for looted stelae in the virtually unknown San Bartolo ruins when he accidentally discovered an extraordinary mural of the Maya creation in a looter's tunnel. The earliest known Maya paintings, dating to 100 BC, they are revolutionizing our knowledge of Maya art and mythology.

Art also became wealth, buried hastily in troubled times, never to be recovered by its owners – to the delight of the archaeologist. Jeremy Hill describes a series of rich Iron Age hoards found in Britain in recent years, while Catherine Johns gives an expert account of the magnificent treasure from Hoxne in eastern England – coins and gold and silver jewelry – buried as the Roman grip on Britain loosened. Some 500 years later, the largest Viking silver hoard ever found was deposited on Gotland, Sweden, as Dan Carlsson recounts. A hoard of a different kind – more than 400 stunning statues of the Buddha from Qingzhou, China – is rated as one of the greatest Chinese discoveries ever made.

At the Origins of Art:
New Discoveries of Decorated Caves

Jean Clottes

In Europe there are almost 400 known sites of engravings and paintings attributed to the Upper Palaeolithic, between 35,000 and 11,000 years ago, ranging from shelters and rocks in the open air to deep caves. It is the latter that have revealed the true glory of this very ancient form of art. Over the last 15 years, more than 30 new decorated sites have been discovered, including three major caves: Cosquer, Chauvet and Cussac.

For almost 25,000 years, men and women went into the darkness of caves to create drawings and to carry out ceremonies, an exceptional phenomenon in the history of humanity. Most decorated sites are minor and contain very few works. Some, however, such as Lascaux and Niaux in France, and Altamira in Spain, have become famous for the quantity, the spectacular nature and aesthetic quality of their art.

We should also mention the discovery in 1994 of a large surface site, with thousands of Palaeolithic engravings at the edge of a river in Foz Coâ, in northeastern Portugal. In Fumane in northern Italy, painted blocks detached from cave walls have been found in an Aurignacian layer dating to 33,000 years. And the first Palaeolithic rock art site to be found in the British Isles was discovered in 2003, at Creswell Crags, northern England: a Magdalenian cave with some engravings, including a fine stag.

The Cosquer Cave

In July 1991, a diver named Henri Cosquer discovered paintings in a cave near Marseilles, in the south of France. The entrance is located 37 m (120 ft) below current sea level, although at the last glacial maximum, 20,000 years ago, the sea was 115 m (377 ft) lower than it is now and the coastline was 5 km (3 miles) away. At the end of the Ice Age, with the rising water levels, four-fifths of the chambers and galleries were flooded. No paintings or engravings have survived on the submerged walls, now completely corroded; the remaining art is found only in the upper chambers that have remained above water.

The cave, studied by myself, Jean Courtin and Luc Vanrell, contains 187 images of animals, tens of geometric signs in various shapes, 65 hand stencils, the image of a dead man and several representations of male and female sexual organs. The most frequently depicted animals are: horses (63); ibex (28); bison and aurochs (an extinct wild ox, 24); and deer (17, including 2 megaloceros). Others are much rarer: 4 chamois, 1 feline, 1 saiga antelope. Sea animals are quite common (17) and include 9 seals, 4 fish and 3 auks. Twenty animals are

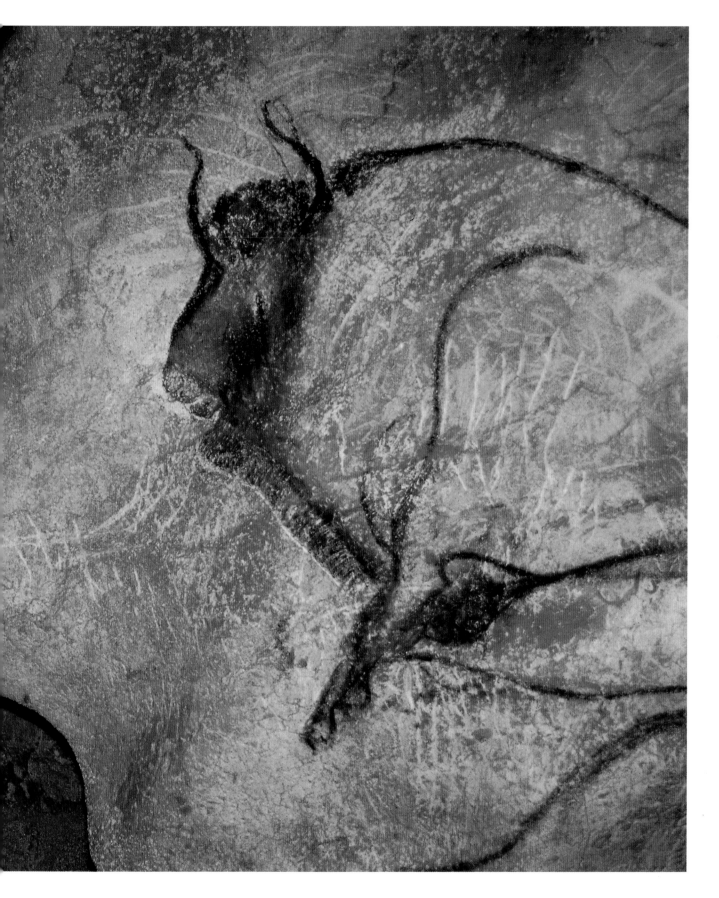

left
*In the Cosquer Cave, near
Marseilles, a number of hand
stencils were made on stalagmitic
draperies at the brink of a deep
shaft.*

below
*Two hand stencils in the Cosquer
Cave, one red on the left, the
other black. The latter was dated
to around 27,000 BC.*

previous pages
*The Chauvet Cave: a horse, in
the background, seems to emerge
from the depths of the cave wall.
The bison in the foreground was
dated to around 30,000 BC.*

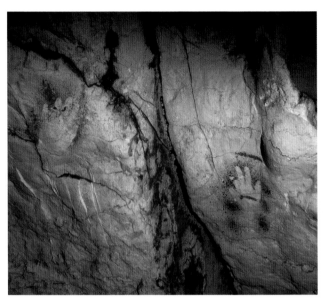

indeterminate and three are composite, that is, they have
characteristics belonging to different species.

The floors of these upper chambers are littered with
charcoal – the remains of torches or fires used to make
the charcoal needed for the drawings. People did not live
in these remote caves: the 27 dates obtained by radiocarbon
dating show that the cave was frequented during two separate
periods, the first around 27,000 years ago and the second
around 19,000 years ago.

Small handprints in the soft and altered surface of the
wall show that children had access to the depths of the cave.
One of them was lifted up by an adult to make a handprint
on the rock surface, 2.2 m (7 ft) from the ground, perhaps
during a ceremony.

The study of fragmented stalagmites and stalactites in
various places has shown that these were intentionally broken
and the pieces removed. In addition, the surfaces of the
accessible walls have been scraped to remove disintegrated
limestone. Ethnological studies have shown that over the course
of history, stalagmites and stalactites were gathered from caves
for medicinal purposes. More than 27,000 years ago, in the
depths of the cave, people scraped off the powdery surface of

the walls and carried it away. They probably believed that these
mineral substances possessed a supernatural power. In Cosquer
therefore, as well as abundant and original rock art, we may also
have found the earliest known evidence in the world for the use
of a specific medicine, calcium carbonate.

The Chauvet Cave

The Chauvet Cave, discovered in December 1994 by cavers
(including Jean-Marie Chauvet, who the site is named after), is
one of the most important and remarkable sites of Palaeolithic
art. Its study by a team of professionals, led first by myself and
later by Jean-Michel Geneste, has been in progress since 1998.

Scattered across the well-preserved floors are the bones of
cave bears and surfaces retain many other traces of their
presence in the form of prints and clawmarks. Prints and bones
also provide evidence of other animals (wolf, ibex). Footprints,
some flints and pieces of charcoal allow us to study human
activity. Bear bones that pre-date the arrival of humans had
sometimes been put to use: two humerus bones were stuck
vertically into the floor some 10 m (33 ft) apart, near to the
entrance; a bear skull had been removed and placed in
spectacular fashion on a large stone in the centre of a chamber.

This image of a panther from the Chauvet Cave is the only one known in the whole of Palaeolithic art.

below

A male lion turns and sniffs at a crouching, snarling female, in a dramatic scene in the Chauvet Cave. The lion's outlines were drawn to make it look as if it is behind some previously drawn horses.

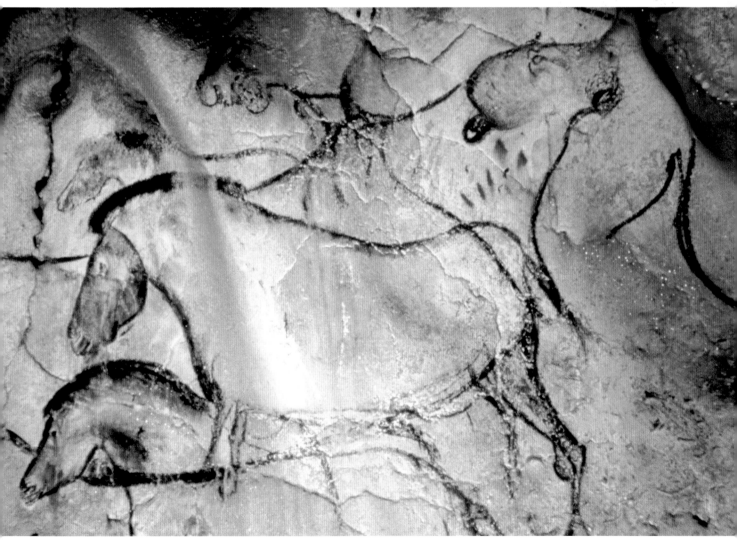

The topography of the cave played a major role in the arrangement of the paintings, with a clear dominance of red drawings in the first part of the cave and black drawings and engravings in the deeper areas.

A total of more than 420 painted or engraved animals makes Chauvet one of the most densely decorated caves known in Europe. The most common subjects are unusual: there is a dominance of mammoths (76), felines (75) and rhinoceros (65). These dangerous animals, which were generally not hunted and also include bears (15), occupy the central position in some of the major compositions, although they are much rarer in the art of later periods. The other species represented here are horses, bison, aurochs, ibex, deer (including three megaloceros) and reindeer, as well as two musk oxen, a long-eared owl and a panther. There are also 78 indeterminate animals and two animals are composite. Geometric signs are relatively rare. As well as six hand stencils and the same number of positive handprints, more than 300 large dots were created by daubing the palm in red paint and pressing it against the wall. There are five representations of female sexual organs. One extraordinary composition links the lower body of a woman and a bison with a human hand.

The techniques used are remarkably elaborate, including attempts to create the visual effect of perspective by various means; shading the inside of the bodies of animals; carefully

scraping away the outside of some figures to emphasize their outlines; and the preparation of the walls by scraping.

These unusual techniques and subjects are of even greater interest now that the Chauvet Cave has been dated more than 50 times. There is evidence of two phases when humans went into the cave: one between 32,000 and 30,000 years ago, and another between 27,000 and 26,000 years ago (from uncalibrated radiocarbon dates). The great majority of the drawings were probably created during the first phase. Their sophisticated nature and elaborate aesthetic shows that during the Upper Palaeolithic, art did not develop in a linear way, as was once believed, but the art of the first European Cro-Magnons – the Aurignacians – had already reached its peak.

The Cussac Cave
The scientific study of this huge cave, discovered at Cussac in the Dordogne region of France by a caver, Marc Delluc, in 2000, has not yet begun. The earliest research, carried out by Norbert Aujoulat and Christian Archambeau, has nonetheless confirmed its great importance for the number, nature and homogeneity of the representations, as well as the presence of half a dozen human skeletons.

The rock art almost uniquely takes the form of engravings, sometimes of large size: one bison measures over 4 m (13 ft). More than 150 figures have been counted, mostly bison, horses and mammoths, as well as some ibex, rhinoceros, birds and fantastic and composite animals. Four female silhouettes recall those found in the Pech-Merle cave in the Lot region. The techniques used, for example for the animals' horns, are similar to those used in Cosquer and Gargas.

There seems to be evidence of only one epoch at Cussac: the Gravettian. This evaluation, based on stylistic criteria, has been confirmed by radiocarbon dating of a human bone, which gave the date of around 25,000 years ago. Seven human skeletons have been discovered in the cave, the first time that burials have been found inside a decorated deep cave, which seem to have a direct relationship with the engravings.

opposite above
Two engraved bison face each other in Cussac Cave. A horse on the right has Y-shaped legs, a common convention used in art at the time.

opposite below
A large bison, also in Cussac Cave, turns to the right and is superimposed on a horse, itself drawn over the hindquarters of a smaller bison turned to the left.

above
This engraved female figure at Cussac Cave in the Dordogne is very similar to one in another French cave at Pech-Merle.

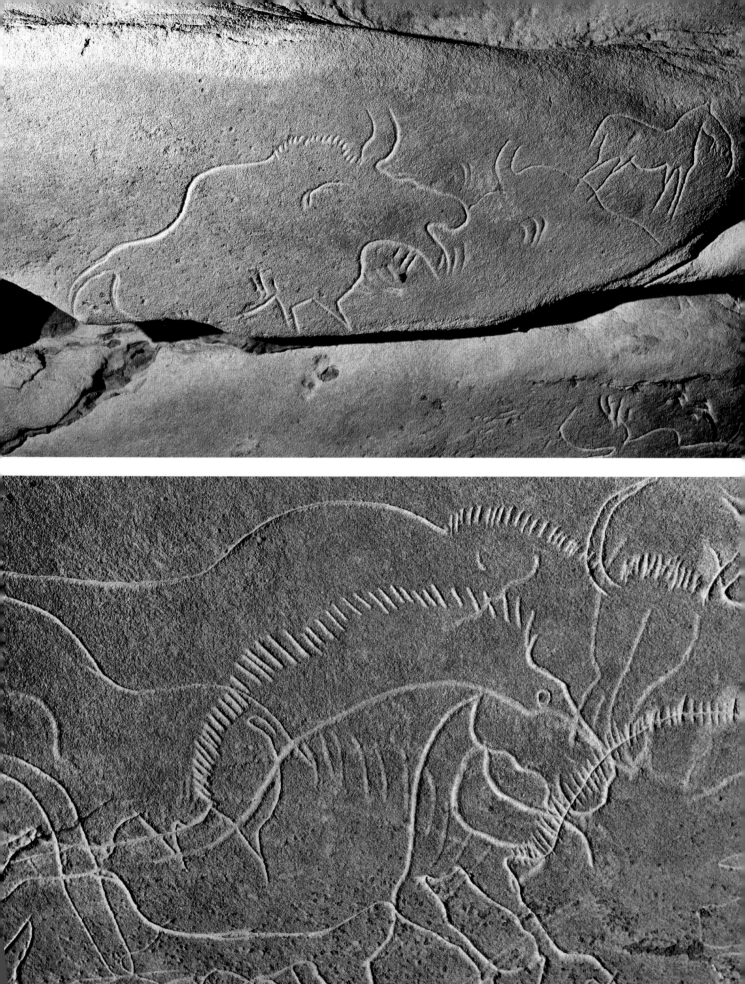

Black Pharaohs: A Cachette of Statues from Kerma, Sudan

Charles Bonnet and Dominique Valbelle

In the ancient town of Pnubs (Doukki Gel), just north of Kerma in Sudan, we made the surprise discovery of a pit containing seven monumental statues representing five rulers of Nubia of the 7th and 6th centuries BC. Though in pieces, these masterpieces of world sculpture could be restored, allowing us to explore the development of an art not yet fully understood. They exhibit the intensity of Egyptian creations, but they also show a stylistic evolution influenced by regions further to the south in Africa.

Some 3 m (10 ft) in diameter, the pit in which the statues had been buried was in an area between two temples, perhaps part of what was traditionally known as the 'Mansion of Gold', where statues were consecrated in ancient Egypt. Five pharaohs are depicted: Taharqa and Tanutamun – the two last rulers of the Nubian, or Kushite, 25th Dynasty of Egypt – and Senkamanisken, Anlamani and Aspelta of the Napatan dynasty, which ruled a territory stretching from the 2nd to the 6th cataract of the Nile. Analysis of the different fragments by our team from the Sudan Archaeological Mission of the University of Geneva has revealed that the sculptures were deliberately broken. The almost perfect condition of the surface shows that the time that elapsed between their destruction and their burial in the pit must have been very short. Why were they broken and buried? One possible explanation is that in around 591 BC, the Egyptian pharaoh Psamtik II waged a military campaign against the Kush sovereigns of the 'Land of Pnubs', a name for the Kerma region. It was probably following these events that the statues were shattered. Aspelta survived this confrontation and continued to reign for some 20 years. He may have been the one who ordered the statues to be buried in the pit, in sacred ground.

Opening an exciting field of investigation, this exceptional discovery is part of a long quest to discover the origins of Sudanese history and the part played by the 'black' Nubian pharaohs in Egyptian antiquity – a quest that has made substantial progress in recent years.

opposite
A reconstructed statue of the pharaoh Tanutamun, one of the Nubian kings who ruled the whole of Egypt in the 25th Dynasty. He is depicted in the traditional style of Egyptian kings, including the double uraeus – two cobras – on his forehead, but also with Nubian features, such as his helmet, in an interesting fusion of styles.

right above
The pit with the statues during excavation: the young boy waits to carry away the soil as it is carefully removed from around the fragments.

right
The head of the statue of Tanutamun, shown opposite, as it was found lying in the pit.

A Celtic Warrior Prince from Glauberg, Germany

Holger Baitinger and Fritz-Rudolf Herrmann

One of the earliest life-size, three-dimensional human representations known from Europe north of the Alps, the Glauberg warrior was found during excavations next to a huge burial mound of the 5th century BC near Frankfurt-am-Main in Germany. The burial mound, or barrow, lay at the foot of a hilltop which was fortified in antiquity, possibly a princely residence.

The statue was found carefully laid down on its back in a ditch, 2 m (6.5 ft) deep, along with fragments of three other life-size statues. Carved from local sandstone and standing 1.86 m (just over 6 ft) high, the carving represents a warrior wearing composite armour of linen or leather. With his left hand he holds in front of his body an oval shield with a prominent spindle-shaped boss. His right hand rests on his breast in a very deliberate gesture. His legs and arms appear naked, but it is probable that they were originally painted to indicate clothing.

As jewelry, but no doubt also as insignia of power, the warrior wears a neck ring with three pendants, an arm ring on his right wrist, a finger ring on his right hand and three rings on his left upper arm. The face is represented in a stylized fashion with large circular eyes, a moustache and beard. On the head there is a so-called leaf crown, consisting of a tight-fitting cap decorated with leaf-shaped patterns and two large protrusions at the sides.

Stone statues in human shape are known from Central Europe from the 7th century BC onwards. However, unlike the older sculptures, the Glauberg statues are finely carved and are fully three-dimensional pieces of work. The only parallel with these pieces is a fragmentary head of red sandstone found in Heidelberg in 1893. This had long been thought to have formed the crown of a pillar-shaped monument, but the new finds suggest a reconstruction as a three-dimensional figure. One other statue from Hirschlanden is around 50 years older.

The Glauberg statues are remarkable for their strict frontality and their flat, almost board-like shape when viewed from the side, characteristics also found in the oldest Greek stone sculptures, such as the Nikandre from Delos of the mid-7th century BC. Given the distances in time and space, these similarities are probably the result not of direct influence but the fact that in both cases existing models were translated into another material. The earliest Greek cult statues were carved from wood (*xoana*), before the first large-scale stone figures appeared around 650 BC, and a similar process must have occurred in early Celtic Central Europe in the 6th and 5th centuries BC, influenced by contacts with the Mediterranean.

Interestingly, the dead man buried in grave 1 of the princely barrow was wearing items very similar to those depicted on the statue and the other fragments, and so it seems likely that they were representations of deified ancestors or heroes.

left
A stone statue known as Nikandre, found on the Greek island of Delos and dating to around 650 BC (1.75 m/5.75 ft high). As with the Glauberg warrior, the statue is flat and board-like when viewed from the side and may have been a translation into stone of earlier cult statues that were carved from wood.

opposite
The Celtic warrior statue from Glauberg (back and front views) was found almost complete and measures 1.86 m (6ft) high. He was carved with the accoutrements of a warrior.

Artistic Splendours from the Greek and Roman World

Mark Merrony

Some of the most compelling and beautiful wonders of ancient art found in recent years come from the Classical world – from ancient Greek marble sculpture in Athens to late Roman frescoes in Budapest. But without a doubt, the most spectacular finds of the past decade are bronze statues and mosaics, often preserved in unusual environments and discovered by chance. The splendour of these works not only reflects supreme artistic skill and style, but also reveals much about different aspects of ancient life, such as religion and patronage, trade and economics.

opposite and above
The dancing satyr, a life-size bronze statue found off the coast of Sicily in 1998 by local fishermen. This exquisite sculpture, with its lively and realistic style, may be the work of the famous Hellenistic sculptor Praxiteles, or is perhaps a later Roman copy; 4th century BC or 1st century AD.

Bronze statues from the deep

It is easy to imagine the astonishment and excitement generated when fishermen off southwest Sicily landed an unexpected catch at the beginning of March 1998. Instead of their usual daily consignment of fish for the local market, they had netted the most extraordinary haul of their careers – one of the most exquisite Classical bronze statues ever discovered. Lost on a shipwreck, this beautiful sculpture, nearly 2 m (6.5 ft) high and weighing 200 kg (440 lb), represents a dancing satyr associated with the cult of Dionysos, the Greek god of wine. Thought to date to the 4th century BC (although some scholars believe it may be a 1st-century AD Roman copy of a Greek original), its high artistic quality has even led to claims that the statue was created by the famous Hellenistic sculptor Praxiteles, who specialized in producing graceful works of this kind.

When it came to the surface, the statue was missing its legs and arms, but by an astonishing stroke of luck, its right leg had been recovered seven months earlier. Meticulously conserved by the Istituto Centrale del Restauro in Rome, the satyr now dances again, nearly 2,500 years after its original creation, on display in the Presidential Montecitorio Palace.

Better preserved is a bronze statue found in 2001 on the seabed near the island of Vele Orjule off Croatia. This remarkable chance discovery was made at a depth of 45 m (148 ft) by Belgian scuba diver René Wouters. Standing 1.94 m (6.4 ft) high, this figure represents an *apoxyomenos* – a male athlete cleaning oil, sweat and dust from his body with a bronze scraping implement (*strigil*). This form is found frequently in Classical figurative art, incorporating a strong sense of realism and freedom of movement.

Radiocarbon dates from organic matter within the statue reveal that the athlete was lost in a shipwreck some time between AD 50 and AD 70. Intriguingly, however, the statue is thought to be significantly earlier, dating to the 4th century BC, and had been purchased or plundered as an antique before it was lost at sea. The Croatian athlete is very similar to a statue found at Ephesus, Turkey, in 1896, now in the Kunsthistorisches

Museum in Vienna, Austria, and it has been suggested that both statues were copied from the same model. But unlike the Ephesus figure, which was found in 234 fragments and cannot be reconstructed with certainty, only the head and base of the new statue had broken off. As a result, its conservators at the Croatian Conservation Department in Zagreb have managed skilfully to reconstruct the figure almost in its entirety.

Masterpieces in mosaic

A comparably spectacular discovery, but in a completely different artistic medium, was made during the excavation of a villa at Wadi Lebda, near the Roman city of Leptis Magna, in Libya, by Dr Marlies Wendowski between 2000 and 2004. While working in the cold-water room (*frigidarium*) of the villa's bath-house, excavators unearthed the most exquisite Roman figurative mosaic of all time. Dating to the 2nd century AD, the pictorial area, 9 m (30 ft) long, is divided into five panels, all relating to public entertainment. The most extraordinary depicts two gladiators, one sitting exhausted and pensive, his slain opponent stretched out on the ground next to him. This panel is of the highest artistic quality: the fatigued expression of the victor and the skilful illusion of foreshortening of his victim are incredibly difficult to achieve in mosaic art. The overall impression is of a realism usually seen only in painting.

above, right and opposite
The apoxyomenos, *a life-size bronze statue found by scuba divers off the coast of Croatia in 2001. A meticulous programme of restoration was necessary to bring this well-preserved work, dating to the 4th century BC, back to its original splendour.*

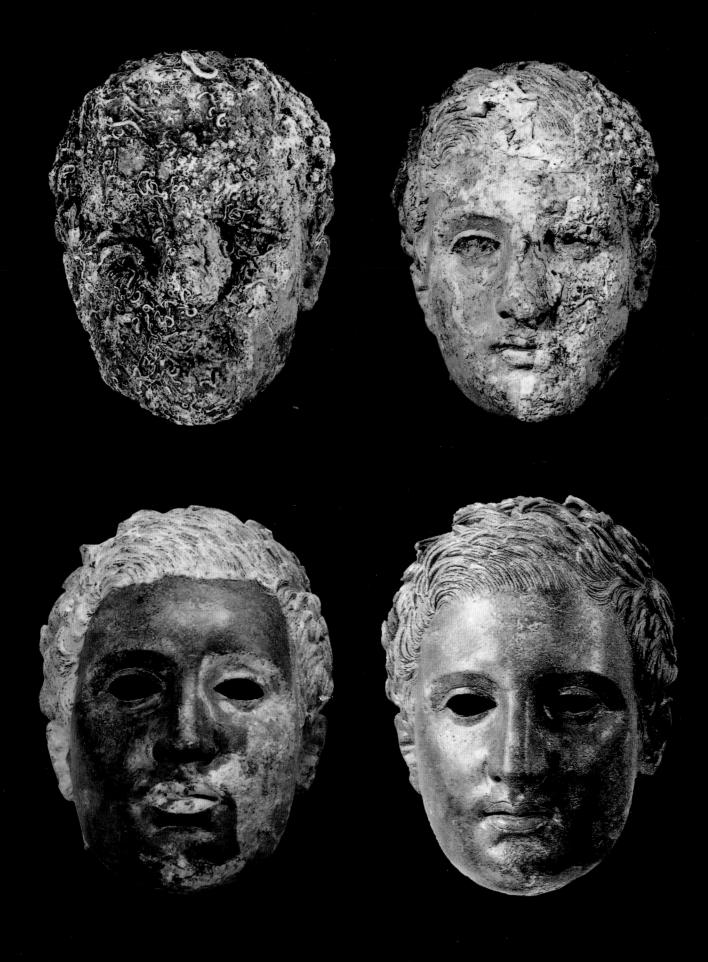

Scenes of public spectacle are a common theme in floor mosaics in the Roman empire, and it is widely accepted that they reflect the sponsorship of games in the arena or circus by wealthy villa owners who were also important city or provincial officials. In this case it is likely that the craftsmen were recreating an eye-witness event at the local amphitheatre in Leptis Magna.

A different style and message is conveyed by another remarkable floor mosaic, excavated in 2005 by Dr Michal Gawlikowski in Palmyra, Syria. This floor belongs to the reception room (*triclinium*) of a Roman villa and dates to the middle of the 3rd century AD. Two large panels form the centrepiece of the floor. One depicts the Greek mythological hero Bellerophon on the winged horse Pegasus slaying the monstrous Chimaera, while in the other an archer on horseback is hunting two tigers with his bow.

Although equal in beauty to the gladiator from Libya, this mosaic is in a very different, much less naturalistic style; this is more a reflection of its period than poor artistic skill. In general, mosaics in the Classical period developed from three-dimensional realism to two-dimensional abstractness – the Palmyran example lies somewhere between the two.

Collectively, these exciting discoveries of statues and mosaics are much more than just beautiful objects of art – though of course they are this too. They are also historical 'documents' in their own right, providing precious snapshots in the long history of Classical art, as well as illuminating the skills of the artists, the financial means of patrons and aspects of the broader, social, economic and religious life of the ancient world.

below
An extremely realistic polychrome mosaic floor from a Roman villa depicting a gladiator sitting looking exhausted and pensive. It was discovered near Leptis Magna, Libya, in 2004 and dates to the 2nd century AD.

Turkey's Pompeii: The Magnificent Mosaics of Zeugma

Robert Early

The archaeological remains of Zeugma, a Hellenistic and Roman city on the banks of the River Euphrates in southeastern Turkey, have rightly been described as 'Turkey's Pompeii'. In 2000, rescue excavations took place as the site was due to disappear under a vast lake caused by the construction of the Birecik hydroelectric dam, representing one of the most extraordinary archaeological challenges of recent years. With the waters rising at a rate of 25 cm (10 in) a day, a multinational team of experts worked around the clock to salvage and record an overwhelming quantity of outstanding mosaics, frescoes, standing buildings and artifacts.

The twin Hellenistic towns of Seleucia and Apamea, together referred to as the city of Zeugma, were founded in the 3rd century BC by Seleucius Nicator, one of Alexander the Great's generals. Located on the fertile plains of the Euphrates, at a strategic location between Syria and Mesopotamia, Zeugma enjoyed rapid commercial development. The pinnacle of the city's prosperity followed the establishment of the 4th (Scythian) Legion at Zeugma in AD 66. Subsequently, during the 2nd and 3rd centuries AD, wealthy Romans, high-ranking military commanders and veteran soldiers settled there, and it expanded to become one of the four most important garrison cities along the eastern Roman frontier. Zeugma's prosperity came to an abrupt end when the Sasanian king, Shapur I, sacked the city in AD 253. Although occupation continued until the 10th century, it was on an increasingly modest scale. The magnificence of the ancient city faded into the landscape as a result of landslides and perhaps also periodic earthquakes and tremors. In the summer of 2000, following reports in the international media that a great archaeological treasure was to be flooded by the lake behind a hydroelectric dam, archaeologists rediscovered the remains of the city protected beneath the 5 m (16 ft) of erosion deposits that formed the pistachio groves and terraces of today.

The rescue excavations were funded by the Packard Humanities Institute. The multinational operation was co-ordinated by Oxford Archaeology, working with the Gaziantep and Sanliurfa museum, David Kennedy, and Catherine Abadie-Reynal, who had first brought the site to the world's attention. Italian restoration expert Roberto Nardi and his team worked to conserve the discoveries. The mission's aim was to understand the topography of Zeugma's lower city, with the excavations carried out over a four-month period, during which temperatures rose to a record 50° C (122° F). As the excavations commenced, the dam locked up the Euphrates, and the waters began to rise. It was a race against time.

left
Detail of a 'cupid astride a dolphin', from a sea scene mosaic, a popular depiction at Zeugma, furnishing an outer reception room of the town house of the Synaristôsai.

opposite
Painstaking excavation being carried out at 5 a.m., as the waters of the lake gathering behind the hydroelectric dam continue to rise.

My first memories of Zeugma were of the frantic efforts to record and retrieve the remains of the Poseidon and Euphrates villa, named after its mosaics, as it was rapidly engulfed by the flood waters. We discovered an opulent 3rd-century AD town house with a colonnaded courtyard and barrel-vaulted chambers decorated with elaborate mosaics and frescoes. Artifacts recovered included a bronze statue of Mars, a bronze support for a candelabrum with three panther feet, and various ceramic amphoras and lamps. At the time, I thought these were the last of the important remains to be discovered, but over the next four months, 19 other areas were excavated by a team of over 120 archaeologists, supported by more than 100 local workers. Overall, the excavations cut a 1-km (0.6-mile) wide cross-section through the lower city. More and more significant finds were unearthed, providing an ever clearer map of the city's history.

By July, the Poseidon and Euphrates villa was submerged, and Catherine Abadie-Reynal's team focused their energies on the terraces above. Here, much of the ground floor of a complex high-status residence was found. It had been built into the hillside by adapting several rock-cut tombs which formed part of a Hellenistic necropolis. It was thus clear that the residence

was part of the 2nd- and 3rd-century Roman expansion of the earlier Hellenistic city. This town house has been named the house of the Synaristôsai ('women lunching together') after a scene from Menander's play of that name which was depicted in a mosaic in a fine *triclinium* (dining room).

Meanwhile, the Oxford and Turkish teams worked together on a terraced headland between two valleys where a public area of the Hellenistic city was discovered. French archaeologists had identified the base of a staircase that rose up to this area from the river valley below. The remains of public buildings and shops were revealed, including what may have been a temple that was later replaced by a commemorative monument or *nymphaeum*. The Turkish team identified 100,000 seal

above
*The extravagantly spacious 2nd-
and 3rd-century AD town house
of the* Synaristôsai, *incorporating
remodelled earlier tombs from a
Hellenistic necropolis cut into the
hillside as a series of chambers.*

opposite
*The spectacular mosaic named
Synaristôsai ('women lunching
together'), after a scene from a
play by Menander of that name.*

impressions during excavations of rooms thought to be part of an archive building, the largest collection of its type ever found. The seal impressions were used to authenticate or validate documents and commodities, and remind us of Zeugma's commercial importance. A customs house found close to the Roman bridge across the Euphrates would have controlled traffic and trade between the Roman and Parthian empires.

In August and September, further richly decorated residences were identified on either side of what seems to have been a piazza. Space close to the piazza was at a premium and here, in contrast to the extravagantly spacious town house of the *Synaristôsai*, Hellenistic properties were remodelled in Roman times and were often tightly packed and had more than one storey. Yet more impressive mosaics were identified. On one occasion the Oxford team worked through the night under flood lights with Roberto Nardi's conservation team to record and save a spectacular mosaic in the loggia of a courtyard house depicting Nereids riding on a sea-monster. By the end

of September the site was submerged and, once again, the historic landscape was transformed.

The Roman mosaics from Zeugma are already recognized as one of the greatest collections in the world, and are now housed in a special museum in Gaziantep. As works of art, these mosaics provide glimpses of the skills of local craftsmen and of the social status and extravagant lifestyle enjoyed by the rich. They include images of divinities and of everyday life. However, possibly of greater significance is the fact that the scale of the excavations in 2000 has allowed these great works of art to be understood in their true context, within the buildings they once decorated. We have a rich picture of what living in this cosmopolitan centre on the eastern edge of the Roman empire might have been like in the 2nd and 3rd centuries AD, and of how Zeugma evolved and eventually declined. The upper levels of the city now sit safe above the waterline, and over the coming decades research excavations here will continue to reveal more and more of the site's history, building on the foundation of our discoveries.

The Maize God and the Mythology of Kings: Maya Paintings at San Bartolo, Guatemala

William A. Saturno

In a remote and densely forested corner of northeast Guatemala, at a site I had not even planned on visiting, I found myself sitting in a dark tunnel made by looters, gazing at murals painted by the ancient Maya around 2,100 years before and completely unknown to archaeologists. The paintings are remarkable not only for their quality and the scenes they depict, but also for their very early date – they are certainly one of the most significant finds in Maya archaeology for many decades.

Nothing comparable had been found for more than 50 years, since Giles Healy had discovered the famous murals at Bonampak in southeastern Mexico in 1946. Painted in the waning years of the 8th century AD in brilliant colour, these depicted the events of the royal court and provided an unparalleled look into the pageantry and warfare of a Maya world on the verge of collapse. The murals at San Bartolo were painted nearly nine centuries earlier, around 100 BC, and show the mythic foundation of the world, at the very dawn of Maya civilization.

In March 2001, in my first year of college teaching, I set off on a short expedition to Guatemala, sponsored by the Corpus of Maya Hieroglyphic Inscriptions of the Peabody Museum at Harvard University. Unfortunately, the two treks originally planned were cancelled at the last minute, and my apologetic guides offered instead another option: three as yet undocumented hieroglyphic stelae recently uncovered by looting only a half-day's journey away.

We departed the next day, following an old logging road northeast from Uaxactún towards the large ruins of Xultún. The guides had estimated that the trip of 40 km (25 miles) would take about two or three hours by vehicle, and the sign marking the entrance of the jungle track reading 'camino en

mal estado' ('road in bad state') did little to dissuade us. As it turned out, the message was a dramatic understatement, and as night fell on the first day we had only reached Xultún. From here we had planned to walk approximately 6 km (4 miles) to reach the new site and its monuments, and though we lacked the appropriate supplies, we decided to press on rather than turn back to re-supply.

The six of us, with no food and very little water, set out on foot early the next day, but again the journey proved to be considerably longer than planned. There are those who say I got lost, but that is not altogether accurate – I was carrying a GPS, so I knew exactly where I was. Unfortunately, as the co-ordinates of the new site were unknown this was of little use in navigating towards it. In addition, travel through the jungle is never direct, but follows paths that criss-cross the forest to each *chiclero* (gum-harvester) camp. Thus, in the end, the route we travelled, recorded by our GPS, took us nine and a half hours through more than 20 km (12 miles) of jungle, before, dehydrated and exhausted, we finally came upon the ruins of a large pyramid, pierced by looters' tunnels, near a camp named San Bartolo.

Imagine our disappointment, then, as we looked around the pyramid to locate the rumoured stelae and found none. Unable to make the return trip without rest, we set up camp. As the guides went off in search of water, my thoughts turned to cooling down. I went to the rear of the pyramid and entered the main tunnel left by looters. Just at the point where the natural light ceased to penetrate, I sat in total darkness, reflecting on how badly the expedition had gone, wondering if we would even survive. Realizing I was sitting in bat dung,

left
*Wall-painting conservators
carefully remove surface debris
and inject lime grouts and mortars
to stabilize areas of fragile plaster.*

I turned on my headlamp to see if any of the creatures remained above me. As I shone the light upwards the beam fell upon the red, Olmec-looking face of the Maya Maize God and then upon the delicate face of a kneeling female attendant her hands stretched out to him. The San Bartolo murals had been discovered.

The excavation of a fragile work of art is never a simple task. I next waited two full years following the murals' serendipitous discovery to begin their excavation, in order to ensure that they wouldn't be damaged by exposure to modern environmental conditions. In this instance, the difficulties of delicate plaster and fugitive pigment were compounded by having to excavate in a tunnel no wider than myself beneath more than 15 m (50 ft) of rubble structure that the Maya had later raised on top of the room containing the murals. As I chipped away to create a tunnel, I hoped the ancient architects and masons knew what they were doing, and that the ceiling would stay up above me. When finished, the tunnel was more than 9 m (30 ft) long and followed the mural while leaving a thin veneer of masonry still covering the paintings to protect them during excavation. With specialists in mural conservation at the ready, I began to remove each stone of the later structure that obscured the mural's surface, and found myself face to face with the ancient gods and their story. The narrative of the mural read like an ancient Maya book whose pages had been spread open before me, recounting the birth of the Maya cosmos and providing a divine charter for the local king.

The epic Maya tale of creation has many chapters, and at San Bartolo we can see a new one beginning in each corner of the rectangular room that we excavated. On the north wall the story begins with the birth of five infants from a cleft gourd. This scene is followed by the emergence of the Maize God and his attendants from Flower Mountain, the place of origins. In all, four ancestral couples, including the Maize God and his wife, are exhaled from the zoomorphic mountain's cave-like mouth, riding on the back of a feathered serpent.

The ancient Maya conceived of a world bounded at the cardinal directions by four sacred trees bridging the gap between underworld and sky. On the west wall, a young lord, the patron deity of kings and the son of the Maize God, stands in flowing water before the first of these trees. He makes an offering of his own blood, let from his genitals, and sacrifices a

above

Accurate photographic documentation of the mural was a difficult task given the close quarters of the tunnel and lighting restrictions imposed for reasons of preservation. A standard flatbed scanner was used to take high-resolution rectified images of the entire mural surface. A composite of these scans is seen here.

left

William Saturno reassembles fragments of the Maya Sun God from the east wall mural that was destroyed in antiquity.

fish on a smoking pyre before the monstrous Bird Deity perched in the tree. As the narrative unfolds, we see the young hero continuing in his journey of creation and sacrifice past the remaining trees. He stands on the ground beneath the second tree, and floats in the air in front of the third, offering a slain deer and turkey respectively. At each sacrifice he also offers his own blood, fuelling the creation as he moves from the watery underworld, through earth and sky, finally to come to rest in the flowery paradise where the sun is daily reborn. Here he makes his final offering of blood, along with the scent of flowers, and in doing so sets the stage for the world the Maya lived in, binding the lives of Maya kings to the ritual sacrifice necessary to maintain it.

Our story continues with the Maize God himself setting up the fifth tree at the world centre, before crowning himself king upon a throne covered in a jaguar pelt. The Maya associated two gods with resurrection, the Sun God, who was reborn each day, and the Maize God, whose life, death and rebirth paralleled the agricultural cycle. For the very first time we can now see this

Maize God cycle depicted in its entirety. We see him first as an infant, born out of water, carried in the arms of another deity. We see him in death, diving back down into the water with hands outstretched. Between his birth and death we see his rebirth, dancing out of the turtle-shaped earth, playing music in front of the gods of rain and standing water, carrying the harvest on his back.

Finally, in the northwest corner of the room, seated upon a wooden scaffold, following the agricultural cycle and facing the mythic coronation of the Maize God, is a king, labelled by the painted text in front of him, receiving his royal headdress. In this artwork he claims no right to rule from his parents as Classic Maya kings later would, but rather shows himself as the inheritor of this divine responsibility from the gods themselves.

The site of San Bartolo continues to undergo intensive investigation, particularly in the pyramid that houses the murals known as Las Pinturas, and certainly much more remains to be discovered. It is clear, however, that these paintings have revolutionized our impression of early Maya civilization.

Torcs, Coins and Gold Cups:
Ancient Hoards from Britain

Jeremy D. Hill

Museums around the world display beautiful and iconic ancient objects, often made of precious materials. Yet sometimes, surprisingly little is known about such 'treasures' – even where they were found. Today, increasing numbers of artifacts are discovered in Britain by members of the public, especially those who use metal detectors for a hobby. Alongside this, new legislation and initiatives to raise awareness mean that frequently these objects can now be properly studied, and so make a greater contribution to our understanding of the past, rather than just being museum show pieces. Several high-profile discoveries illustrate this trend, as well as all being important finds in their own right.

The Snettisham hoards

The hoards of torcs excavated at Snettisham (Norfolk) are one of the most important discoveries in recent years dating from the European Iron Age. Impressive torcs, or neck rings, made from alloys of gold and silver, had been found sporadically at Snettisham between 1948 and 1973, including the 'Snettisham Great Torc', perhaps the most famous object from the British pre-Roman Iron Age. Limited archaeological investigations at the time found no other objects or archaeological features at the site, so little was known about how or why these objects were deposited. Then, in 1990, Charles Hodder made a new discovery of cut up torcs and ingots in the same field, while out metal detecting. His unexpected find led to systematic large-scale excavations by the British Museum, directed by Ian Stead, which located and investigated five discrete groups of complete torcs, buried tightly packed in small pits. This brings the total of hoards from the site to around 11, including 75 complete torcs – more than doubling the number of these objects found in Britain.

Yet the importance of this discovery is not just in the numbers found, it is that this was the first time that these iconic

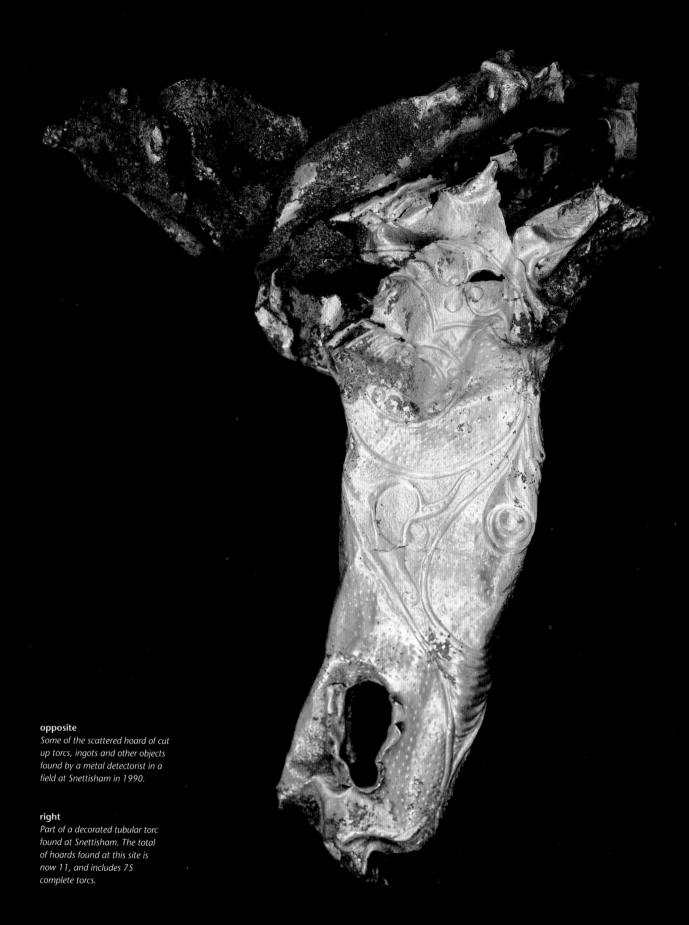

Iron Age objects have been excavated by archaeologists in the United Kingdom. One reason for this is that, like many prehistoric metal objects across northern Europe, they were deliberately deposited in the landscape, away from settlements or burial places, and were later found by chance. Interpretation of why these objects were deposited in such places has been hampered by the fact that little was known about the exact circumstances of their deposition. At Snettisham no evidence was found for large structures or archaeological features, though this absence is itself of interest. It appears that the neck rings were deliberately buried on a prominent hilltop in the open air, some considerable distance from the nearest settlements. In addition to the hoards of complete torcs, there were also 'scrap' hoards of cut up torcs and ingots, and coins. Some archaeologists suggest these hoards are wealth stored for safekeeping, although most Iron Age specialists today would see them as ritual deposits, perhaps made over a long period of time (c. 150–50 BC). Research on the torcs themselves is continuing, with detailed scientific examination revealing the surprisingly complex metallurgy and technology used in their construction.

The Winchester hoard

When other pre-Roman Iron Age torc-like objects were discovered near Winchester (Hampshire), in 2000, by another metal detectorist, Kevan Halls, a similar approach was taken. After he reported his first find of an unusual, very massive gold necklace and gold brooches, its location was investigated. Although no further objects or archaeological features were found, important details about the precise location of where the ornaments were deposited – a small hilltop with prominent views – could be recorded that would otherwise have been lost.

The Winchester hoard contains two unique gold necklaces, along with two pairs of gold brooches. Gold Iron Age brooches are extremely rare in Britain – only two were known before this. The necklaces are comparable in size and mass to the Snettisham torcs, but made using a completely different technology. Detailed examination showed that high-quality goldworking techniques from the Roman and Hellenistic worlds were employed in their manufacture, but applied to necklaces of a style, shape and massiveness never produced in the Mediterranean region. They were also made of refined gold, which was not used in pre-Roman Iron Age Britain. The evidence suggests that these objects are the equivalent of an indigenous traditional torc, but made by Roman or Hellenistic craftspeople. Who owned them and why they were made is unclear. The brooches suggest a date in the 1st century BC for the hoard, a period of growing political contacts between important individuals in Britain and the Roman empire. These unique objects might thus be gifts made for high-status Britons in a Roman workshop.

The East Leicestershire hoards

The East Leicestershire hoards are an even more recent discovery that shed new light on contacts between native British elites and the Roman world around the time of Roman annexation of southern Britain from AD 43 onwards. In 2000 Ken Wallace discovered large numbers Iron Age 'Celtic' coins while following up a survey by the local archaeology group of which he is a member. Excavations over several years uncovered 15 hoards of Iron Age coins, still in their original context. A number of very ephemeral archaeological features were also found, including a trench for a palisade. Just to one side of the entrance through

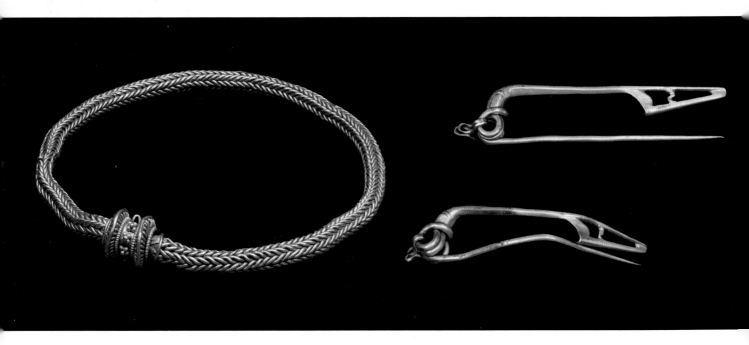

this lay a cluster of 13 coin hoards, while not far away was a large area of shallow pits packed with pig bones – providing an unusual picture of events accompanying the deposition of the coins. Close to the entrance, a further coin hoard was found with a corroded helmet. Carefully lifted on site and excavated in the laboratory, this turned out to be a Roman cavalry parade helmet covered with gilded decorated silver sheet. The one cheek-piece so far exposed has an image of a Roman imperial figure in triumph, with a defeated barbarian trampled beneath his horse's hooves. This extremely rare object was perhaps worn by a high-ranking officer in a Roman cavalry unit and was buried just before or during the time of the Roman annexation of southern Britain. That this Roman officer may have been a Briton from the local area remains a distinct possibility.

The Ringlemere Cup

From an earlier period, the Ringlemere Cup dates to the Bronze Age. It was found by Cliff Bradshaw in 2001 near Sandwich (Kent), badly crushed by modern farming machinery. Even in this state it was recognizably similar to another gold cup found at Rillaton (Cornwall) in the 19th century. The bodies of both were carefully raised out of single ingots of gold, strengthened with corrugations in their thin walls. The Ringlemere Cup has a pointed base, while that of the Rillaton Cup was flattened after it was discovered. Only four other such cups, all made around 1700–1500 BC, are known from elsewhere in northern Europe, pointing to long-distance contacts across Europe at this time. The findspot of the Ringlemere Cup, close to the shortest sea crossing between mainland Europe and the British Isles, suggests the importance of this area in these links.

Excavations at the site have revealed that the cup came from close to the centre of a large circular burial monument, over 40 m (130 ft) across and with ditches 4–5 m (13–16 ft) wide, now almost invisible on the surface of the field. This monument was first built as a henge monument in the Late Neolithic, which was reused much later with the construction of a mound. The cup on its own provides new information about these beautiful and enigmatic objects, but, like the other objects described here, set in the context of the excavation of its findspot and a reconsideration of its place in time, it can provide a much richer story about the past.

above
Some of the over 5,000 Iron Age coins from the East Leicestershire hoards site.

opposite
One of the unique heavy necklaces or necklace torcs found near Winchester in 2000, with two of the 1st-century BC style gold brooches (not to scale).

right
The Ringlemere Cup, badly crushed by modern farm machinery but recognizably of Early Bronze Age date.

above
The statuette of a leaping tigress, 15.9 cm (6.25 in) long, was made as a handle for a silver vase, but the vase itself is not present in the treasure. Cast in silver, the tigress's stripes are inlaid in black niello.

right
The silver half-figure of a richly dressed and bejewelled late-Roman lady is functional as well as decorative. The 10.3-cm (4-in) high figure was designed to contain and dispense ground pepper or other spices at table.

far right
There are 19 gold bracelets in the treasure. This one is ornamented with openwork foliate patterns and a good-luck wish to its owner, 'domina Iuliane' – 'the Lady Juliane'.

The Hoxne Treasure: A Late Roman Hoard

Catherine Johns

The Hoxne treasure is the most spectacular, important and largest late-Roman hoard ever discovered in Britain. Though it fits into a pattern of valuables buried for safety at the time when Roman authority was breaking down in the province, the sheer size and quality of the hoard make it exceptional. It contains many objects of rare or previously unknown types which enhance our understanding of the art and wealth of the late 4th century AD.

On 16 November 1992, Eric Lawes was metal-detecting in a Suffolk field when he found the first coins. After filling two carrier-bags with coins, gold chains and silver spoons he stopped digging and, together with the tenant-farmer, Peter Whatling, informed the authorities of his find. Fortunately, this meant that the bulk of the hoard was excavated by professional archaeologists employed by Suffolk County Council, and thanks to Mr Lawes's responsible conduct we have detailed information about the way in which these valuables were concealed. The whole hoard had been carefully packed into an iron-bound wooden box, with some objects evidently enclosed in textile wrappings or in smaller boxes within it. Though all the wood had decayed, the size of the original treasure-chest, about 60 x 45 x 30 cm (24 x 18 x 12 in), could be inferred.

The treasure contains 15,234 gold and silver coins, of which 579 are gold *solidi*, and over 14,000 are small silver *siliquae*. There are also some larger silver coins (*miliarenses*) and a few bronze ones. All belong to the later 4th century AD and the early 5th century, and the presence of coins of the British usurper emperor Constantine III (r. 407–11) establishes that the hoard must have been hidden after 407–8.

The jewelry comprises 6 chain necklaces, 3 finger rings, 19 bracelets and a body-chain. The necklaces are simple chains, lacking the pendants that would have hung from them in use, and the three rings are missing their gemstone settings, which were perhaps removed for use in new ornaments. The body-chain, an exceptionally rare and valuable ornament, is a gold 'harness', its chains passing over the wearer's shoulders and under her arms, decorated with a gem-set mount at the front containing an amethyst and four garnets, along with four empty settings for additional stones. At the back, the clasp contains a coin of the emperor Gratian (r. 367–83) mounted in a decorative gold frame. Among the bracelets, in flamboyant late-Roman taste, are many featuring openwork pierced patterns – one with a good-luck wish worked into its design to '*domina Iuliane*', 'the Lady Juliane'. All the jewelry is of fine workmanship and the metal is of very high purity, averaging 95 per cent gold.

Including the coins, there are about 24 kg (53 lb) of silver present in the shape of small items of tableware, toilet utensils and mounts from boxes or furniture. There are nearly 100 silver

above
A few of the coins from the treasure: the gold ones are solidi, *the smaller silver ones* siliquae, *and the large silver coins are* miliarenses.

left
A detail of the gold body-chain, showing the jewelled mount where the chains cross on the wearer's chest. The amethyst and four garnets survive; the missing stones may have been pearls.

spoons and ladles, many decorated and partly gilded, and some inscribed with personal names – by far the largest collection of such late-Roman spoons yet found. Larger table vessels include 5 plain bowls, 4 small containers for pepper or other valuable spices, and the detached handle of a vase, cast in the form of a rearing tigress, her stripes inlaid with black niello. The pepper pots are charming small statuettes, the largest of which represents a half-figure of an aristocratic Roman lady. Even small objects such as toothpicks are made in decorative shapes incorporating birds and dolphins, and are elegantly embellished with gilding.

Spillings: The World's Biggest Viking Silver Hoard

Dan Carlsson

In July 1999, more or less by chance, the biggest silver hoard from the Viking world ever found was discovered in a field at a farm at Spillings on the island of Gotland, Sweden.

In fact there were two separate deposits, some 3 m (10 ft) apart, together weighing around 67 kg (148 lb), both deposited under the floor of a Viking Age house. No evidence of any containers was found, but the form of the hoards suggests that the silver objects were held in bags of leather, textile or skin. In one of the deposits were the remains of a small wooden box, which had contained coins.

A further surprise came when a third deposit was discovered just 2 m (6.5 ft) away from the two silver hoards, this time purely of bronze objects. Weighing some 20 kg (44 lb), it consisted mostly of pieces of jewelry originating in the Baltic area. The three deposits were found in the same building – probably a barn or a storehouse – and there were even signs that there had been a fourth hoard that must have been removed at some time in the past.

In all, the silver deposits contain some 14,300 coins, almost all Arabic. So far, only 5,000 coins have been closely examined, but they give a good indication of the content of the hoards. The oldest coin is from AD 539 and the youngest from AD 870/871. Four coins were minted in Hedeby, a trading town in southern Denmark (today northern Germany). One coin from around AD 830 was minted for the Emperor Theophilus

at Constantinople. Such coins are not unusual finds in Viking Age hoards on Gotland, but there was one exceptional coin, with the inscription '*Musa rasul Allah*', Arabic for 'Moses is the envoy of God'. Intriguingly, the coin is a counterfeit, minted illegally by someone who wanted to take advantage of the good reputation of Arabic coins. Who this was is not certain, but a good candidate is the king of the Khazars, living near the mouth of the River Volga where it enters the Caspian Sea.

Besides the coins there were 486 arm rings, 25 finger rings, 34 ingots and a huge amount of spiral rings and broken pieces of raw silver. Many of the spiral rings were bundled together to a specific weight, and there are clear signs that this material should be seen as a huge deposit of payment silver – during the Viking Age the value of silver was by its weight, not the denomination stamped on the coins.

Gotland, Silver Island

The Spillings hoard is just one of around 700 Viking Age hoards found on the island of Gotland during the last 100 years, dated to between AD 800 and 1140. The end of this period coincides with the first minting of coins on Gotland; from then on, silver by weight no longer functioned as the currency in trading. Every year at least one new silver hoard is discovered. In some cases, several hoards come from the same farm, perhaps indicating that each generation on the farm had its own hoard.

This wealth of silver raises many questions. The Gotlanders must have engaged in successful commercial activity, and one prerequisite would have been a stable society. It seems that the Gotlanders made treaties to ensure that their trading was safe and prosperous, and there are no signs of internal problems. Society was based on free farmers who met every year at the Allthing to settle matters; there is no evidence of any king or a feudal upper class, though some farmers were wealthier than others. Being the middleman meant being the link between the Arabic area and the western Viking world – Sweden, Denmark and Norway. Gotland was thus a natural stepping stone in the long-distance trade between East and West at that time.

left and opposite
Besides some 14,300 coins, the hoard also contained some 500 arm rings. These were not used as bracelets but were a kind of payment. On the left is a piece of the hoard during excavation; opposite, some of the finds after conservation.

above
The most remarkable coin from the hoard is this one with an Arabic text 'Musa rasul Allah', meaning 'Moses is the envoy of God'. The coin is obviously a counterfeit, probably minted by the king of the Khazars.

Portraits in Pottery: Ceramic Vessels from Lake Titicaca

Antti Korpisaari and Martti Pärssinen

*We are accustomed to learning about people in the past from their physical remains,
or from statues or paintings, but in an unexpected find, we discovered pottery
portrait vessels made with such a high degree of technical and artistic skill that they
have completely revolutionized our understanding of how an ancient people
dressed and what they looked like.*

A team of Finnish and Bolivian archaeologists working on the island of Pariti in Lake Titicaca in 2004–05 found fragments of around 500 ritually broken ceramic vessels in two offering pits almost 2 m (6.5 ft) deep. More than 400 vessels have now been reconstructed, of which 32 are astonishingly naturalistic and lifelike portraits. They represent people of the Tiwanaku culture, who lived in this area between around AD 500 and 1100. The pits have been radiocarbon dated to approximately 1000, and so our finds prove that, contrary to previous theories, material of high quality was manufactured up until the final phase of the Tiwanaku culture.

Written records of the 16th and 17th centuries inform us that at the time of the Spanish Conquest, the Bolivian high plateau was inhabited by the speakers of three distinct languages: Aymara, Uru/Uruquilla and Pukina. The diverse facial features, hairstyles, clothing and ornamentation of the Pariti portraits strongly point to the existence of various ethnic groups in the high plateau also in the earlier Tiwanaku period.

Excavations had been carried out on Pariti in 1934, but a 70-year gap separated this pioneering effort from our own investigations. At the beginning of our fieldwork, we could not possibly have imagined that our excavation would produce some of the most sensational discoveries of modern Bolivian archaeology.

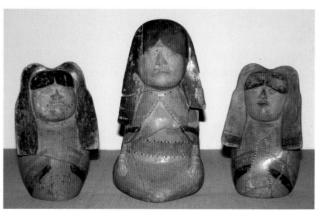

opposite

Above: Two vessels in the form of seated males, probably members of the elite. The older man is realistically portrayed with a lined and wrinkled face.
Below left: The 'Mona Lisa' of the Andes. The naturalism of this piece can be compared to that of some of the finest works of European and Asian masters who were contemporary with the Tiwanaku potters.
Below right: This anthropomorphic vase portraying a broad-faced man with earplugs and a labret is one of the very few Pariti vessels to have remained intact.

right above

The first Pariti offering pit under investigation in August 2004. Two archaeologists are excavating at the bottom of the pit, while one of our local helpers looks on.

right

Three pottery vessels representing elite Tiwanaku women. The clothing they are wearing closely resembles that depicted in the early 17th-century drawings of the native chronicler Guaman Poma de Ayala.

Statues of the Buddha from Qingzhou, China

Jan Stuart

In 1996, a trove of medieval Buddhist sculpture was unexpectedly unearthed in China's northeastern Shandong Province in the city of Qingzhou. The statues' stunning visual impact and the evidence they offer about early Buddhist practices earned the discovery recognition as one of the most significant archaeological events of 20th-century China, on a par with excavating the terracotta soldiers from the tomb of Qin Shihuangdi, China's First Emperor.

The Qingzhou hoard came to light when workers levelling a school sports field stumbled upon a pit more than 1.5 m (5 ft) below ground, filled with thousands of fragments of broken limestone sculptures. Luckily, the local museum was directly next door, and its staff rushed in to begin a 10-day excavation – under armed guard as a deterrent to theft. After years of work reassembling the stone pieces, the museum experts restored more than 400 statues of Buddhas and bodhisattvas (enlightened beings who help guide other sentient creatures to enlightenment). Most of them had been carved between the AD 520s and 570s and many presented imagery seldom or never before seen. Evidence showed that the cache had been buried in the early 12th century on land belonging to the long-disappeared and forgotten Dragon Rise Temple (Longxing si).

Everything about the Qingzhou hoard is noteworthy: the great number of statues; their overall excellent condition; the impressive quality of the carving and complex imagery; and the circumstances of their deliberate burial more than 500 years after the majority of the sculptures were carved.

Colour and style

Although broken, the Qingzhou statues are remarkably well preserved. Most striking is the generous amount of surviving antique pigment and gilding, much more than is usually found, which affords a rare opportunity to envisage the dazzling impact of brightly embellished Buddhist sculptures in dim, smoky temple interiors. Remnants of carefully applied gold leaf on areas corresponding to the faces, arms, hands and feet indicate that the sculptors gave visible form to the belief that Buddha emitted a golden light. As the Qingzhou treasures reveal, vivid colour has a strong effect, and its liberal use on the sculptures no doubt was to help empower them in their role as icons to mediate communication between believers and the sacred realm.

The beauty, maturity and variety of styles of the Qingzhou sculptures attest that during the 6th century Shandong was a major, innovative centre of Buddhist belief and imagery; yet prior to the Qingzhou discovery, the province was usually dismissed as a backwater in terms of Buddhist tradition. Sculptors working in Shandong simultaneously practised several styles of imagery and also created breathtaking new models,

fusing elements from multiple sources. Cushioned between the distinct traditions of a politically and culturally divided north and south China in the 6th century, it seems the province's location proved invigorating. Moreover, the Shandong sculptors received foreign stimulation via the Silk Route from India and Central Asia, and by sea from India and Southeast Asia.

North China experienced three brutal dynastic takeovers by foreign rulers in the 6th century, generating conditions that created two contrasting sculptural styles. Under the Northern Wei rulers (386–534) the Buddha was no longer shown in Indian-style dress, but instead wore voluminous Chinese robes depicted in a manner to conceal the sense of the body beneath. The Northern Wei images exude a sense of strict formality and their attenuated proportions and small pursed lips give the figures an otherworldly, elegant aloofness.

above
Members of the excavation team at work in the pit where the broken statues were found, led by Wang Huaqing, then the director of the Qingzhou museum.

opposite
A triad of two bodhisattvas and Buddha with a mandorla (halo), 1.2 m (4 ft) high. The aloof, otherworldly demeanour of these elegantly attenuated figures is typical of the Wei period, as is the voluminous Chinese style of the Buddha's attire.

The Eastern Wei (534–50) witnessed a gradual shift towards more sensual, human figures, but the period was transitional. Spectacular changes occurred in the Northern Qi (550–77), when sculptors crafted images showing the Buddha wearing Indian-style monastic garments that exposed more flesh and clung to the body. Bodhisattva images were decorated with elaborate jewelry as a sign of their sanctity and divinity. Sculptors created figures with softly rounded abdomens and articulated limbs – foreign-inspired traits – and they carved fleshy, full faces with broad lips and down-cast eyes, imbuing the statues with a more humanly compassionate appearance than previously seen.

The burial of the statues

Several facts suggest that the burial of the Qingzhou sculptures was carefully planned and not hurriedly executed. The date of the burial is provided by coins scattered in the pit, probably as good luck symbols, which were minted in a reign between 1102 and 1107. As to why they were buried, some scholars hold the brief waves of anti-Buddhist sentiment in China responsible.

But the damage to the Qingzhou hoard does not fit the usual pattern of iconoclastic destruction. Rather, the breakage is more likely the result of exposure to natural and manmade disasters. Occasional earthquakes recorded in Qingzhou could have toppled the large images. Others bear char marks and may have been partially destroyed during the infernos that were not infrequent in ancient wooden temple halls. Several sculptures bear signs of ancient repairs.

The sculptures' entombment is thus more convincingly explained as the result of a newly understood 12th-century religious practice in Shandong. An important clue comes from an inscription by monks living near Qingzhou, dated to 1004, in which they describe collecting damaged sculptures from various temples in order to give them a ceremonious burial; it seems that they wanted reverentially to lay to rest outmoded, damaged icons that were no longer useful as active ritual objects, but which were too sacred to summarily discard – a practice for which the modern world is thankful, as it has preserved for us a truly remarkable output of human faith and artistry.

Lost Cities

previous pages and right
One of the many mysteries surrounding the building of the gigantic pyramids at Giza, Egypt, is where the work-force who laboured on them lived. Mark Lehner has now discovered their city, in the shadow of the pyramids themselves.

right
Sometimes the past is literally beneath our feet: archaeologists discovered traces of Saxon London in one of the busiest parts of the modern capital: Covent Garden. Excavations at the Royal Opera House took place under a temporary shelter.

right
Curved wall trenches and an accompanying moat mark out one of the cannon positions at James Fort, Virginia. It had been thought that all traces of this fort had been eroded by the James River, but William Kelso's researches led him to find the remains of the fort exactly where he predicted.

DESPITE NEARLY TWO CENTURIES of archaeological excavations, there are still unknown cities to be found. At Caral, in the Supe Valley north of Lima in coastal Peru, Ruth Shady discovered a vast complex of plazas and pyramids that date to about 2600 BC, much earlier than other Peruvian cities. Astonishingly, Caral's pyramids are as old as those by the Nile. Caral was part of a dense concentration of coastal farming and fishing settlements, one of several still-unexplored early cities in the region.

Even at such a well-known site as the pyramids of Giza, there has always been a puzzle. Where did the thousands of artisans who must have laboured on these colossal monuments live? Mark Lehner has solved the mystery, by finding the pyramid city right under our noses on the Giza Plateau itself.

In China, the kinds of huge urban excavations that used to take place in the Near East are now proceeding in advance of construction work. One of the most exciting developments has been the discovery of previously unknown early civilizations in the Sichuan Basin, western China. At Jinsha, a 3,000-year-old political and economic centre, Chinese archaeologists have dug up over 5,000 luxury objects, many made of gold, bronze and jade, as well as thousands of elephant tusks and pottery vessels.

By contrast, much of today's urban excavation is often on a more limited scale, though the results can be equally spectacular. Eilat Mazar, working in eastern Jerusalem, believes she has uncovered the palace of King David. Ronnie Reich and Eli Shukrun, in the same city, are revealing the history of the Pool of Siloam, where Jesus cured the blind man.

Roman London was a substantial city whose location has never been lost. But where was its Saxon counterpart, Lundenwic? Only in recent years has the puzzle been solved. Excavating in 1996 at the Royal Opera House in Covent Garden, Robert Cowie and his colleagues uncovered dwellings, workshops and narrow gravel streets from the long-vanished trading centre.

An equally fine piece of archaeological detective work has taken place across the Atlantic. The year 2007 marked the 400th anniversary of the Jamestown settlement in Virginia, birthplace of the United States. Most people believed that the original fort was lost to the river. But William Kelso thought otherwise and, after 12 digging seasons, triumphantly exposed the fort's foundations, many of the buildings and over half a million artifacts.

Caral: The Oldest Civilization in Peru and the Americas

Ruth Shady

The sacred city of Caral, in Peru, is the most important settlement dating from the beginnings of Andean civilization, thanks to its large extent and architectural complexity. Occupied and continually remodelled between 3000 and 1800 BC, its antiquity can be compared only with the pristine centres of civilization known in the Old World. When the pyramid of Saqqara was being built in Egypt, or the Sumerian cities occupied in Mesopotamia, the inhabitants of the city of Caral, in isolation from the rest of the world, were constructing and shaping a complex of pyramidal buildings.

I became interested in the arid valley of Supe, 185 km (115 miles) north of Lima, when I came upon reports of many archaeological sites there with monumental architecture whose age had not been established. After two years prospecting in the valley, from 1994 to 1995, I and a team of Peruvian archaeologists decided to start excavating in 1996, in one of the 18 sites that showed similar architectural patterns. We had no idea how old they were or who had built them, and we selected Caral because of its enormous size and architectural complexity.

Caral turned out to comprise eight settlements and was the largest, most complex city of the period, with evidence of careful urban planning. The city was situated in the Supe Valley, 26 km (16 miles) from the Pacific and 350 m (1,150 ft) above sea level. The buildings extend over 66 ha (163 acres), distributed in a nuclear zone divided into two halves with monumental structures. Among the various architectural groups of Caral, the most impressive in terms of size are the 29-m (95-ft) high Greater Pyramid, and others of lesser height, ranging from the Pyramid of La Huanca (18 m/60 ft) to the Amphitheatre Temple (8 m/26 ft). In addition to these pyramidal buildings, there were open spaces for mass public meetings, as well as 26 other public buildings; two sunken circular plazas; residences of government officials; workshops; a Greater Residential Complex in the Upper Half of the city covering over 20,000 sq. m (215,285 sq. ft); a Lesser Residential Complex in the Lower Half with an area of nearly 5,000 sq. m (53,800 sq. ft); and houses grouped rather like an archipelago on the outskirts of the city.

The inhabitants combined inshore fishing with river valley agriculture. The trading of dried anchovies and shellfish for cotton and other agricultural produce set an extensive trading chain in motion to the benefit of the city's rulers; indeed, from this local economy, the trading activity grew to include regions in the Andean highlands and jungle. All the regions formed a great trading network and exchanged goods. In this hierarchical social system people held different positions created by the unequal distribution of goods. They periodically participated in group building projects such as pyramid construction, or the cleaning and maintenance of the irrigation system. Group tasks were carried out in association with trade fairs or markets, often coinciding with festivals, public ceremonies and rituals.

Interestingly, we found two sets of musical instruments: one group of 38 small horns made out of the bones of camelids and deer; and another set of 32 flutes, fashioned from pelican and condor bones. A pelican-bone *quena* (Andean flute) was also found, as well as four pan-pipes. These instruments point to elaborate musical practices, which assumed great importance during Caral's ritual activities.

The recent find of a quipu (knotted string) and pictures of them painted on some stones in the city walls are proof that the recording of information, as well as other cultural elements traditionally attributed to the Incas, had already been developed and used by this complex society at the dawn of civilization. This remarkable discovery confirms that the roots of Andean civilization lay as much as 5,000 years ago in the remote past.

Our multidisciplinary team has been working continually since 1994, not only at Caral but also on four other settlements in the Supe Valley. Our discoveries have enabled us to identify Caral-Supe as the first civilization in Peruvian history. This remarkable coastal society established the basic institutions of Andean civilization that flourished from its beginnings until the Inca empire, 4,440 years later.

opposite above
The small plaza of La Huanca, presided over by a pyramidal building with superimposed platforms and a central stairway leading up to rooms on the top of the structure.

opposite below
The 'Greater' pyramidal building, with its sunken circular plaza.

Pyramid City, Giza

Mark Lehner

The pyramids at Giza were the most massive building projects of the ancient world. Among many puzzles about them, one aspect in particular stands out – where were the settlements to support such a huge enterprise and what might they tell us about how the pyramids were built? For around 17 years I have been leading a team trying to resolve such questions. We have revealed precocious town planning, 2,000 years before the Greeks, paved streets, Egypt's oldest columned hall, barracks and bakeries, all buried for 4,500 years beneath the sands of Giza.

Groups of mud-brick houses had already been found in the 20th century at two different areas on the Giza Plateau. But working there over the years, I began to sense that there must have been much more settlement attached to these Old Kingdom pyramids, both during each king's lifetime when his pyramid was under construction, and afterwards. Estimates of the numbers of workers and support staff, running into the tens of thousands according to modern Egyptologists, are comparable to the populations of sizeable cities in the Near East at this time. Where were such numbers housed and fed? What could scientific excavation tell us about how the Egyptians organized their society for this colossal task, and what effect did pyramid building have on the development of Egypt as a nation? If the royal household moved to a site like Giza for three generations, then the butchers, the bakers, the sandal makers, and all the rest of the dependent work-force and its activities – to say nothing of the other officials and their households – must have amounted to a kind of city. Where should we look for it?

Mapping the Giza Plateau

I began by mapping the wider area of the Giza Plateau and thinking about how, around 2500 BC, the pyramid builders would have distributed their work-forces across the landscape. The whole chain of supply had to ascend the southeastern slope of the Giza pyramid plateau, from a harbour near the Sphinx, through a wadi approach, into the quarries and on up to the pyramid. The area east of the plateau must have been a vast delivery zone, with waterways leading to the valley temples of the pyramids of Khufu, Khafre and Menkaure. A huge limestone

left
View of the site of the Giza Pyramid City, as cleared in spring 2001. The surface of the ruins of Gallery Sets II and III appear in the centre of the cleared area to the lower right of the end of the Wall of the Crow. The Sphinx can be seen to the north, with the pyramids of Khufu (right) and Khafre (left).

wall, called the Wall of the Crow, 200 m (656 ft) long and 10 m (33 ft) high, forms the southern border of this zone. My interest was thus drawn to the area south of this giant wall as the place to look for the pyramid workers' accommodation.

We have tested this hypothesis over 17 years and 16 field seasons of survey and excavation, through the Giza Plateau Mapping Project (GPMP). The good news is that we found ample evidence of substantial pyramid-age settlement. More daunting is the fact that borings and trenches for sewage pipes during the installation of an extensive modern sewage system along the base of the plateau hinted at a virtual Lost City of the Pyramids, mostly irretrievable under the modern city of Cairo, 3–6 m (10–20 ft) below ground level over a 3-sq. km (1.2-sq. mile) area.

It soon became clear that the pyramid settlement at Giza was more than a small cluster of houses attached to the valley temples. Excavating south of the Wall of the Crow into the Pyramid Age settlement, every trench we dug into the sand and modern dumps revealed thick mud-brick and fieldstone walls, as well as intact bakeries, workshops and the remains of Egypt's

oldest columned (hypostyle) hall. As one of our graduate students said, 'something really big is lurking down there'. In 1999 we began a 'marathon' of much longer seasons and by 2005 we had mapped the largest exposure of 3rd millennium BC settlement anywhere in the Nile Valley. The urban footprint is a kind of circuit board of how the Egyptians organized themselves for the special, massive purpose of building the giant pyramids.

Bread and barracks

At the far southeast of our site lie the remains of a large enclosure that I dubbed the Royal Administrative Building because of evidence of storage and administration activity. The thick fieldstone Enclosure Wall runs from the southern face of the Wall of the Crow south and then east to enclose the central part of the site. Within a sweep of the Enclosure Wall are four great blocks of galleries, 50 and 35 m (164 and 115 ft) long, extending 185 m by 75 m (607 x 246 ft). Bakeries, cooking chambers and a small overseer's house take up the rear of each gallery; a long colonnade of slender wooden columns fronts on

to the street. A series of sleeping platforms along the colonnade in the one gallery we excavated entirely led us to suggest that each gallery may have housed a contingent of from 40 to 50 workers. The Gallery Complex was thus a vast barracks, either for workers or a royal guard that monitored work on the pyramid. Three streets cut west to east through this complex. 'Main Street', running 160 m (525 ft) through the city centre, is amazingly modern, with a bedding of crushed limestone and clay and a central drain, with paving of grey mud instead of asphalt.

We found dozens of additional bakeries and other food-processing facilities flanking the Gallery Complex on three sides, in effect the catering service for the corvée labour force that rotated on the royal project. In the Royal Administrative Building is a sunken court of large round silos, probably the central grain store, as well as small chambers and courtyards for administration, evidenced by numerous clay sealings, many with the names Khafre and Menkaure, builders of the second and third Giza pyramids.

In the Eastern Town, a dense cluster of small houses east of the Royal Building, people of low status ground the grain into flour, as shown by scatters of grinding stones nearly exclusive to this area of the site. Administrators of high status, with titles such as 'Royal Scribe' recorded on clay sealings, occupied much larger house compounds to the west of the Royal Building. This Western Town extended at least 200 m (656 ft) south of the Enclosure Wall – we have yet to find the end of it. A broad street connected the Eastern and Western Towns, whose inhabitants appeared to have been strictly segregated from the people in the Gallery Complex.

Altogether we have exposed around 7 ha (17 acres) of this urban centre, and this is possibly only a part of the pyramid cities of Khafre and Menkaure. Our deep probes tell us that a major earlier organization lies under the urban footprint we have mapped, possibly the phase of the pyramid city during the reign of Khufu, builder of the first pyramid at Giza.

Our intensive retrieval and analysis of plant and animal remains, and other material culture, reveal that the inhabitants consumed unusual quantities of prime beef – male cattle under two years of age – as well as sheep, goat, pig and fish. Using GIS (Geographic Information Systems) we can begin to discern patterns of distribution across the site. Those in the larger houses consumed the best meat and fish – cattle and perch – while the occupants of the Gallery Complex consumed more goat and those of the Eastern Town more pig, a typical village animal.

This sprawling heterogeneous urban centre may have been just part of the Giza pyramid city when the plateau teemed with the thousands who built the pyramids – no doubt under the supervision of the royal house operating from a residence somewhere within the greater urban layout. When the Giza dynasty ended, succeeding pharaohs built much smaller pyramids at Saqqara and Abusir further south that probably required less infrastructure and smaller 'company towns'. Pyramid City Giza must have shrunk into the smaller villages attached to the valley temples.

Jinsha: Changing the Map of Ancient China

Jay Xu

Within the last two decades, several great discoveries in the isolated Sichuan Basin in western China have dramatically altered the map of ancient Chinese civilizations. Most recently, excavations at the site of Jinsha, which thrived around the beginning of the 1st millennium BC in a region that was previously considered a cultural backwater through much of the Bronze Age, have revolutionized our understanding of ancient Sichuan.

Like most major finds in China, the discovery of the Jinsha site was a by-product of construction work. On the afternoon of 8 February 2001, workers bulldozing a ditch in the village of Jinsha in the western suburb of Chengdu, capital of Sichuan province, turned up fragments of elephant tusks and a few jade artifacts. Archaeologists of the Chengdu Municipal Institute of Archaeology quickly moved in, starting work at the site the next day. It immediately became clear that the find was important, and they decided to conduct large-scale excavations, which continue to this day over an ever-expanding area. Jinsha is now estimated to cover more than 5 sq. km (nearly 2 sq. miles), but the archaeologists have yet to determine its limits.

Finds and features

So far, archaeologists have excavated at more than 20 locations, with a total area approaching 10 ha (25 acres), uncovering building foundations, pottery kilns, burial grounds, refuse pits and pits containing precious materials. Remains of sizeable buildings are concentrated in the northern sector of the site, with the largest measuring over 430 sq. m (4,630 sq. ft), though foundations of smaller structures are found across the site. All revealed traces of post-holes for wattle-and-daub walls. Several burial grounds, usually in areas of abandoned buildings, have also been excavated, revealing more than 1,000 graves, the majority poorly furnished, with no burial goods or merely a few pottery and stone artifacts.

The finds of precious materials that make Jinsha such an archaeological sensation came largely from the initial discovery at the site. At present, some 5,000 luxury artifacts have been unearthed, including hundreds of ritual objects made of bronze (1,200), gold (200), jade (2,000), stone (1,000) and animal bone, in addition to approximately 1,000 elephant tusks, thousands of boar tusks and deer antlers, and some 10,000 pottery vessels and fragments. The luxury artifacts take the form of both implements and ornaments, though some of the tools are decorated with the same motifs found on the ornaments. Iconography at Jinsha is comparable to that known from the famous site of Sanxingdui, discovered in 1986 about 40 km (25 miles) northeast of Chengdu, showing that the cultures represented at these two sites were related, but strikingly

top
View of the excavation grid at the location of the initial find, at the central eastern sector of the site.

above
A pit containing tusks of Asian elephants, measuring 1.2–1.8 m (4–6 ft) long. They were neatly deposited in eight layers, with bronzes and jades beneath.

opposite
A stone kneeling figure with long braided hair and hands bound behind his back, 21.72 cm (8.5 in) high. This is one of 12 such figures found so far.

left
*A circular gold foil with four birds
and a whirling pattern consisting
of 12 strands, 12.5 cm (5 in) in
diameter and dating to around
1000 BC.*

opposite
*One of 10 stone crouching
tigers, with traces of red pigment
highlighting facial features.
This one measures 28.44 cm
(11 in) in length.*

different from any outside the Sichuan Basin. At Jinsha, the most
outstanding examples of representational images include human
figures, birds, tigers and other creatures, whose styles are
unparalleled elsewhere beyond Sichuan.

The archaeologists found that objects of the same type tend
to be concentrated in particular areas – for instance a collection
of unfinished stone implements, and elsewhere boar tusks and
deer antlers, elephant tusks and jades, and a small assemblage
of turtle shells that were possibly used in ritual divination for
foretelling the future. Occasionally objects were deposited in
pits, as in the case of a cache of elephant tusks.

Dating Jinsha

The depth of the deposits excavated at Jinsha – 4 to 5 m (13–16
ft) – as well as the types of pottery, bronze and jade found there,
indicate that the site was occupied continuously for a relatively
long time, roughly from the second half of the 2nd millennium
to the beginning of the 5th century BC. The abundance and
richness of the finds from the mid-11th to the early 9th centuries
show that this is when the site reached its peak, though remains
datable to earlier times, corresponding to the last phase of the
Sanxingdui site, are also well represented. In the 9th century,
Jinsha apparently went into a sharp decline.

What kind of site was Jinsha?

The nature of Jinsha is far from clear at this early stage of
fieldwork. The archaeologists conjecture that the cluster of
large-scale buildings might represent a palatial compound,
with a numerous population of low social status occupying
other parts of the site, as indicated by the cemetery with poorly

furnished graves and the clusters of modest buildings. As for the scattered yet concentrated distributions of particular objects, the excavators interpret these as the remains of sacrificial activities, though this may not be true for all of them. It is possible that some areas are the remains of workshops, for instance for making stone implements, as shown by material in various stages of manufacture. The elephant tusks at Jinsha showed no signs of burning, unlike those at Sanxingdui which had apparently been consumed by fire as a sacrificial offering; moreover, in addition to whole tusks there are also neatly cut chunks that were perhaps on the way to being made into ivory artifacts.

In a regional context, Jinsha was perhaps a secondary settlement to Sanxingdui, which covers 12 sq. km (nearly 5 sq. miles) and includes a walled enclosure of 3.5 sq. km (1.35 sq. miles), though their exact relationship is not clear. After the site at Sanxingdui was abandoned, the situation must have changed radically. Before the discovery of Jinsha in 2001, around a dozen other places with similar cultural remains had been found in its general vicinity, on the western and southern edges of Chengdu. However, the ritual objects and large-scale buildings at Jinsha set it apart from those sites, which are smaller in scale and yielded few luxury objects. Jinsha appears to have become the major centre in the region, and it may have been from this site that Chengdu began its rise to its pre-eminent position in Sichuan.

As fieldwork constantly generates new information, our understanding of the Jinsha site will no doubt evolve. However, this much is certain: Jinsha, together with Sanxingdui and other discoveries, attests to a wealth and a level of cultural brilliance in the Sichuan Basin that had previously been unknown and unsuspected.

Towards a New Jerusalem

Roberta L. Harris

In the past few years two 'rescue' excavations have led to momentous discoveries in Jerusalem's City of David. The first, at the top of the hill overlooking the Kidron Valley, is a monumental building that Eilat Mazar, the excavator, has identified as the palace of King David and his successors. The second, below the southern scarp of the city, is the Pool of Siloam of the Herodian period, where Jesus cured the man blind from birth. Together these two discoveries, respectively from the First and Second Temple periods, are adding an enormous amount to our knowledge of the biblical city.

The Palace of David

Recent excavations have led to the discovery of a huge expanse of ancient masonry atop the hill of the City of David, close to the Stepped Stone Structure excavated by Yigael Shiloh in the 1980s. Investigations by Dr Eilat Mazar are revealing a structure monumental enough to be called a palace, and finds of pottery dating to the 11th and 10th centuries BC are enough for her to feel justified in calling this the palace of King David and his successors. If this is indeed the case, then the ability of a ruler of this date (the 10th century BC is the era to which the reigns of David and Solomon are assigned) to build such a substantial edifice surely casts doubt on the assertions of some scholars who think that David and Solomon were no more than clan chieftains and not the great kings whose history is detailed so carefully in the Hebrew Bible.

The Pool of Siloam

Both the Hebrew Bible (the Christian Old Testament) and the New Testament mention the Pool of Siloam, the existence of which was confirmed by archaeologists, who discovered it as long ago as the 19th century. The Gihon Spring was the only source of fresh water for the City of David and the Canaanite town of Jebus which preceded it, and the inhabitants had climbed down rock-cut stairs and walked through an underground tunnel to fetch their water from a pool fed by the spring from as early the 19th or 18th century BC.

But at the end of the 8th century BC King Hezekiah, knowing that he was under threat of imminent attack by the Assyrians, channelled the water of the Gihon to the southern end of the city. A tunnel was cut through the living rock by two teams of miners, who hewed their way towards each other from both

ends at once using a natural pre-existing fissure in the limestone
to guide them. Once the Gihon's water had been deflected into
the new Siloam Pool, the growing number of citizens of
Jerusalem had easy access to it.

But this was by no means the end of the story of the 'waters
of Shiloah that run softly'. In the 1st century BC King Herod the
Great, for instance, paid detailed attention to the provision of
a good water supply for the Temple ritual and for the people
of Jerusalem; Jesus would have known the pool as it had been
in Herod's day. It would also have been the general water supply
and perhaps even used for laundering clothes and bathing.

Ronnie Reich and Eli Shukrun of the Israel Antiquities
Authority are now investigating the history of this pool and its
surroundings. It was approached by three flights of five shallow
stairs which would have been underwater if the winter brought
much rain. The north side of the pool was some 68 m (225 ft)
in length and the angles of both excavated corners were more
than 90 degrees, revealing that the pool was not a regular
shape. Column bases show that it was surrounded by a
colonnade of Ionic columns and from the northwest corner
a flight of stairs gave access to a piazza and a street which,
so the excavators believe, led up the steep slope of the central
valley of Jerusalem to the Temple Mount.

Some years ago excavation revealed the northern end of
this street at the point where it opened into the great piazza
at the southern foot of the Temple Mount. Here pilgrims
gathered before their ascent to the Temple itself. Archaeology
is thus revealing significant information about Jerusalem's water
supply, an extremely important element of the city's history
throughout the ages.

Saxon London, Concealed Beneath the City Streets

Robert Cowie

For many years Lundenwic (Saxon London) was an enigma to modern scholars. One of the first towns to be established in Britain after the end of Roman rule, Anglo-Saxon sources suggested that it had been a substantial settlement and a major river port. Yet its long-forgotten site, somewhere beneath the buildings and streets of the modern capital city, eluded discovery.

By the late 1970s numerous archaeological excavations had shown that it did not, as had been assumed, lie within the walls of the former Roman city of Londinium (now the City of London). The first breakthrough came in 1984 when Martin Biddle and Alan Vince independently suggested that Lundenwic lay about 1 km (0.6 miles) to the west, along a Roman road (now Strand). Their theory, based on local topography, a place-name and a few chance finds of Saxon artifacts, was confirmed the following year when Rob Whytehead discovered remains of the settlement during the redevelopment of a site in Covent Garden. I was among the small team of enthusiastic young archaeologists that, during a few days of frantic digging, salvaged enough evidence to convince all but the most hardened sceptics that Lundenwic had been found. Since then further remains have been unearthed, showing that the site of the settlement covers over 55 ha (136 acres) extending from Aldwych to Trafalgar Square.

But most subsequent excavations on the site of Lundenwic were small and afforded only the briefest glimpse of the Saxon townscape. All this changed in 1996, when I and my co-directors, David Bowsher and Gordon Malcolm, conducted a large excavation at the Royal Opera House in Covent Garden which enabled us to see the clearly delineated layout of building plots and narrow gravel streets. The buildings, on average about 11.5 m (38 ft) long and 5.5 m (18 ft) wide, often served as both dwellings and workshops. They were made of timber and were probably thatched; most had wattle-and-daub walls, which were sometimes whitewashed, earthen floors and hearths made of stones or reused Roman tiles set in clay.

Buildings and streets were kept fairly clean, but yards and open areas were often strewn with rubbish. Here pits were used as open latrines and for the disposal of household and industrial waste. Fly pupae and faecal matter containing worm eggs suggest that standards of hygiene were low and intestinal parasites widespread. Wells, which were simply deep pits lined with wattle or barrels, were often located amid such squalor.

Lundenwic's rubbish has provided much information about daily life in the settlement. Plant and animal remains show that the inhabitants were supplied with cereal grain (chiefly wheat and barley), pulses, fruit, nuts, eels, fish, oysters and meat (mainly beef, but also mutton and pork). Most foodstuffs would have been brought in from the surrounding countryside and rivers, but honeybees, poultry and possibly pigs were kept in the settlement. Other imported goods included pottery from various parts of England (especially Ipswich), antler, for making double-sided combs, wool and metals. Pottery, glass vessels, rotary querns, whetstones and wine were shipped across from northern France, the Low Countries and the Rhineland. In return, Lundenwic may have exported woollen clothing, for most households in the settlement spun and wove. A reference by the 8th-century monk and historian Bede to the sale in London of a Northumbrian prisoner to a Frisian also suggests that the port was a market for slaves.

Tools and waste from bone- and antler-working and metalworking are widely scattered across the settlement, although occasional concentrations of slag and other debris indicate the sites of smithies and workshops. During this period London was an important Anglo-Saxon mint, and the discovery at the Royal Opera House of two or three silver discs, possibly blanks, suggests that coins may have been struck in Lundenwic. However, only one known coin bears an epigram specifically mentioning the trading port: DE VICO LVNDONIAE 'from the wic of London'.

opposite above
Reconstruction of Lundenwic looking east – the large gravel pits in the foreground were found beneath Trafalgar Square.

opposite below
A hearth made of clay and re-used Roman tiles under excavation.

right
Coin of the Mercian king Coenwulf with an inscription mentioning the port of London, found next to the River Ivel in Bedfordshire.

Jamestown:
The Fort that was the Birthplace of the United States of America

William M. Kelso

As early as the 1960s, I felt sure that digging at Jamestown, Virginia, near the site of a 17th-century church tower, would turn up some traces of James Fort, the 1607 nucleus of the first permanent English settlement in North America, and arguably the birthplace of the United States. For over two centuries, visitors, most scholars and other people interested in the place where Captain John Smith and Pocahontas once trod, thought that the site was long lost to erosion of the James River shoreline. So it is difficult adequately to describe my emotions when, after 12 digging seasons, our archaeological team found on dry land almost all the foundations of the James Fort walls, as well as some of its buildings and structures, and over a half million related artifacts.

On 14 May 1607, just over 100 men and four boys chose to settle on an island some 56 km (35 miles) up the James River in Virginia and began to seek the means to show a profit for their sponsor, the Virginia Company of London. Their mission was primarily to establish a permanent base from which they could search for gold, find a short western route to the Orient, and convert the Virginia Indians to Christianity. Hostilities with the Indians, shortage of food and the alien environment quickly took the lives of half the colonists immediately after they struggled to construct a timber-walled fort. With better weather in the fall, game plentiful and food from the Indians, the colony began to take root under the leadership of Captain Smith. But conditions grew worse in the winter of 1609–10, a period known as the starving time, resulting in a move to abandon Virginia and sail home. Within a matter of hours, however, the first resident Virginia Company governor arrived with fresh supplies and a contingent of men, women and children to re-energize the venture; enough to ensure that Jamestown would live on to be the capital of Virginia for almost a century. Much of the archaeological remains we recently found offer vivid proof of these early struggles for survival and new insights into the effort it took for the colony to succeed.

I began the project not in the ground but in the library. There I found eyewitness accounts, mostly written by John Smith, and a Spanish spy map, which served to guide our shovels. One report suggested that if traces of the fort survived, then we should uncover narrow trenches that would form a triangle. The Spanish map – it seemed nothing more than a sketch – and Smith's description suggested the colony's church was near the centre of the triangle. Assuming then that the current church tower was a later addition to an original building, the first shovel went into the ground between the tower and the river shore where the south wall would likely be. Success! Within hours artifacts old enough and military enough to be signs of James Fort appeared, and within weeks a section of the line in the clay left from the decay of an upright timber palisade wall appeared. But one line could not prove that we had found the whole triangular James Fort. Arms, armour, coins, pottery and glass, all datable to the late 16th to early 17th centuries found in context with the wall line were, nonetheless, tantalizing signs that we were digging somewhere within the 1607 enclosure.

left
This facial reconstruction of an unearthed Jamestown settler based on forensic sculpting is shown on the drawing of an early 17th-century soldier. He wears a breastplate and holds a helmet and matchlock musket found at the James Fort site.

opposite
Dark soil found in a palisade wall trench parallel to the cobblestone and brick foundations of the 1611 governor's house are both signs that, after struggling for years, the Virginia Company invested more seriously in this venture.

opposite
A digital reconstruction of James Fort based on the recently uncovered archaeological remains and documentary evidence of the fort walls, buildings and an extension, as they probably appeared in 1610–11.

The first discovery served to anchor the south wall, but the rest could be located in any one of three remaining directions. But by September 1996, we had discovered a ditch-like moat and curved wall trench and segments of a palisade trench extending to the north. These features appeared to form a corner of the fort (a bulwark for mounting cannon), thus anchoring the plan to the east. These latest discoveries proved that the fort did indeed exist on land and that most of it could be uncovered in time. Still the extent of the fort to the north and west remained unknown. Painstakingly and methodically, over a span of 12 seasons, up to 2005, all the angles and corners found on the ground transformed the model from an educated guess to the real thing.

Excavations located evidence of five James Fort-period buildings including a barracks, the governor's and councillor's row houses, and the factory (trading post/workshop) to the east. The foundations of the row houses showed that these buildings, probably built by the resident governors c. 1611, were of cobblestone-based timber-frame construction, with timber and clay chimneys based on brick foundations. The later move to a more permanent box-frame construction was a clear sign that the Virginia Company was committed to a lasting Jamestown.

While we now know 17th-century Jamestown from a combination of written fact, architecture and artifacts, we have also come face-to-face with its people by recovering burials from the early Jamestown period (1607–30). Their meticulous analysis leads to a richer understanding of the colony's population. The mystery surrounding the discovery of the remains of a young colonist who died from a gunshot was especially revealing about dangers in the settlement. Studies of other unmarked graves tell of the lives of a woman labourer, some of the original gentlemen and a Captain, probably Bartholomew Gosnold, the prime moving energy behind the planning, financing and planting of the colony. Study of over 70 other burials from an unmarked burial ground on the western end of the island revealed a cross-section of the population in the first 25 years of settlement. Analysis indicated that most men died at about 25, women lived a few years longer, four men were shot, there was a mixture of 'proper' ceremonial graves with some coffins and a number of hasty burials, interred in times of mass sickness or starvation.

Archaeological remains at Jamestown and the sense of reality they convey reflect the buried truth about modern America's birthplace. There is evidence of a better life for some. There was usually not that chance for the Virginia Indians who met them. But the combination of evidence we found at Jamestown leaves no doubt that the American dream began in earnest on the banks of the James River.

Enigmas of Ritual and Religion

previous pages
The Pyramid of the Moon and the Pyramid of the Sun in the ancient city of Teotihuacán, Mexico: recently the Moon Pyramid yielded some of its dark secrets when archaeologists excavated tunnels into its core and found burials of humans and animals.

right
One of the oval enclosures with extraordinary carved megaliths found at Göbekli Tepe, Turkey, by Klaus Schmidt. This sanctuary dates from the dawn of agriculture.

right
Excavating lost megaliths that were once part of an avenue leading to Avebury, in southern England. The Beckhampton Avenue had been mentioned by William Stukeley, an antiquarian, in the 18th century, but had disappeared – until rediscovered by archaeologists.

right
A painted relief depicting a Spider Decapitator, from Huaca Cao Viejo. The Moche of Peru, who created this mural, frequently portrayed supernatural beings and religious rituals, often of a sacrificial nature, in their art. Steve Bourget found rare archaeological evidence of human sacrifice at Huaca de la Luna.

THE REALMS OF RELIGION and ritual remain some of the profoundest mysteries of the past. It is only when we uncover a complete shrine that we can glimpse the shadowy world behind the material remains of the Stone Age past. The extraordinary sanctuary at Göbekli Tepe found by Klaus Schmidt in southeastern Turkey is an expression of the intricate beliefs that sustained the lives of hunters and farmers in the early centuries of agriculture nearly 11,000 years ago. The multiple circular enclosures set on a hill, the benches and dramatically carved megaliths, the clear isolation of religious activity and sacrifice from the outside world, all define a unique sacred place.

Some 8,000 years later, early farmers in Britain were setting up another type of ritual enclosure – so-called 'henges'. Mike Pitts describes the discovery of the largest wood henge ever seen at Stanton Drew in southern England using the latest in subsurface detection technology, as well as the finding of the famous 'Seahenge' wooden circle on the east coast that also shows how little we know about the complex relationships between ancient communities and their ancestors.

Sometimes, cosmologies and rituals come down to us in distinctive art traditions, which enabled knowledge to be passed from one generation to the next. The Nebra Sky Disc of 1600 BC from Germany is the oldest known guide to the heavens in the world, thought to depict the celestial bodies and represent a kind of calendar.

In neighbouring France, Christophe Maniquet and his colleagues have made one of the most outstanding finds from the Celtic period – a ritual hoard at the sanctuary of Tintignac containing numerous helmets, war-trumpets, swords and spearheads.

Religion and power went hand in hand among the ancient civilizations. Saburo Sugiyama and his colleagues have found dedicatory burials of foreign war captives and caged animals under the Pyramid of the Moon at the great city of Teotihuacán, Mexico, emphasizing the authority and militarism of the rulers there. In coastal Peru, the Moche state of the 1st millennium AD carried out rituals that revolved around war and human sacrifice. Steve Bourget's excavations at the Moche ceremonial centre of Huaca de la Luna revealed the remains of some 70 sacrificed male warriors scattered around a ritual precinct.

For all these finds, we will never fully comprehend the true extent of the grip of the supernatural world on our ancestors, but enough has survived to show that the forces of the intangible shaped human history in profoundly important ways.

Carved Creatures from the Dawn of Agriculture: Göbekli Tepe, Turkey

Klaus Schmidt

A question that has exercised the minds of generations of archaeologists is why did people give up hunting and gathering and start to domesticate plants and animals? In other words, why did the Neolithic Revolution – a transition that first occurred immediately after the end of the last Ice Age, during the 10th to 8th millennia BC in the Near East – take place? New discoveries of carved pillars and ritual enclosures at Göbekli Tepe, in southeastern Turkey, have produced evidence for explanations that are quite different from the generally accepted view.

My own research had been focused on this very question, and in 1994, having been led there by a survey report, I arrived at Göbekli Tepe. I knew immediately that this site would occupy the rest of my scientific life. It was obvious that it was an enormous mound dating to the Neolithic period before the use of pottery – thousands of flint tools were visible on the surface, but there were no traces of ceramics or other items of later date. But most exciting was another observation: all over the site were large smashed limestone slabs, many of them carefully dressed.

Now, after 12 campaigns of excavations, we know enough to show that this is one of the most important archaeological sites in the world – one that challenges received ideas about the origin of the Near Eastern Neolithic. Compared to other Early Neolithic sites, Göbekli Tepe is unique in its location: on top of a huge hill it forms a landmark overlooking the surrounding plains. The distinct character of the site is underlined by its architecture and art objects, ranging from small stone figurines through sculptures and statues of men and animals, to large decorated megaliths. The society that lived at the site was still on the level of hunter-gatherers. There are no cultivated plants and the fauna included only wild species such as gazelle, wild cattle, wild ass, red deer and wild pig. Fox, wolf and leopards and several species of birds are recorded too.

Most characteristic of Göbekli Tepe are the megaliths in the form of T-shaped monolithic pillars, which stand in situ several metres high and weigh up to 10 tonnes. The largest, not yet fully excavated, seems to be as much as 5 m (16.4 ft) high. An example left in the quarries at the nearby limestone plateau is nearly 7 m (23 ft) long, and weighs approximately 50 tonnes.

Interestingly, the vertical element of the pillars sometimes shows a pair of arms and hands in low relief, implying that the pillars represent stylized humans, the horizontal and vertical parts respectively being the head and body. It seems the pillars were 'beings' of some sort. Many are also embellished with

above
The front face of one of the T-shaped pillars, with an enigmatic series of reliefs showing animals and symbols. These spectacular motifs have been called 'Stone Age Hieroglyphs'.

opposite
A wild boar and other animals in relief on one of the pillars of enclosure C. Many pillars are only partially excavated. In this case, soon after the pillar was erected a bench had been built which covered the body of the fox but left its head visible.

left
*On this T-shaped pillar a bull,
a fox and a crane are carved in
relief. The top of the pillar had
been destroyed just before our
excavations began. Fortunately,
we could prevent further damage
and the reliefs were preserved in
good condition.*

opposite
*One of the so-called lion pillars.
It belongs to the building phases
of the 9th millennium BC, when
the installations and their pillars
had been drastically reduced in
size. This lion pillar is 1.5 m
(5 ft) high.*

breathtaking carvings of lions, foxes and gazelles, wild boars and wild asses, aurochs (wild cattle), snakes and birds, insects and spiders. There are non-figurative carvings too, such as H-shaped symbols, circles and crescents. In addition there are also sculptures of animals, largely boars and other dangerous beasts, that seem to have been placed on top of the walls, perhaps 'guarding' the interior of the enclosures.

All the animals depicted are recorded in the faunal assemblages, but there seems no close connection between them. Animal symbolism in the Neolithic Near East was clearly very complex, and anthropologist Claude Lévi-Strauss's expression, that animals that are 'good to eat' are not necessarily 'good to think', seems to be confirmed at Göbekli Tepe.

Excavations revealed that the pillars had been arranged purposefully to delineate round or oval structures, and that a single circle may include up to 12 pillars that are interconnected by stone benches. The central part of each enclosure is dominated by two pillars, which are larger than the surrounding ones and of a superior quality.

During the Neolithic, for reasons unknown to us, settlement refuse was deliberately dumped on to Göbekli Tepe's megalithic architecture, which, as a result, was sealed and protected until we discovered it in the mid-1990s. A geomagnetic survey shows that there are not only the four enclosures under excavation,

but numerous similar structures inside the mound. At least 20 enclosures with more than 200 pillars in total can be expected. A huge amount of labour over many decades must have been expended in the making of the Göbekli Tepe structures. Yet there is, so far, no evidence for a large settlement. Nor is there any suggestion that the enclosures were residential.

Göbekli Tepe was thus not a settlement site, rather it was a sanctuary. Perhaps the people who maintained it may have lived there permanently, but this was for reasons very different from the causes of early village life. One such early village was Nevalı Çori, where I had in fact excavated 20 years before. A small sanctuary in that village also contained T-shaped megalithic pillars and life-size limestone sculptures of humans and animals, showing that Nevalı Çori and Göbekli Tepe shared a common symbolic language, but the two sites were otherwise very different. Nevalı Çori was a village; from such settlements people would have gone to Göbekli Tepe, perhaps seasonally, to cut pillars from the plateaus, drag them to the building site, carve them with reliefs and erect them in the oval arrangements. Having completed one structure, the people filled it in after some time – and then began to build another one.

What took place in the enclosures before the backfilling? As the excavations are far from complete it is still a mystery, but it seems to us that Göbekli Tepe was a place made not for the living, but for the dead. Funeral customs could account for the enormous amount of work undertaken for just one enclosure. We haven't yet found the burials, but we expect they will be located beneath the benches or behind the walls.

Several hundred people must have gathered for many months for the construction of each of the circular enclosures. For non-food producing communities such ritual imperatives must undoubtedly have caused problems of subsistence – how could all these people be fed? Could this possibly have led to agriculture? My conjecture is that construction at Göbekli Tepe was accompanied by efforts to develop innovations to provide subsistence for the workmen occupied in the quarries and in building. Thus we have evidence that archaeologist Jacques Cauvin was correct when he expressed the view that belief and social systems changed *before*, not as a result of, shifts in the economic systems of life.

Stanton Drew Stone Circles

Interpretation of magnetometer surveys

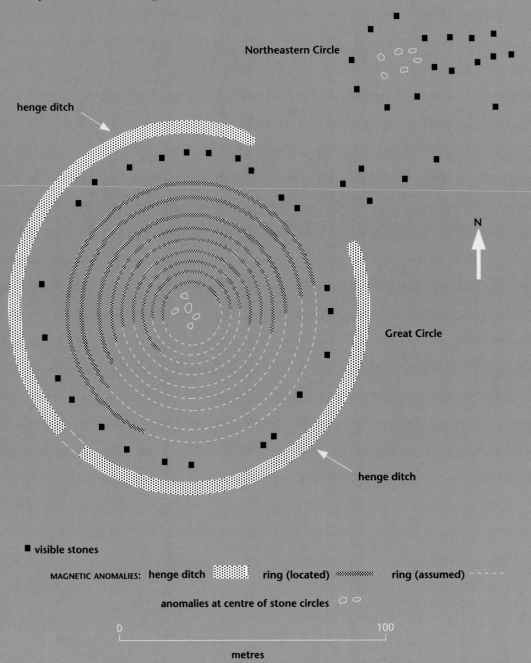

Northeastern Circle

henge ditch

N

Great Circle

henge ditch

■ visible stones

MAGNETIC ANOMALIES: henge ditch   ring (located)   ring (assumed)

anomalies at centre of stone circles

0   100

metres

Secrets Revealed at Britain's Henges

Mike Pitts

In 1723 a friend wrote to William Stukeley, Britain's greatest antiquary, then working up his Stonehenge surveys. 'We shall have you come home', he said, 'like another Columbus from the discovery of a new world.' Which he did, with news of an ancient Britain peopled by Druids and decorated with mysterious monuments. Today it seems we are on a second such adventure, so many are the continuing revelations concerning what we now regard as the end of the Neolithic era, around 3000–2000 BC.

Three spectacular discoveries in particular illustrate these exciting developments. The first transformed a stone circle mapped by Stukeley. The second would have delighted him: no doubt he would have called it a Druidic grove. He actually found the third, but few believed him and it had long been lost.

Stanton Drew

At Stanton Drew, Somerset, in southeastern Britain, are three little-visited stone circles. In 1997 English Heritage scientists undertook a geophysical survey there, the first investigation in modern times – and they were not alone in being astonished by the results. Unexcavated and undated, Stanton Drew suddenly entered the world of Stonehenge and the famous Wessex wood 'henges'. Unique to Britain and Ireland, henges are ritual earthworks with a ditch outside the bank (hence not defensive). Sometimes enclosing standing stones or rings of oak posts, they seem to have been places where crowds of people gathered for ceremonies, feasting and, occasionally, disposal of the dead.

The first thing the Stanton Drew survey revealed was that the great stone circle stood inside a circular ditch, 135 m (443 ft) in diameter, with a single gap facing – as at Stonehenge – the general direction of midsummer sunrise (there may be a small gap opposite, facing midwinter sunset). The ditch was so close to the stones that the now-vanished bank must have been on its outer edge, making this earthwork by definition a henge.

That alone made Stanton Drew almost unique: a large circular henge enclosing a large stone circle. Yet this was not the most surprising discovery. Inside the circle of stones the survey showed nine concentric rings of closely spaced spots. There was only one likely explanation. Here was the largest wooden henge ever seen: the pits for 400 or 500 oak posts formed circles 19 to 92 m (62 to 302 ft) across – twice the size of Woodhenge, the most famous site of this type.

opposite
Routine geophysics at Stanton Drew in 1997 – the results of which are seen here – revealed a distinct circular ditch and rings of post-holes at the largest stone circle, making the greatest wood 'henge' known.

right
In 1998 a ring of posts around an earthfast, upturned tree stump (here covered in green weed) appeared at Holme-next-the-Sea on Britain's east coast. The timbers were lifted for preservation.

Seahenge

So far there has been no excavation at Stanton Drew. There might have been none at Holme-next-the-Sea, on Britain's east coast, either, if protesters had got their way. Here, what was once, long ago, scrubby woodland and freshwater swamp had been buried by sand. But the dunes were now eroding, and in 1998 John Lorimer was shrimping on this wide Norfolk shore when he noticed an upturned tree stump.

A year later the press announced 'Seahenge', by then exposed as a ring of oak posts nearly 7 m (23 ft) across, with the stump in the centre. Public interest exploded. The Norfolk Archaeological Unit asked Mark Brennand to excavate. Self-proclaimed pagans tried to stop him, and even some archaeologists argued the remains were better left to erode into the sea. Nonetheless, the ring of 56 posts and the stump were lifted for preservation.

The reward was a detailed story. From tree-ring study and radiocarbon dating, we know construction began in spring or early summer 2049 BC. A honeysuckle rope was looped through a hole in the stump to help drag it to the site. Posts were hammered into the wet ground with their split faces inwards, their sides touching, with a single gap formed by a forked branch on the solstice axis. Study of marks left by bronze blades

suggests over 50 axes were used to make Seahenge, perhaps representing an entire community. We have no further clues as to its function, though few doubt it was ceremonial. A larger, less well-preserved ring has since been found nearby, with two parallel logs lying flat on the mud. For both, it is imagined the central timbers supported a coffin or body. These sites, dating from after the great era of henge construction, c. 3000–2200 BC, and linked to a later tradition of burial beneath small round mounds, are thought to be places for laying out the dead.

Beckhampton Avenue

Meanwhile, as Brennand attempted in 1999 to rescue Seahenge from the tides and didgeridoo-wielding pagans, that powerful alliance of William Stukeley, English Heritage and modern archaeologists was making another discovery, in Wiltshire, southern England. Avebury is famous for its vast megalithic monuments: a stone ring 350 m (1,148 ft) across inside a massive but irregular henge (enclosing two further stone rings), and the West Kennet Avenue, 2.3 km (1.4 miles) long, leading to the Sanctuary. Few knew that Stukeley had recorded a second avenue, leading west. Even as he looked, the last few stones had been removed by local farmers. Generations on, his observations were dismissed as fantasy.

So when another geophysical survey by Andrew David's team at English Heritage suggested Stukeley might have been right, archaeologists Mark Gillings, Joshua Pollard and David Wheatley

opened trenches near the hamlet of Beckhampton. Their work in 2000, 2002 and 2003 uncovered four buried megaliths as well as the pits that once held 14 others. The Beckhampton Avenue ran from Avebury for 1.3 km (0.8 miles). At its end first stood three widely spaced stones, and later a more compact group of four huge megaliths, each over 60 tonnes. One of these still stands, along with what is now seen to be the last true avenue stone. Here, the southern row ran beside an older earthwork enclosure, whose bank was levelled when the avenue was built.

What were these avenues for? Perhaps the concept originated in older 'cursus' monuments, long processional ways marked out by ditches and banks dating from *c.* 3500–3000 BC. Unique to Britain and Ireland, over 100 of these are now known, mostly discovered by air photography, with the first recognized by Stukeley near Stonehenge.

Avenues imply ceremonies and movement across wide areas. New research is exploring this engagement with the landscape, including a programme at Stonehenge directed by Mike Parker Pearson and colleagues. The aim is to see how the great monuments related to each other. Excavation began at Durrington Walls (Britain's largest henge) in 2004, continued at Woodhenge and will visit other locations. Quantities of artifacts and faunal remains have been found outside the henge at Durrington associated with apparent houses, as well as a track leading to the River Avon. Further significant discoveries are expected. A new world indeed.

The Nebra Sky Disc: The Oldest Representation of the Heavens

Harald Meller

The oldest representation of the heavens known in the world, the Nebra Sky Disc fundamentally changes our picture not just of the European Bronze Age, but of the history of all mankind. Although stylized and encoded, its astronomical statements can be read and reveal a precise knowledge of the movements of the celestial bodies.

The Nebra Sky Disc was discovered and unearthed illegally in 1999 on the Mittelberg Hill near Nebra, in Germany, by two treasure hunters using metal detectors. Sold on through art market fences, news of it slowly began to emerge, and after lengthy undercover efforts it was offered to me for sale in Switzerland. Secured by the police authorities, it is now housed in the State Museum of Prehistory in Halle. Both the original location and the authenticity of the Sky Disc, as well as the unity of the complete find – it also included two swords, two axes, two arm-rings and a chisel – were established beyond all doubt through forensic police work, archaeological investigations and scientific analyses. On the basis of the associated artifacts and radiocarbon dating, we can now say that the hoard was deposited around 1600 BC in a shallow pit on the Mittelberg.

The iconography of the Sky Disc at first glance seems straightforward – gold decorations in the form of the sun or full moon, and a crescent moon and stars, with curved bands at the edges – but closer inspection reveals it be mysterious and strange. It finds no parallels either in the prehistoric iconography of Europe, nor in the slightly later painted sky ceilings of tombs in Egypt. So how should we interpret the image? Looking closer at the gold appliqués on the now greenish and corroded, but originally darker, disc we notice that changes have been made, apparently in prehistoric times. Three different types of gold were used for those elements which had clearly been changed.

The first version seems clear: it shows 32 stars, a crescent moon and a full moon or the sun. The group of seven stars is probably the Pleiades; no other constellations can be identified. But a complex and elegant coding of astronomical knowledge lies hidden behind this simple appearance. On the one hand, the position of crescent and full moon in relation to the Pleiades accurately represents the declination phenomena to the precise day in the western evening and the eastern morning sky on 10 March and 17 October – dates which frame the rural year. But there is also concealed a celestial mechanical leap rule, allowing the harmonization of the shorter lunar year with the longer solar year, resulting in a serviceable calendar showing the day, week, month and year. A Babylonian source (8th century BC) describes the conjunction of the moon and Pleiades in spring: a narrow new moon near the Pleiades means the solar and lunar year are synchronous; and if a moon of 4½ days' thickness stands near the Pleiades, a lunar month must be included – precisely the picture represented on the Sky Disc. The number of stars – 32 – as well as the full moon, incorporate the leap year rules and the beginning of spring in further codings.

This first version of the Sky Disc thus both recorded extremely valuable knowledge and allowed it to be passed on in times before writing. That this failed is illustrated by subsequent changes made to the disc. Two lateral bands were attached that covered or repositioned older stars, thereby completely or partially obscuring the older meaning. The lateral bands mark the annual celestial cycle of the sun between summer and winter solstice in central Germany. At least two further dates are thus fixed by the extremities of the bands – 21 June and 21 December.

The next change to the Sky Disc was more drastic. A golden arc bordered by fine lines was attached near the rim between the horizon bands. This is probably a stylized representation of a ship. In the Nordic Bronze Age, the ship is a key symbol in an emerging religion whose central myth relates to the journey of the sun by ship through night and day. The Sky Disc – perhaps thus far kept hidden and used only by a few – now becomes a mythologized and cult object. The addition of perforations around the edge of the disc may have allowed it to be mounted on a support and perhaps publicly displayed. Finally, after the removal of one horizon band, the disc was interred with the other objects in a ritual act – a precious sacrifice to the gods.

left
Diagram showing the five stages of changes to the disc.

opposite
The Nebra Sky Disc is now greenish and corroded, but was originally a much darker colour.

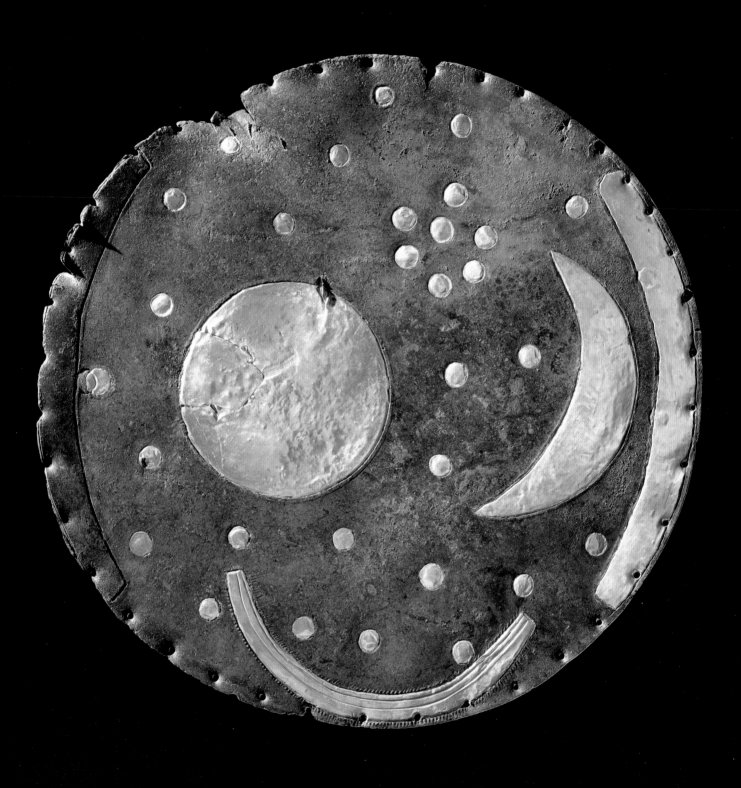

Helmets and War-Trumpets:
A Ritual Hoard from Tintignac, France

Christophe Maniquet

The cult site of Les Arènes de Tintignac in France is located in the territory of the Celtic people known as the Lemovices, on the southwestern edge of the Massif Central. I and my team have been excavating at this important Gallo-Roman sanctuary each summer since 2001, but it was not until September 2004 that we discovered one of the most extraordinary finds of the Celtic period brought to light in the last 20 years.

The sanctuary takes the form of a large square area surrounded by ditches which perhaps held a palisade enclosing a space around 24 m (79 ft) across. Almost in the centre of the platform, a collection of post-holes marked the presence of a circular wooden building. In the northeast corner of the sacred enclosure we uncovered a small pit, only about 1.3 m (4.3 ft) square and just 0.3 m (1 ft) in depth, which we were astonished to find contained a remarkable quantity of iron or bronze objects.

Among the 492 objects we recovered from the pit, 148 have been identified as fragments of iron sword sheaths; there are also 42 pieces of sword blades, 11 fragments of spearheads, including some complete, 1 shield boss and 33 fragments of helmets. There were also 4 animal heads made of cast or sheet bronze and some 10 bronze pieces from the bodies or feet of animals. To this can be added a complete cauldron, 2 horse bits

and 7 bronze discs. Of the helmets, 10 were complete but badly damaged. Nine are of bronze, mostly of a fairly simple shape, though one was decorated with a network pattern, the spaces originally filled with small pieces of gilded metal and probably enamel. One helmet was made of iron, with a bronze crest and added decoration. A final helmet was uncovered on the floor of the pit. This is the most remarkable – nothing similar has ever been found. Made entirely of bronze, it is in the shape of a swan, the body of which forms the skullcap. Because of the unusual nature of some of the helmets we wondered whether they were worn in combat or were instead ceremonial objects used in a ritual context.

What makes the Tintignac hoard even more astonishing, even unique in the Celtic world, is the presence of fragments of seven carnyxes. The carnyx was a large war-trumpet which was

used by the Gauls, according to the Classical authors Polybius and Diodorus Siculus, as part of the 'tumult of war'. These trumpets were held vertically and their upper end was cast in the shape of an animal's head with open jaws, through which the sound emerged. Until our discovery of this hoard, such war-trumpets were known primarily through depictions on Gallo-Roman triumphal monuments or coins – examples of actual carnyxes were limited to a few dozen fragments, including two mouths, from across the entire Celtic world. At Tintignac, the carnyxes were among the first objects placed in the pit. Two boar's heads in cast bronze may have been mouths; four other fragments of varying sizes, also decorated with stylized boar's heads, are probably parts of war-trumpets, as is a fifth decorated with a serpent's head. The mouths are all wide open. One straight carnyx mouthpiece was also found in the pit; this is exceptional because it is the only one of its kind discovered to date.

After the initial excitement of the discovery itself, we now have to try to determine the reason for the presence of a pit of this kind in the corner of the sanctuary of Tintignac. The various objects in it were clearly placed there at the same time. Based on the stratigraphy and the date of items found in layers above the pit, we know that the objects were deposited in the 2nd or 1st

century BC, following a major rebuilding of the sanctuary. However, stylistic features of several of the finds seem to belong instead to a period between the 3rd and the mid-2nd century BC. We think the weapons and instruments may have been displayed within the sanctuary before they were buried at a later date.

Could the objects found in the Tintignac hoard have been pieces of ritual equipment used during a ceremony? The Tintignac finds certainly seem to be sacred in nature and may have been used during initiation rituals for warriors. Perhaps they were then buried during a troubled period, or when a change in rituals occurred due to Romanization.

The discovery of such a rich collection of objects, deliberately placed within such a context, is unprecedented. Interpretation is at an early stage, and the objects are still undergoing restoration, but it is certain that the contribution of the Tintignac hoard to the study of Celtic civilization will be considerable.

opposite
The unusual helmet shaped like a swan required meticulous excavation, with several team members on hand to support it as it came out of the ground.

below, left and right
A boar's head in cast bronze and fragments of war-trumpets still in situ as found at the bottom of the pit, with the lines of the excavation grid visible.

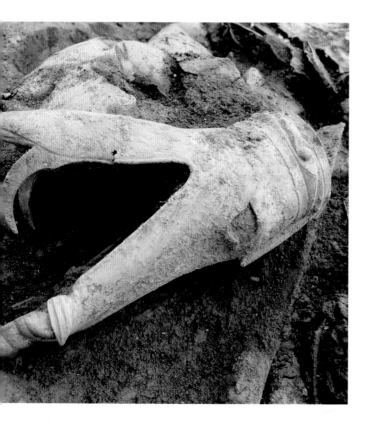

Symbols of Religion and Power:
The Pyramid of the Moon, Teotihuacán

Saburo Sugiyama

Recent tunnels excavated into the core of the Pyramid of the Moon at Teotihuacán, Mexico's greatest and most mysterious ancient city, have yielded extraordinary information about sacrificial rituals carried out by the rulers here. Specially chosen people, perhaps war captives, were buried deep inside the monument, along with bound or caged animals and exceptionally rich offerings, to consecrate newly constructed pyramids.

Teotihuacán, which flourished between the 1st and 6th centuries AD, became the largest and most populous urban centre in the Americas, with an estimated population of 100,000 to 150,000. It was the most influential state in Mesoamerica until its intentional destruction by unknown people around AD 600. Despite generations of research, the city remains an enigma. Who built it? What was the function of its major monuments? Written records and royal graves have yet to be found, but our recent discoveries are at last providing new perspectives.

Dedicatory burials

Teotihuacán was a highly planned city, with the giant Pyramid of the Moon, 46 m (151 ft) high, rising at the northern end of the city's main axis, the Avenue of the Dead. A joint project from 1998 to 2004 with Mexico's National Institute of Anthropology and History, co-directed by Rubén Cabrera and myself, systematically explored the pyramid complex, especially its nucleus, with 345 m (1,131 ft) of tunnel excavations. We discovered seven superimposed buildings, indicating the importance of this location from the time of the city's foundation. Constant rebuilding represented changing social and political fortunes. For instance, the enlargement of what we named Buildings 4 and 6 apparently symbolized an expansion of state power around AD 250 and 350 respectively. We also discovered, and completely excavated, five burials (Burials 2 to 6), containing 37 human sacrificial victims, mostly adult males, associated with animals and extremely precious objects. All the graves lay on the axis of the Moon Pyramid as dedicatory offerings to newly constructed monuments. Their locations, the graves, the people buried and the associated objects varied significantly.

Burial 2 dedicated the construction of Building 4. The construction level included one sacrificed person and sacred animals, including 2 pumas, 1 wolf, 9 eagles and several

left
The Pyramid of the Moon formed the principal monument of the Moon Plaza complex located at the north end of the Avenue of the Dead in Teotihuacán. It is the only major monument located on the central axis of the city, and measures about 149 m (488 ft) by 168 m (550 ft) at its base.

opposite
A greenstone figure of a man in a seated position was found at the centre of Burial 5. The figure was associated with beads and earspools, as well as obsidian miniatures, shells and a large amount of perishable materials. It may represent an ancestral person of extremely high social status rather than a god.

rattlesnakes, some probably buried alive. The symbolic offerings include greenstone human figures and personal ornaments; obsidian knives, spears, arrows and figures; shell ornaments; pyrite and slate disks; and ceramic jars depicting the rain god, Tlaloc. Two further dedicatory burials were then incorporated into a new monument, our Building 5, some 50 years later. One of these (Burial 3) was set under the back wall, with four other sacrificial victims and a rich variety of lavish offerings. In the other burial (6), 12 people were sacrificed and buried together with rich offerings and animals near the centre of the building; 10 had been decapitated. More than 40 complete and incomplete animals were also sacrificed and consecrated.

Two more burials were later dedicated to Building 6, one of which (Burial 4) consisted of 17 human heads without bodies or offerings, while the other (Burial 5) was placed on the upper floor of Building 5 just prior to the construction of Building 6. This included three individuals who were buried with great respect. They lay with exceptionally precious ornaments indicating their high social status, including Maya-style jadeite pendants symbolizing rulership. This discovery unexpectedly confirmed Teotihuacán's direct intervention into major Maya centres in the lowlands.

Religion and politics

The Moon Pyramid excavations confirmed that the major monuments at Teotihuacán were actively rebuilt or enlarged throughout their history and that sacrificial burials were often integrated into the nucleus of the pyramids during construction. We also believe that the Teotihuacán rulers symbolically expressed their military power and authority through these dedicatory burials. Isotope analyses of the victims' bones show that most of them were foreigners from different regions of Mesoamerica – perhaps war captives. They represent a range of social status, from high-ranking dignitaries to the lowest social classes or ethnic groups humiliated with extreme violence during the consecration ceremonies. Apart from the skeletal evidence, the importance of warfare was consistently proclaimed through weapons, warrior paraphernalia, conquest trophies such as necklaces crafted from human upper jaw bones, sacrificial knives and bound or caged animals such as pumas and eagles symbolically associated with military institutions.

Our project reaffirmed the ancient Mesoamerican tradition of integrating religion into politics – the burials, with their unique ritual paraphernalia and symbolic objects, show that the two were fundamentally and explicitly intertwined. The Maya,

and later the Aztecs, also merged politics and religion by framing their military campaigns in a fundamentally religious manner. Although Teotihuacán was long believed to have been a sacred, even legendary place governed by anonymous, collaborative leaders, our new discoveries suggest that this society, like other Mesoamerican city-states, also carried out military campaigns, perhaps under the leadership of charismatic rulers whose bodies are likely to be uncovered or identified in future investigations.

opposite

The builders of the Moon Pyramid apparently placed or dropped without care 17 severed human heads, along with rocks, while constructing the north wall of Building 6.

above

One complete skeleton of a puma was found inside a wood cage in Burial 2. A coprolite discovered near its tail indicates that it was still alive during the mortuary ritual.

right

Ten of 12 people sacrificed and buried in Burial 6 were missing their heads and first cervical vertebrae. They were evidently victims of a decapitation ritual carried out nearby or inside the chamber. They had no ornaments, suggesting that they were victims stripped of any attire to humiliate them.

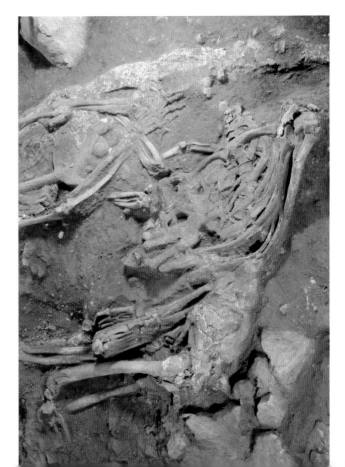

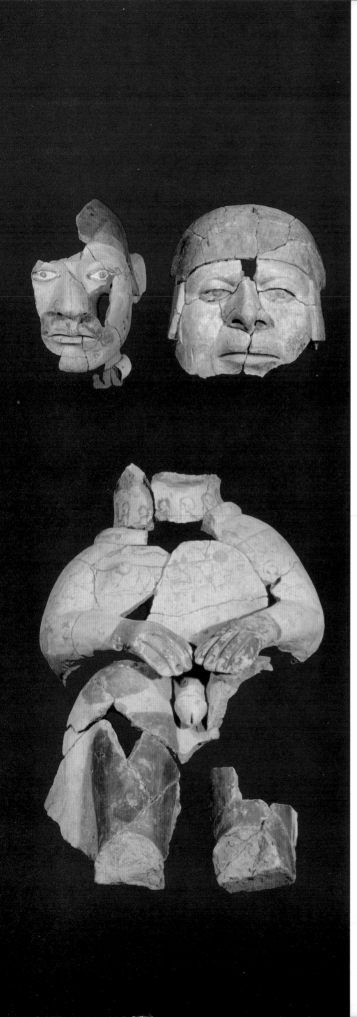

Moche Ritual Sacrifice at Huaca de la Luna, Peru

Steve Bourget

Human sacrifice has apparently been part of the development of numerous complex societies throughout the world. Yet archaeological confirmation of such practices is rare. The sacrificial contexts I discovered in 1995 at the Moche site of Huaca de la Luna, in Peru, are providing tantalizing clues about the nature of religion and political authority in an early state society.

In the early 16th century, when Europeans were first coming into contact with indigenous peoples in the Americas, human sacrifices appear to have abounded there. Soldiers, explorers and clergymen, mostly Spanish, repeatedly recorded that state-level societies such as the Aztec and the Inca carried out such activities. Early accounts are filled with horrific descriptions of people being burned alive, flayed, decapitated or simply thrown down the steps of temples. Yet physical evidence to support these descriptions is extremely rare, and without this crucial information it is difficult to fathom the motivations for such rituals. Were some of these sacrifices meant to establish a connection with the gods? Were they an instrument of the state to instil terror into people's hearts and minds, and to maintain the power of the ruling elite? My excavations formed a unique opportunity to study these rituals and to provide some answers.

The Moche

The Moche (see also p. 87) were an early state-level people who did not possess a writing system or a clearly defined market economy, but they established their presence in at least 10 coastal valleys of the Peruvian north coast and created some of the most outstanding temples of ancient Andean Peru. Building on the religious and political traditions of earlier societies, the Moche developed lavish rituals, an elaborate ruling elite and a social system of great complexity. They depicted the political authority of their rulers and their religious traditions and rituals – often of a sacrificial nature – in the form of remarkable ceramic vessels, metallic objects, wooden sculptures, textiles and painted walls. A significant part of Moche visual culture is dominated by representations of warfare, capture and sacrifice.

At the Huacas de Moche site, which was probably their most important political and ritual centre, the remains of an elaborate

left
These clay statuettes of naked males decorated with patterns were deliberately destroyed and were found with the sacrificial victims in Plaza 3a.

left
The skeletons of human sacrificial victims, spreadeagled in the mud in Plaza 3a, Huaca de la Luna.

below
A painted relief from the Great Patio in Platform I, Huaca de la Luna, in the Moche Valley. This fearsome creature is an octopus surrounded by stylized catfishes.

city dominated by two monumental structures have been under continuous investigation since 1991. The diverse archaeological investigations here at the Huaca de la Luna (Temple of the Moon), under the direction of Santiago Uceda (Universidad Nacional de Trujillo) and Ricardo Morales, led to the discovery of outstanding polychrome murals, complex architectural features, burials of high-ranking individuals and elaborate sacrificial practices.

The sacrificial site

While investigating a plaza in a secluded part of the temple, I made the extraordinary find of an extensive and complex sacrificial site. Plaza 3a was built sometime in the 6th or 7th century. In this precinct, surrounded by high adobe walls, some 70 male warriors had been sacrificed and in many cases dismembered in the course of at least five distinct ritual events. After the sacrifices, the remains of the victims were scattered around the ritual precinct. They were sometimes accompanied by clay statuettes portraying naked males with their bodies covered with intricate symbols. These statuettes are in fact three-

dimensional renditions of the individuals depicted in fineline paintings. Evidence suggests that at least two of these rituals took place during torrential rainfalls brought by El Niño events.

This sacrificial context has generated much scholarly debate. Some suggest that the victims had been provided by the military activities of the state – Moche polities fighting against other Moche polities, or Moche against other groups. Although such interpretations remain possible, the facts of the architecture solely devoted to these activities, the El Niño conditions of certain rituals and the clay statuettes clearly associated with the iconography suggest that another explanation must be sought.

Sacrifice and authority

At the beginning of the investigation, I suggested that these sacrificial rituals may have been aimed at placating the cataclysmic El Niño events. Human sacrifices would have been performed as a means of establishing contact with the forces responsible for the occurrence of these disastrous conditions and attempting to appease them. Ritual battles would have provided a method for selecting the eventual sacrificial victims. This rather mechanistic position can no longer be supported by the mounting evidence that demonstrates that El Niño events were in fact fully integrated into Moche religion and ideology.

High-ranking individuals, like those found in the sumptuous burials excavated by Walter Alva and Luis Chero at Sipán, or in the looted context at La Mina, wore large pectorals, bracelets, and nose and ear ornaments decorated with various animal species. The most prominent creatures depicted on these objects, and on ritual vessels, are those that accompany the El Niño sea current, such as the Peruvian eagle ray (*Myliobatis peruvianus*) and swimming crabs. The nobility also adorned themselves with depictions of local species that were directly affected by the changing conditions that El Niño brought, such as octopuses, catfish, spiders, seabirds and sea lions. The temple walls of Huaca de la Luna and Huaca Cao Viejo among others are also covered with painted reliefs of animal species clearly associated with El Niño events.

Thus the response of Moche rulers to the threat posed by El Niño would have been to associate their authority with its awesome power – its frightening capacity to transform the familiar sea into a completely different marine environment. The iconography depicted on temple walls, on ritual ceramics and on the objects worn by high-ranking individuals would have served to display and reiterate this intimate relationship. Joined to a religion and a political system centred around the practice of human sacrifice, the effect of these devastating conditions would not have been to diminish or challenge the rulers' power but rather to reinforce it. Human sacrifices and the incorporation of El Niño events into the ritual sphere would have been some of the devices used to foster and maintain social solidarity around Moche rulers even during cataclysmic conditions.

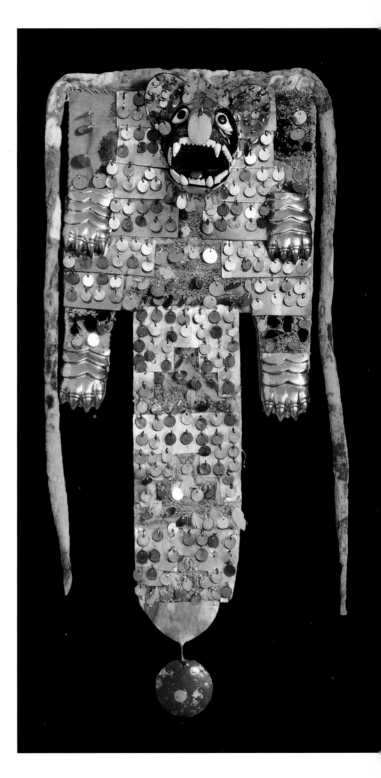

above
A strange animal effigy covered with discs of gilded copper, from Platform I, Huaca de la Luna.

Discoveries from the Deep

previous pages
Eerily lit by the divers' torches, a statue of a robed priest and two sphinxes loom out of the underwater darkness in the harbour of Alexandria.

right
Ships moored in the desert: the world's oldest built vessels were discovered, each in its own grave, at Abydos in Egypt, dating from the 3rd millennium BC.

right
A colossal statue of a pharaoh raised from the seabed from a temple of ancient Heracleion, one of the submerged cities rediscovered by Franck Goddio in Aboukir Bay.

right
The USS Monitor was an ironclad built as part of the arms race in the American Civil War. Its massive gun turret was located on the seabed and later raised to the surface, providing new details about how it rotated.

ANCIENT SHIPWRECKS laden with cargo are among the most exciting of all archaeological discoveries. But the most unexpected find of recent years came not from the seabed, but from the Egyptian desert. Matthew Douglas Adams and David O'Connor describe how they unearthed the oldest wooden vessels in the world from the royal cemetery at Abydos, Egypt. The 14 planked boats lay in the sand, ready to assist one of the very earliest Egyptian rulers in his journey in the afterlife.

Little remains of Hellenistic Alexandria, one of the greatest cities of antiquity, founded by Alexander the Great in 332 BC. Franck Goddio has rediscovered the submerged remains of the city's harbour, using geophysical technology to identify and map the harbour's temples and shipyards. He has also brilliantly researched and found the long-lost ancient cities of Canopus and Heracleion in Aboukir Bay, the latter the main port-of-entry for Egypt before Alexandria. Ancient ports such as those of Pisa in Italy were bustling, crowded places, where ships from distant lands unloaded exotic cargoes. One of Pisa's naval ports, uncovered during construction work, was on a now-silted up tidal lagoon. Italian archaeologist Stefano Bruni describes remarkably well-preserved Roman boats and ships buried in the silt, dating between the 1st century BC and the early 6th century AD.

Many details of even well-documented events such as the mutiny on the *Bounty* come from the seabed. The frigate HMS *Pandora* sailed from England in search of the *Bounty* mutineers in 1790, but foundered on the Great Barrier Reef off northeastern Australia. Peter Gesner guides us through the wreck excavation, an underwater Pompeii of late 18th-century naval life.

Underwater archaeology also carries us into the fury of US Civil War conflict. Robert Neyland describes the search for two historic Civil War warships, the *Monitor* and the *Hunley*. The ironclad USS *Monitor* fought the previously invincible Confederate ironclad *Virginia* to a standstill in Hampton Roads, Virginia, on 9 March 1862. Several months later the *Monitor* sank in a storm. Its turret was recovered in 2002. The Confederate submarine *Hunley* was lost in 1864 after sinking the Union ship *Housatonic*, an exploit that caused hasty changes in US naval tactics. The submarine was discovered in 1995 and raised in 2000, a converted steam boiler armed with a spar torpedo attached to the bow. Neyland tells us how he felt a human and personal connection with the trapped crew.

The World's Oldest Boats, from Abydos, Egypt

Matthew Douglas Adams and David O'Connor

Significant archaeological discoveries are at their most exciting when totally unexpected. Tutankhamun's spectacular tomb, discovered in 1922, had been specifically sought for, but the identification of the world's oldest surviving built vessels (rather than dugouts) at Abydos, southern Egypt, in 1991 was truly a 'bolt from the blue'. Their discovery (each embedded in its own brick-built grave structure) resulted from systematic excavations, but the existence of boat graves at the site was completely unsuspected.

For 20 years we have been systematically investigating the early royal mortuary monuments in north Abydos, a series of mud-brick enclosures (some quite large, occupying as much as 1 ha, or 2.4 acres), in work sponsored by the Institute of Fine Arts, New York University, the University of Pennsylvania Museum and Yale University. Most were built for individual kings of the 1st and 2nd dynasties (*c.* 2950–2650 BC), who were buried about a mile to the south in tombs that were initially excavated in the 1890s. Although physically separated by a considerable distance, tomb and enclosure together conceptually comprise the whole of the two-part mortuary complexes of these early kings. Despite the earlier excavations, much about the function of these large enclosures, the walls of which originally rose impressively as high as 11 m (36 ft), remained mysterious when we began our work.

In 1988 our excavations at the enclosure of King Khasekhemwy of the 2nd Dynasty encountered a strange, rounded, buttress-like construction in mud brick, 2 m (6 ft) outside the wall. This did not resemble any known 1st and 2nd Dynasty feature at Abydos, and, since the surrounding cemetery is filled with later graves, and even Coptic (Christian) structures, this enigmatic feature was originally thought to be relatively late. However, further study showed it instead to be contemporary with the enclosures, and we thought it might be an unusual example of the same type of structure.

Puzzlingly, as we expanded our excavation in 1991, multiple wall lines emerged, though this initially was interpreted to mean the assumed enclosure had been rebuilt several times. Soon,

left
Five of the boat graves at Abydos. Behind them is the enclosure of Khasekhemwy. The boat graves probably belong to an earlier 1st Dynasty enclosure, not seen here.

left

Excavation of subsidiary graves belonging to an early 1st Dynasty enclosure uncovered donkey, rather than human, burials.

below

The preserved planks of one of the Abydos boats inside its brick grave structure.

opposite

Artist's reconstruction of the creation of the boat graves at Abydos. On the left is the 1st Dynasty royal enclosure to which the boat graves probably belonged. The reconstruction depicts the various stages involved in building the boat graves. In the distance, a boat is being dragged on to the site. In the foreground, both the preliminary and the final stages involved in the construction of the boat graves are shown.

however, 12 low but very long (on average 25 m/90 ft) cigar-shaped brick structures emerged (two more were found in 2000), with rounded buttress-like features at each end. We immediately recognized them as boat graves, from smaller examples found elsewhere.

We had not anticipated finding such boat graves, because no traces of any had been found in earlier, sometimes quite extensive, excavations at Abydos, and, in any case, where boat graves had been found at other sites, they were associated only with tombs. Our boat graves, however, appear to be linked to a king's enclosure of perhaps late 1st Dynasty date. We can now see that the boats, like the sacrificed courtiers and retainers found associated with other enclosures at Abydos, had also been 'sacrificed' and ceremonially buried, so as to pass into the afterlife to serve the dead king. Similarly, near another enclosure that we discovered in 2003 were subsidiary graves containing 10 donkeys, rather than humans.

It is unlikely that either boats or donkeys were intended for the relevant king's personal use; rather, they would have been utilized by rowers or riders (some perhaps in nearby subsidiary graves) to provide services required by the king in the afterlife. The 14 boat graves now discovered, each built in the shape of a boat and covered with a mud-plastered and whitewashed brick structure, would have appeared as a fleet moored in the

desert. Some even had what appears to be a mooring stone or symbolic anchor.

If the discovery of the boat graves themselves was exciting, equally if not more so was what we subsequently found inside them. In 1991 we recorded a cross-section of a wooden boat inside one grave, and in other, as yet unexcavated, boat graves, the outlines of the tops of similar wooden boats are visible in the partially eroded tops of the mud-brick structures. Much more revealing was the actual excavation of part of one of the boats in 2000: it proved to be a fully assembled and functional vessel.

Although the wood of the boat had been heavily damaged by insects and later pitting and was extremely fragile, much of the fabric of the hull remained. As the debris left by insects was removed, the individual planks that made up the hull could be defined. They appear to have been fashioned from local wood, perhaps tamarisk, and varied in size and shape, having probably been individually cut to fit as the boat was constructed. Parallel rows of mortises had been cut in the planks, through which rope lashings had been threaded. When pulled tight, these would have closed the seams between the planks and held the hull together.

The boat was shallow in draft, only around 60 cm (2 ft), and the longitudinal profile of the hull was a convex shallow

arc – slightly higher at the ends than in the middle. The outside of the hull was plastered and had been painted a deep yellow.

Based on the evidence from the partially excavated boat and careful examination of the other graves, it appears that each boat was probably brought to the site overland, a significant achievement in itself since each hull weighed as much as a ton; it was then set into a shallow trench in the sand. The trenches were not deep enough to support the hulls fully, as in some cases it is clear that the boats warped significantly and large stones were used to prop up sections. Once the boats were in place, the exteriors of the hulls were encased in brick masonry, and the interiors were also filled with brickwork. Finally, each boat grave was plastered and whitewashed.

The implications of these extraordinary boat graves and their contents extend well beyond the early period to which they belong. They clearly anticipate the spectacular boat burials and boat-shaped graves associated with some later royal pyramids of the 4th to the 12th dynasties (c. 2575–1755 BC), especially the royal ships of King Khufu, found buried in pits next to his Great Pyramid at Giza. In addition to their symbolic significance, however, the Abydos boats also provide a revealing insight into the earliest boat-building techniques documented anywhere in the world.

Alexandria Underwater:
Greek Cities Beneath the Sea in Egypt

Franck Goddio

On 1 August 1798, the British fleet under Admiral Lord Nelson sailed into Aboukir Bay, 25 km (15.5 miles) east of Alexandria, to attack the French ships anchored there. None on board realized they were sailing over the ruins of two lost cities – Canopus and Heracleion. Referred to by numerous ancient authors, their location remained a complete mystery until we started a long-term exploration project along Egypt's northern coast.

The work began in 1992, when the Institut Européen d'Archéologie Sous-Marine obtained permission from Egypt's Supreme Council of Antiquities to investigate both Alexandria's ancient port and Aboukir Bay. This area had suffered from numerous natural disasters, which had submerged the *Portus Magnus* of Alexandria and the cities of Heracleion and Canopus without trace.

Alexandria's *Portus Magnus*

The first focus of our investigation was Alexandria, one of the great cities of antiquity, founded by Alexander the Great in 332 BC and a cosmopolitan trading hub and centre of Classical learning. Alexandria's lighthouse, the Pharos, was one of the Seven Wonders of the World, but little was known of the ancient city's now-submerged harbour. The port presented major challenges. The work was certainly on a different scale from other projects we had developed our techniques on – in addition to wrecks, there were thousands of stone blocks, some weighing several tons, scattered across the seabed. Rather than lifting each one, we decided to record them and any inscriptions in situ. In addition, fine silt and pollution from the city complicated the diving, which was all at depths of less than 5 m (16 ft).

Information was gathered from Classical authors and epigraphic documentation, and this, together with our underwater work, led to unexpected results which have revolutionized our knowledge of the eastern port of Alexandria.

right
Laid out on a barge after they had been raised from the seabed are the colossal triad of the Temple of Heracleion, together with the assembled fragments of a huge stela. The pharaoh, the queen and the god Hapi, dating to the 4th century BC, are carved from red granite and are all over 5 m (16 ft) high. The red granite stela was found in 17 pieces and is 6.1 m (20 ft) high. It dates to the 2nd century BC and bears hieroglyphic and Greek inscriptions from the time of the pharaoh Ptolemy VIII.

opposite
Franck Goddio and divers from his team inspect the colossal statue of a pharaoh carved from red granite (also visible on the left on the barge in the photograph on this page). It was found close to a large temple in the sunken city of Heracleion.

We were able to draw up a detailed map of the *Portus Magnus*, both of its outline and of the structure of its facilities, located near the city's palaces – the royal harbour, the Roman general Mark Antony's retreat, the Timonium, and the island of Antirhodos, where there once stood a royal palace.

Canopus and Heracleion

We next moved on to Aboukir Bay, stretching eastwards from Alexandria, an area that promised to reveal significant finds. A long-term survey begun in 1996, together with electronic devices, allowed us to locate major archaeological deposits and the course of the former western branch of the Nile. It appears that a large triangle of low-lying coastline became submerged as a result of gradual subsidence and collapse of the shoreline. It was here that the cities of Canopus, Heracleion – a city sacred to the mythical hero Heracles – and Menouthis once thrived.

One concentration of ruins was discovered over 6 km (3.7 miles) from the coast. Our excavations found the boundary wall of a temple more than 150 m (492 ft) long and also a *naos*, the monolithic chapel that once contained the image of the god, dedicated to 'the Amon of the *gereb*'. This, along with literary and epigraphic evidence, proved that these were the ruins of Heracleion. A gold plate with an inscription declaring that King Ptolemy III had founded or renovated a sanctuary dedicated to Heracles in this general area confirmed the identification.

right
The Stela of Heracleion (1.9 m/6.2 ft tall) was ordered by the pharaoh Nectanebo I (380 BC). The place where it was intended to be erected is explicitly mentioned: Thonis. This enabled us to identify the Greek city of Heracleion as the Egyptian Thonis.

far right
Statue of a priest of Isis holding an Osiris-jar, found on the sunken island of Antirhodos in the harbour of Alexandria. Carved from black granite, it stands 1.22 m (4 ft) high.

opposite
A diver examines a colossal red granite statue of the god Hapi, from the temple of Heracleion. The god of the Nile inundation has never before been found represented on such a large scale, which points to his importance for the Canopic region.

Another extraordinary discovery was an intact black granite stela on which the text mentions the Egyptian name of the site, Thonis, showing that Greek Heracleion was the Egyptian *Thonis*.

The site was once a peninsula confined between several port basins on its eastern side and by a lake stretching westward. Thus, the city with its bustling port controlled access to the Canopic branch of the Nile. Finds include more than 700 anchors of various shapes, as well as 21 wrecks dating from the 6th to the 2nd centuries BC. Dozens of small votive anchors of bronze, lead and stone remind us of the offerings sailors made to the gods. A large channel passing through Thonis-Heracleion linked the port basins to the western lake. Lavish ritual offerings, including many of statuettes connected with ceremonies of the god Osiris-Dionysos, show the sacred nature of the waterway.

Part of Canopus lies west of Thonis-Heracleion and about 2 km (1.2 miles) east of the modern port of Aboukir. A line of ruins, 150 m (490 ft) long, along with other structures, was dated by jewels, crosses, coins and seals to the Byzantine period, and belonged to a Christian institution. Broken shafts of pink granite columns lie mingled with a maze of limestone building blocks. To the north, foundations of a temple boundary wall lay under 2 m (6 ft) of sand. Measuring 103 m (338 ft) long, this is the largest Egyptian sanctuary so far discovered in the region. Between this temple and the Byzantine complex we found a dumping ground where statues had been discarded, most likely to be cut up and their stone reused. Pieces of granite engraved with hieroglyphs came from the famous chapel called *Naos of the Decades*. A remarkable marble head of the god Serapis, dating to the Ptolemaic period, once belonged to a statue over 4 m (13 ft) tall. Ancient texts tell us that pilgrims flocked to the Serapeum of Canopus, sometimes from far away, to visit its god with miraculous healing powers.

The Heracleion and Canopus excavations form an immense research project involving two entire ancient cities, in working conditions where the visibility underwater on a good day is a mere 2 m (6 ft). We are uncovering an incredible snapshot of Egyptian life, not only spectacular sculptures and objects, but also ships and remains of trading activities. Hundreds of coins tell us much about economic conditions and the trade patterns of the day in cities that were untouched by either contemporary looters or modern robbers.

The Ancient Port and Ships of Pisa

Stefano Bruni

In December 1998, construction work in an area of Pisa just to the west of the famous Piazza del Duomo stumbled upon the remains of an ancient harbour, dating to the Etruscan–Roman era. From the outset we realized it was a highly significant find, and ongoing excavations have uncovered the remains of more than 15 well-preserved ships and revealed part of the harbour of one of the greatest Classical ports of the Mediterranean.

Since antiquity, the environment and geography of the port of Pisa have changed dramatically: the ancient coastline was considerably closer to the city, but has since retreated as the River Arno silted up over the centuries with alluvial deposits. Other features of the ancient landscape have also altered over time. This is the result of continual flooding of the area as water defences were abandoned, together with a rise in sea level, as well as water pollution caused by Pisa's political, economic and demographic crisis in Late Antiquity, and land reclamation works carried out from the Middle Ages onwards.

In the Etruscan and Roman period, Pisa grew up around a complex coastal lagoon system, very like Venice, with two rivers, the Arno and the Auser (which no longer exists), as well as canals and minor watercourses. The city had a number of ports

left
One of the best preserved of the Pisa boats, labelled ship D, has much of its hull and deck surviving. It perhaps dates to the early 2nd century AD, and will be able to tell us much about shipbuilding techniques at the time.

above
The site is strewn with remains of the cargoes and equipment of the ships, well preserved in the silt and mud.

and landing places, including the harbour we uncovered during our excavation. This lay at a deep meander of the northern branch of the Auser, within a populated area that had been settled since at least the end of the 9th century BC, though our finds date only from the end of the 6th century BC up to and including the 5th century AD – when the Roman urban system collapsed.

During its long period of use, the harbour was subjected to numerous modifications: the southern section of the area under investigation gradually silted up, and as a result the dock basin shrank. This is how various remains came to be entombed, including parts of a ship's hold from the Etruscan period, buried beneath an area where a port structure existed from the late Republican age. We also found a collapsed pier from the end of the 5th century BC, and the tip of a jetty together with the wreck of a Campanian cargo ship dating to the first decades of the 2nd century BC. Several boards of the latter's planking and other structural elements have been recovered, as well as numerous items from the ship's cargo and equipment.

A phenomenal amount of artifacts has been recovered from the Roman layers of the harbour basin – ceramics, amphoras and archaeological materials of every type, including organic materials that are not normally preserved, such as ropes and baskets, as well as ships' cargoes, from wine and olives to fruit. All the finds are either connected with the life and trade of the port, or came from the many ships that used Pisa's harbour but sank to the bottom for whatever reason. Most remarkable of all, however, was the unexpected discovery of more than 15 ships, as well as fragments of numerous others, which have been exceptionally well preserved owing to the conditions of their burial.

Although study and conservation of the ships is still continuing, of special interest are the remains of three cargo ships and a rowing boat, as well as three vessels that appear to have been used for navigating rivers.

One was discovered completely capsized and covering the remains of another vessel. The ships differ in their type of construction, and this, together with stratigraphy, associated finds and other research, has allowed us to date the vessels to various periods, ranging from the end of the 1st century BC to the end of the 5th or beginning of the 6th century AD.

The best-preserved vessel was ship D, which is around 14 m (46 ft) long, with much of its hull and deck surviving. The rowing boat (ship C), which was found buried under the seabed still anchored to its mooring post, is particularly interesting. The hull, which consisted of a load-bearing shell with connecting rods and treenails – a sort of wooden pin – is 13.3 m (44 ft) long and 2.68 m (8 ft) wide; it was propelled by six pairs of oarsmen who sat on a rowing bench and each held an oar, and a sail that was fixed to a mast. The mast was supported by three shrouds (pieces of rigging) on either side, which were attached with iron stays. The ship's prow has a rather sophisticated breakwater, reinforced by a metallic coating, and there is a primitive support on the stern. On top of the caulking (made from a glue-like substance of natural origin) the planking was painted in white and red, numerous traces of which are visible above the waterline.

To date no other vessel has been found that compares with this boat, a type of small pilot, with the exception of examples depicted in several frescoes in Rome and Pompeii. On the basis of associated materials, it is thought to date to the first 30 years of the 1st century BC.

The remarkable finds of both harbour remains and ships – possibly the largest number of ancient vessels found in one place – will tell us much not only about ancient shipbuilding techniques and the maritime history of Pisa, but also about trade in the Mediterranean from the 6th century BC to the 5th century AD. A purpose-built museum is now under construction so that the public will be able to see and enjoy the ancient ships of Pisa.

right
This small marble statuette came from the upper levels of the excavation.

opposite above
A Roman coin and a glass bowl, found in the area between ships B and E, are just some of the range of artifacts recovered.

opposite below
An enormous task awaits the archaeologists – sorting, studying and classifying the huge amount of material found with the ships.

HMS *Pandora*:
The Ship Sent to Find the *Bounty* Mutineers

Peter Gesner

The Royal Navy frigate HMS Pandora *sailed to the South Pacific in November 1790 under Captain Edward Edwards. Its mission was to capture and bring to justice the 25* Bounty *mutineers who had cast adrift their captain, William Bligh, but it ended in disaster when the ship sank. The wreck of the* Pandora *offered a unique opportunity to recover material evidence of the Grand Age of Pacific exploration, and I have been privileged to be a member of all the expedition teams that have explored it. Over the years I have dived and worked with a wide range of remarkable and interesting people.*

After 10 months at sea, having failed to find the *Bounty* and the mutiny's ringleader Fletcher Christian, the *Pandora* sailed for home with 14 prisoners caught in Tahiti who were locked in 'Pandora's Box', a makeshift cell on the quarterdeck. In late August 1791 the ship was reconnoitring a passage through the Great Barrier Reef towards Torres Strait when it ran aground. It was refloated, but despite the crew's best endeavours, the stricken frigate sank the next morning and settled on to a soft sandy bottom at a depth of 33 m (108 ft); 35 people perished, among them four *Bounty* prisoners.

The wreck was rediscovered in 1977 with the assistance of a Royal Australian Air Force *Neptune* aircraft equipped with a magnetometer. Since then Australian maritime archaeologists and the Queensland Museum have investigated it in nine major expeditions, in two stages. In the first stage we established that approximately 30 per cent of the original hull was preserved in a recognizable state, buried in about 2.5 m (8 ft) of sand and silt. After probing the stern section, I hypothesized that the ship disintegrated in three stages that destroyed the spars and rigging, the quarter- and main decks, and the forecastle. The collapsing debris and accumulating sediment buried and preserved intact much of the lower hull, including the starboard lower deck, the starboard platform deck and the fish and spirits rooms inside the hold. Little of the port side remained.

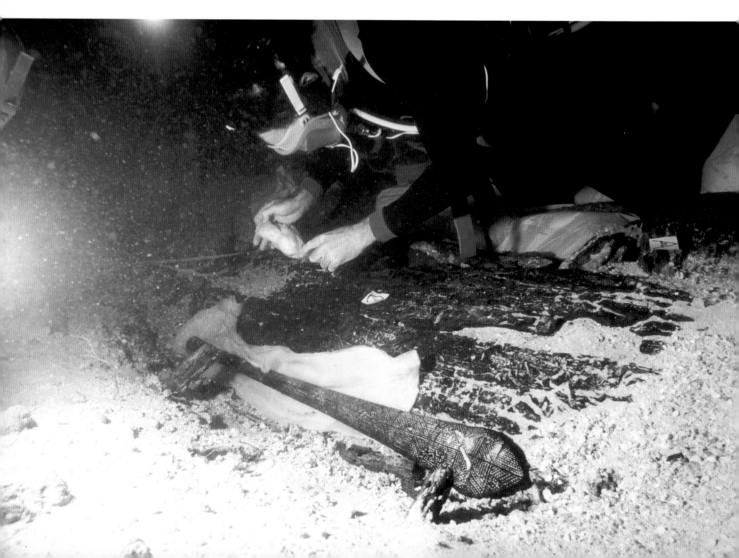

But fieldwork on the *Pandora* ground to a halt because of
inadequate funding, until 1993, when a far-sighted Queensland
Arts minister organized a $1-million subsidy that encouraged
the Pandora Foundation based in Townsville to raise an extra
$2.25 million for additional research. The Foundation supported
four major expeditions between 1996 and 1999 and – just as
important – helped to fund on-going conservation and display
of the artifacts brought to the surface. I worked with an
international team of up to 45 people spending five weeks on
site every season. We expanded the stern trench begun in the
1980s and also dug a new cutting in the bow area adjacent
to the remains of the galley stove.

The stern trench yielded a broad array of artifacts, mainly personal and professional possessions belonging to the ship's officers. These included several intriguing ceramic and semiprecious stone intaglio seals, perhaps talismans hung on fob-watch chains. Some depicted gods of the ancient Greek pantheon; one seal bore the French motto *'Il ne change qu'en mourant'* ('Nothing changes until death') – a rather dire prediction for its owner!

Life on board the *Pandora*

Captain Edwards' private storeroom was found completely intact. It contained a full, entirely unused creamware dinner service thought to be Wedgwood, as well as fine glassware and porcelain and plain crockery. Like the earthenware crockery in the adjacent lieutenants' store, the service had been packed in sawdust in custom-made wooden 'bins' stored on sectioned-off shelving.

The seamen slung their hammocks in the bow sections of the ship, where the excavations recovered cooking utensils of all kinds. These included copper cooking pots, bottles – including a complete one-gallon 'case gin' bottle – storage jars and a spoon; there was also an unusual ceramic wine jar which may have been taken on board in Tenerife or at Rio de Janeiro during the *Pandora's* passage out to the South Pacific.

Both officers and seamen traded for Polynesian indigenous artifacts, or 'artificial curiosities', presumably with the intention of selling them on their return as curios to collectors or their agents to supplement their meagre wages. The bow trench yielded stone adze blades, fishing lures, carved wooden war clubs, coconuts and shell collections.

The *Pandora* excavations revealed a typical array of late 18th-century British shipboard material and nautical technology. For instance, the officers' quarters were adorned with brass cabin fittings, including an ornate fireplace in the Great Cabin. Initially, our studies focused on the artifacts owned by the officers and the surgeon George Hamilton, but we've since turned our attention to the petty officers and seamen. The *Pandora's* muster roll reveals a typical, late 18th-century Royal Navy crew. Some were volunteers, but most had been pressed into service; many came from Orkney, off the north coast of Scotland, and were between 17 and 20 years old. A few were pressed at sea from Greenland whaling ships based at King's Lynn and London, while others came from Great Yarmouth and Shields in eastern England. Of the officers, third Lieutenant Thomas Hayward was handpicked because he had served with Bligh on the *Bounty*.

We recovered three seamen's skeletons from the wreck, one of them thought to be the purser's steward, Robert Bowler. Identifying the three dead men – affectionately nicknamed 'Tom, Dick and Harry' – has been a project involving historical, genealogical and scientific detective work. Forensic experts analyzed Harry's bones, made a facial reconstruction and established he was at least 28 years old. Recently discovered documents indicate that Robert Bowler was 29 at the time the *Pandora* sank. A slow process of elimination has reduced the list of 31 known casualties down to only four or five names. One day, future advances in DNA technology using waterlogged bones may allow us to make a positive identification.

Our excavations have kept up with new technology in both diving and in communications. In 1997, the Pandora Project went on-line, with the expedition team posting daily updates from the wreck site on the Queensland Museum's website. However, the most exciting development was undoubtedly the Queensland government's commitment to a new wing of the Queensland Museum's Museum of Tropical Queensland, which opened in June 2000 in Townsville. A large amount of exhibition space is dedicated to the *Pandora's* story, while museum researchers continue to preserve the recovered artifacts and conduct further investigations to unravel the secrets of the *Pandora's* last voyage.

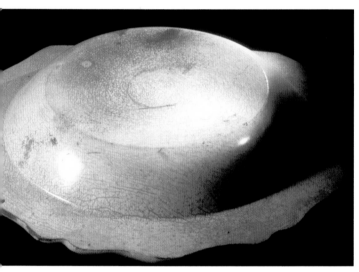

above

'Cream-ware' crockery from the captain's store: a soup tureen (top) and a soup plate with a 'C' scratched on the bottom, probably by the steward to indicate it was for use at the captain's table.

right, above and below

A so-called transfer-printed blue-and-white saucer of British manufacture (above). By the late 18th century such wares were flooding the British and world markets as substitute 'china'. Nevertheless real porcelain bowls were also used in the officers' mess (below).

Submarine and Ironclad: American Civil War Wrecks

Robert S. Neyland

Rarely do archaeologists study something that was the first of its kind, the prototype of a major technological innovation. The American Civil War ships the **H.L. Hunley***, the first submarine to sink an enemy ship, and USS* **Monitor***, the first-built turreted ironclad to fight in the Civil War, are exceptional underwater discoveries. The recovery and excavation of both ships yielded not only weapons and machines, but also the men who manned them.*

History remembers the USS *Monitor* and *H.L. Hunley* as products of the Union and Confederate arms race. The Union believed that USS *Monitor* could counter the fearsome Confederate ironclad CSS *Virginia*, while the Confederates calculated that submarines and mine warfare would break the Union's blockade of southern ports. On 8 March 1862, the seemingly invincible CSS *Virginia* destroyed two Union vessels in a fierce battle, completely demoralizing the Union fleet at Hampton Roads, Virginia. A day later the Union's reply, the ironclad USS *Monitor* arrived. Its battle with *Virginia* ended in stalemate – like fighters too equally matched, both gave up in exhaustion, steaming away without finishing off their opponent. They would never fight again. Although neither side had won, Hampton Roads stayed in Union hands and the blockade remained in effect. The *Monitor* would survive this famous conflict for nine months, only to sink in a gale 26 km (16 miles) off Cape Hatteras, North Carolina, on 31 December 1862, while under tow.

Artifacts and parts of the *Monitor*'s hull began to be brought to the surface in 1977, but the culmination of its recovery was the US Navy's lift of the massive rotating turret in 2002, under the direction of John Broadwater, underwater archaeologist with NOAA (National Oceanic and Atmospheric Administration). Recovered with the turret were the well-preserved skeletal remains of two sailors. I visited Dr Broadwater and gazed into the conservation tank containing *Monitor*'s upturned turret, with its load of cannon, gun carriages and artifacts – all still encrusted with a concrete-like layer of corrosion and sediment. I could see that *Monitor* did not settle peacefully to the bottom, but rolled over, sinking with a violent tumbling of heavy iron. The two

crewmen trapped in the turret as the ship sank not only faced drowning, but were also violently tossed around among the massive machinery and cannon. Although plans and drawings survive for *Monitor*, the recovered turret, cannon and engine provide missing details about how the turret was rotated and the guns fired.

The submarine *H.L. Hunley*

During the Civil War, Confederates successfully countered Union ships with submarine and mine warfare. In these situations, submarine sailors delivered torpedoes directly to the enemy ship. On 17 February 1864, the 12-m (39-ft) long submarine *H.L. Hunley* thrust a barbed spar with a 60-kg (135-lb) black powder torpedo into the giant, 63-m (207-ft) long, USS *Housatonic*. The ship sank, along with five sailors, in minutes. The *Hunley* thus entered the history books as the first sub to sink an enemy ship. After the explosion, watchmen on shore stoking a bonfire to guide the *Hunley* back to port spotted the blue light signalling from the sub. But then something went terribly wrong, and Charleston harbour would not see her boys home for another 136 years. Identifying and understanding what happened on that night is a mystery that continues to haunt archaeologists.

opposite
The gun turret of USS Monitor *breaks the surface. The turret was discovered inverted and lying underneath the hull of* Monitor, *so US Navy divers and NOAA scientists had to slide it out from under the hull to raise it, along with two Dahlgren cannon.*

right
USS Monitor *crewmembers cooking on deck, in the James River, Virginia, 9 July 1862. The crew was of volunteers – many were emigrants from northern Europe, some were African American, and all were between the ages of 18 and 38. The sailor standing atop the turret is holding a telescope. Note the cookstove supported on bricks on the left and the awning above the turret.*

left

H.L. Hunley *stored in a tank of water before archaeologists opened the hull and excavated the interior. This view is from the port side of the bow, looking aft. The hole in the forward conning tower is a broken viewing port; at one time it was thought to have been shot out by Union gunfire, but archaeologists found no evidence to support this speculation.*

below

Interior of the Hunley *after excavation of the sediment. Seven crewmen sat on the wooden bench on the port (left) side. On the starboard (right) side is the hand crank. Lt Dixon's command station is at the far end, directly underneath the forward conning tower. Dixon sat on a crude wooden plank, which rested on the forward ballast tank pump. From this position he could direct the ship by observing through several glass ports, while manning the rudder and dive planes.*

far right
*Lt Dixon's gold pocket watch.
The hands of the watch stopped
between 8:22 and 8:23 local
Charleston time. The watch bob
revealed that Dixon was a mason
and member of the Mobile,
Alabama, lodge.*

right
*Lt Dixon carried his wealth in
his pocket. This diamond ring is
small, probably for a woman's
hand, and it may have been
a gift for his young sweetheart,
Queen Bennett. It was found
with a diamond brooch.*

I took charge of the *Hunley* project in 1998 and oversaw its raising from the seabed in 2000. Although I had excavated many shipwrecks as the Navy's Underwater Archaeologist, when diving on the *Hunley* I felt for the first time a human and personal connection with the determined and courageous Lt George Dixon and his crew, whose remains and stories waited behind the closed hatches. None of the crew escaped the submarine; their ship had become their coffin. We do not often have the opportunity to understand the actions of men, and the outcomes of leadership, determination and courage in battle; in *Hunley* we had that chance. After lifting the sub and re-submerging it in our conservation lab, we strategically drilled out rivets to remove four of the upper hull plates and expose the silt-filled casket. All the histories I'd read led me to believe that I would find nine crew members; however, to my surprise, there were only eight skulls and eight pairs of shoes – there could only have been eight men present. The historians had got it wrong.

Forensic anthropologists literally put faces to history through the reconstruction of not only facial features but also entire lives. Doug Owsley, Smithsonian physical anthropologist, reads bones using subtle diagnostic features on skeletal remains such as chipped teeth, broken bones and stress lines to re-create the hard life of Civil War sailors. It was clear which of the men were pipe-smokers – they had grooves worn in their teeth from the long periods of clenching their pipe stems as they worked. Genealogist Linda Abrams chased documents across the United States for other fragments of these men's lives.

Entombed inside the sub, the eight crewmen were still at their stations, with their personal effects. With the remains of Lt Dixon was a gold pocket watch, its hands still recording the moment that time stopped for the *Hunley* and her crew, between 8.22 and 8.23 p.m. Charleston time. Unlike many other sites I've investigated, here we can glimpse the names and faces and the actions of the men. *Hunley*'s crew was cosmopolitan and varied – we discovered from carbon isotope analysis that at least half of the crew was European. Ages ranged from early 20s to mid-40s. There was also great disparity of status and wealth between the crew and the commander, Lt Dixon. Besides his gold pocket watch, Dixon also had a diamond brooch and ring, as well as other luxurious personal effects. By comparison the seven crewmen had between them only a few tobacco pipes, two pocket-knives, their canteens and the clothes on their backs.

Hunley's recovery is also answering detailed questions about how this early sub functioned; seven men sat on a bench on the port side to operate the hand cranks while Dixon positioned himself directly under the forward conning tower. Steering was by a joystick-like handle; ballasting was of iron, but water could also be let into forward and after ballast tanks to allow the sub to dive. We settled once and for all that the spar that delivered the torpedo was positioned on the bottom end of the bow, rather than attached along the upper edge of the bow. One big mystery that remains is why the sub sank. And we are just beginning to find clues that may answer this question. It is possible that the forward hatch of the sub was slightly open when she sank.

The successes of both *Hunley* and *Monitor* in the Civil War resulted in more than just battles won and lost – the technology and conduct of battle at sea were transformed. Traditional ethics and customs of warfare, developed over the centuries, would never be the same again, with combat now capable of devastating ships and crews entirely. The Civil War is identified as the first modern war on both land and sea. *Hunley* and *Monitor* represent the most prominent archaeological examples of Civil War innovations that changed naval warfare for ever.

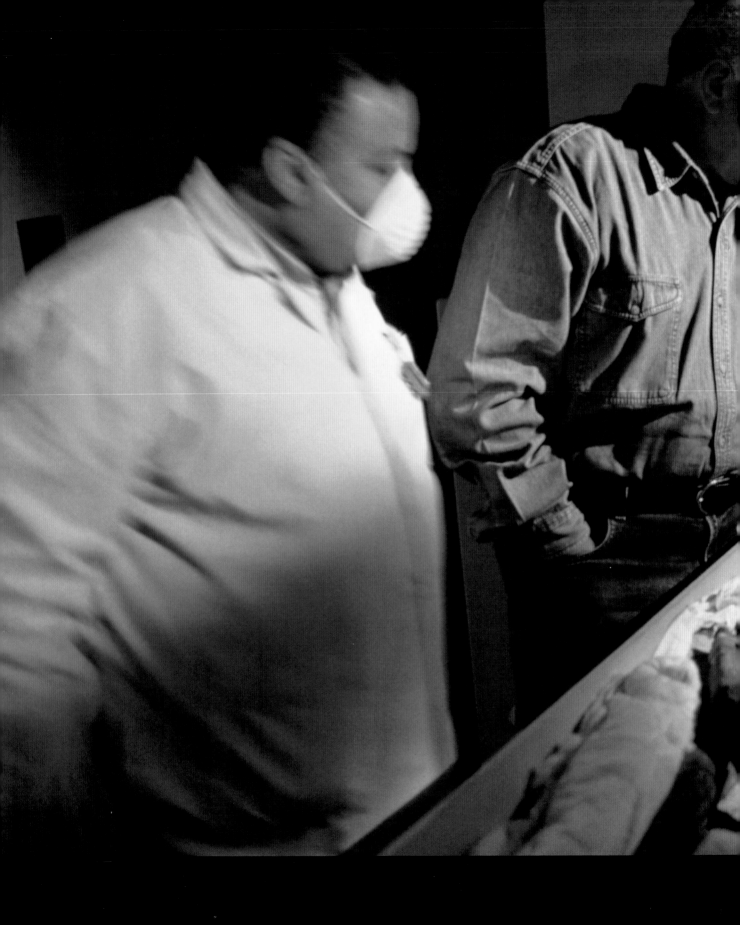

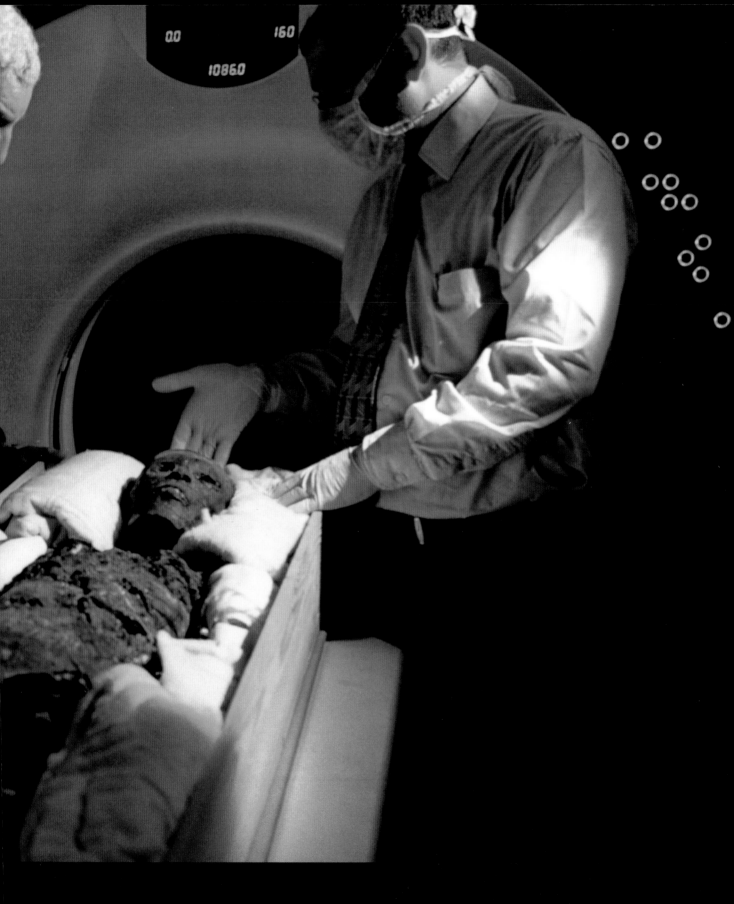

Scientific Discoveries

previous pages
The mummy of Tutankhamun was removed from his tomb in the Valley of the Kings and examined using a CT scanner, watched over here by Zahi Hawass. The scan revealed new details about the boy-king's death and allowed a facial reconstruction to be made.

right
Climate change in the past has had devastating effects on human populations. Tree-ring research has shown that the abandonment of Pueblo Bonito, Chaco Canyon, in the American Southwest, coincided with an extended period of drought.

right
Skeletons can sometimes be documents of past lives, revealing disease and episodes of violence. At Driffield Terrace, York, a Roman cemetery was discovered which contained the skeletons of 30 men who had been decapitated. This man wore shackles on his legs and his skull had been placed near his feet.

right
Bone labels found in a royal tomb at Abydos, Egypt, inscribed with the earliest known hieroglyphic writing. They were attached to a box or jar, and described its contents or owner.

DNA, CT SCANS, ICE CORES: science has revolutionized our knowledge of ancient humanity. Our own bodies and ancient bones are becoming the archaeological sites of the future. The genetic revolution began in the 1980s, with mitochondrial DNA research that identified an 'African Eve' in Africa some 200,000 years ago. We follow a new generation of research into early modern humans, Svante Pääbo's DNA sequencing of Neanderthals and the spread of the first farmers across Europe.

Global warming is on everybody's minds, but few people realize that humans have lived through such dramatic climatic shifts in the past. Brian Fagan describes how ice cores provide a chronicle of 420,000 years of Ice Age climate. Deep sea and lake cores, also tree-rings, provide insights into such events as the collapse of Classic Maya civilization, the destructive power of major El Niños on coastal civilizations in Peru, and droughts that affected the Ancestral Pueblo of Chaco Canyon, New Mexico.

We are what we eat and drink. Patrick McGovern takes us into the esoteric realm of organic residues recovered from ancient containers. He reconstructs the history of beer and wine, as they became an integral part of human life. Human bones also chronicle history.

Major battles were brutal events, where thousands died or were maimed. Medical science records the savage injuries suffered by men who died in northeastern England's Battle of Towton in 1461. Charlotte Roberts guides us through advances in facial reconstruction – including of Tutankhamun, the boy-king – recent studies of tuberculosis and ancient syphilis, and treatments of disease and often severe injuries.

Finally, we learn how a new generation of research into the origins of writing is challenging long-held perceptions. Toby Wilkinson describes the earliest hieroglyphs from an Egyptian royal tomb of 3150 BC. Two inscriptions from Dan and Ekron in Israel throw fresh light on King David and King Hezekiah. Wang Tao surveys some of the important Chinese manuscript discoveries of recent years, found in tombs and wells, many of them written on bamboo or wooden tablets. David Stuart, the leading decipherer of Maya script, gives us a privileged insight into the staggering advances made recently. The Incas of the Andes never developed writing. Instead, they used quipus, knotted strings. Gary Urton tells us how he has made a breakthrough in their decipherment. And Michael Coe describes a newly found incised tablet from the Olmec culture of lowland Mexico that bears the oldest script from the Americas, dating to 900 BC.

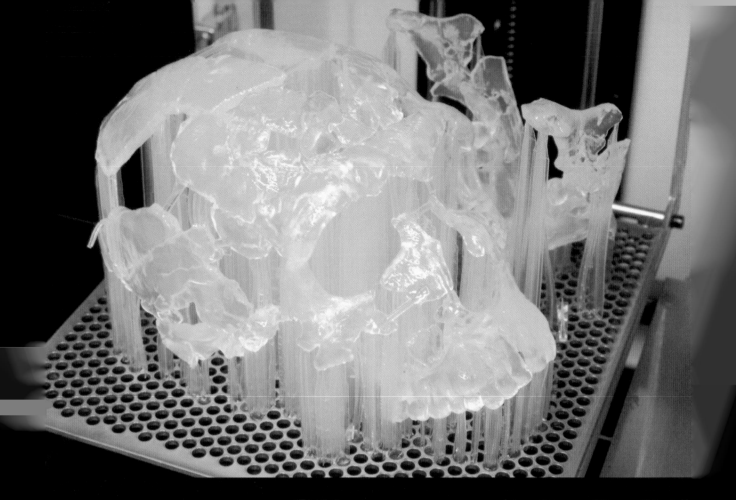

top and opposite
A computer-generated resin cast
of a Neanderthal skull and a
computer model of a Neanderthal
child's skull from Gibraltar
(opposite left) compared to the
skull of a modern human child
(opposite right) – examples of new
technologies that are allowing
scientists to look more closely at
the lives of archaic humans.

above and right
Reconstructions of a Neanderthal
man, based on a skull cast (left)
from the La Ferrassie rockshelter
in France, and of a Neanderthal
child's skull discovered on
Gibraltar in 1926.

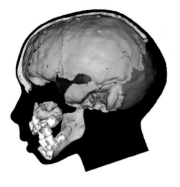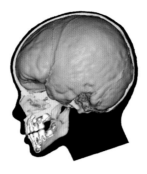

DNA and Archaeology

Brian M. Fagan

Molecular biology has played an increasingly important role in the study of ancient times since the development of the first molecular clock for human evolution during the 1960s. Recent advances in the study of DNA mean that our own bodies and the remains of our remote ancestors are becoming the archaeological sites of the future.

The geneticist Morris Goodman refined the molecular clock in 1999 using beta globulin genes, whose rate of change appears to be different among some primate lineages. On this basis he dates the split between chimpanzees and humans to about 6 million years ago.

Another biologist, Rebecca Cann, used mitochondrial DNA (mtDNA), which is inherited through the female line, to argue that all modern humans derived from an ancestral African population some 200,000 years ago, then spread throughout the world. A storm of controversy erupted over this so-called 'African Eve' hypothesis, but research since 1990 has collected data from the entire mtDNA genome. Africans display more diverse types of mtDNA than any other present-day populations, indicating that they had more time to develop such mutations. The process of the origin and spread of humans is turning out to be more complex than originally thought. Max Ingman and his colleagues believe the three 'deepest' branches of the DNA tree were exclusively African. The next deepest, resulting from a small migration, saw a mixture of Africans and non-Africans, which they date to about 171,500 years ago. A rapid expansion followed. For years, scientists have divided into two camps: those who believe that modern humans (*Homo sapiens*) evolved separately in Africa, Europe and Asia; and those who believe in a solely African origin. The discovery of the Herto skulls in Ethiopia has recently produced solid evidence for anatomically modern people in Africa before 150,000 years ago, and tends to confirm the 'Out-of-Africa' hypothesis.

DNA studies of Neanderthals and the first Americans

In 1997, geneticist Svante Pääbo sequenced mtDNA from Neanderthal fossils, discovering that they were genetically dissimilar to modern people, with only a minimal overlap in the sequence. More recent research shows how the Neanderthals underwent a long period of evolutionary divergence over as much as 500,000 years. It seems they did not contribute DNA to the contemporary human gene pool. Whether the genetic difference between Neanderthals and modern humans was too profound for the two to produce fertile offspring is still an open question.

Genetics are also playing a significant part in another controversial area of study – the first Americans. Genetically, native Americans fall into five main groups with common ancestors which seem to cluster in Siberia. MtDNA from living native Americans is rooted in Mongolia and Siberia, with such a degree of genetic similarity that one major dispersal from Asia perhaps played the most important role in peopling the Americas. Genetics do not date first settlement, however. In 1999 geneticist Ryk Ward argued that there are genetic grounds for believing that humans have only been in the Americas for 800 generations, about 16,000 years. Others disagree and place the event as early as 20,000 years ago, although there are no archaeological finds to support the earlier date.

Farmers

DNA studies are revealing new information about the ancestry, age and place of origin of domesticated animals, cattle and plants. For example, research in the 1990s has pinpointed the Karacadag Mountains in the Urfa region of southeastern Turkey as the original homeland of domesticated einkorn wheat – the same area where the German archaeologist Klaus Schmidt has excavated remarkable early shrines (p. 180).

Another controversial subject that DNA is casting light on is the spread of farming across Europe, and whether agriculture was accompanied by movements of population or was adopted by the people already living in the region. It is now generally agreed that it advanced from southeast to northwest at a rate of about 1.3 km (0.8 mile) a year. Using the DNA of living Europeans, geneticists have established that about 80 per cent of them have genetic roots among people who settled there during the late Ice Age, over 15,000 years ago; only the remaining 20 per cent came from more modern population movements, some associated with the spread of farming. Studies of the Y-chromosome, restricted to males, show a gradient of frequency of 'farmers' genes from Greece northwest across Europe, perhaps the result of male newcomers marrying indigenous women. At the moment the DNA research is based on modern humans, but perhaps one day we will find ancient skeletal material to work with.

Ice Ages, Floods and Droughts:
The Impact of Climate Change in the Past

Brian M. Fagan

Ice Ages, floods, droughts and global warming: our forebears confronted climatic conditions as unpredictable and violent as those of today. Thanks to ice cores, deep sea and lake corings, and tree-rings studied since 1990, we know that climate change was a powerful factor in human history.

Ice cores and sea levels

Ice cores reveal long-term trends in climate. The Vostok core from Antarctica goes back 420,000 years, revealing cold, cyclical oscillations about every 100,000 years in the layers formed by each year's ice. In contrast, Greenland cores track rapid warming immediately after the late Ice Age and document the 1,000-year cold snap of 10,800 BC that plunged Europe into near-glacial conditions and triggered a savage drought over southwestern Asia. Arid conditions coincided with a changeover from hunting and gathering to agriculture in that region, well documented by archaeologist Andrew Moore at Abu Hureyra in Syria.

Global sea levels rose steadily after the Ice Age. In about 5500 BC, the rising Mediterranean broke through a land barrier and flooded the brackish Euxine Lake within months, creating the much larger Black Sea. This huge natural disaster, known

from sea cores drilled in the 1990s, must have played havoc with the farming communities around the lake and may have been a factor in the spread of the first farmers into temperate Europe.

Lake and sea cores and Maya civilization

The collapse of Classic Maya civilization has defied explanation for generations. Now we know that drought may have been a significant player. Climatologist David Hodell drilled cores into Lake Chichancanab in the Yucatán in Mexico and used the oxygen-isotope ratios in shell carbonate to track rainfall shifts. He found evidence of a severe drought from AD 750 to 1025, which coincided with the Maya collapse in the southern lowlands. Fine-grained sediments found in a core sunk by an international team into the Carioco Basin off Venezuela in the southeastern Caribbean refine the drought event even more.

left
Ice cores are a major source of information on ancient climate change. Here, scientists collect a section of core drilled near the Rothera Research Station in the Antarctic.

opposite
Aerial view of Pueblo Bonito, Chaco Canyon, New Mexico, one of the great houses that flourished there between the 9th and 12th centuries AD. Studies of tree-rings have revealed correlations between periods of building and higher rainfall – and that the end of construction at the site coincided with a major drought.

The core identifies four dry spells within Hodell's drought, at about 40-year intervals. No one suggests that droughts were *the* cause of the Maya collapse in the south, but dry cycles may have helped topple powerful Maya city-states already reeling from reduced agricultural yields and social disorder.

The destructive force of El Niños and droughts

El Niño, the 'Christmas child' (from the time of year it occurs), is a phenomenon originating in the southwestern Pacific and only second to the seasons in its impact on human societies. During the mid-6th century AD, a strong El Niño brought torrential rains and catastrophic flooding to the Moche culture on Peru's North Coast. Dykes burst their banks; heavy rain and mountain runoff swept away irrigated fields; houses collapsed, thatched roofs floated downstream. Huge Pacific swells from the storms pounded the beaches and piled up sand dunes that blew inland, burying farmland and blocking river valleys. And 30 km (19 miles) inland, Moche lords looked down on a world devastated by torrential rainfall. We don't know exactly when the great El Niño struck, but ice cores extracted by palaeoclimatologist Lonnie Thompson from Andean glaciers tell us that it was in the middle of a 30-year drought between AD 563 and 594. The dry spell reduced mountain runoff, shrank crop yields and probably led to widespread malnutrition. Desperate rulers moved upstream to a new capital that lay close to the major intakes of all major irrigation canals. But another catastrophic El Niño descended on Moche domains a century later and the state collapsed.

Dendrochronology – tree-ring dating – was originally confined to the North American Southwest. In recent years, however, it has been successfully applied in Europe and the eastern Mediterranean. In the Southwest, tree-ring research has thrown light on the dramatic abandonment of the great pueblos at Chaco Canyon, New Mexico, during the 12th century AD. As many as 2,200 people may have lived there during Chaco's 11th-century apogee, many more at the times of major seasonal ceremonies. Tree-ring samples from Chaco pueblos, accurate to within a year, show a striking connection between major building periods and higher rainfall. Even more dramatically, as a half-century drought settled over the canyon and the Southwest in 1130, all pueblo construction ceased. Chaco's inhabitants dispersed within a decade. By 1140 Chaco was finished.

Dramatic changes in climate are thus nothing new in history, often with disastrous results to human civilization. Our understanding of the causes – and effects – of such events is now increasing, thanks to advances and new discoveries in scientific archaeology.

Ancient Wine and Beer

Patrick E. McGovern

Recent research on ancient organic residues at the molecular level has transformed our knowledge of very early alcoholic beverages. We now know that in the past humans around the world fermented available sugar sources into alcoholic drinks, shedding important new light on cultural innovation and development, agricultural and horticultural skills, and technologies for making special vessels to serve, drink and present the beverages ceremonially.

Neolithic experimentation

The Neolithic period was the first time that all the necessary pieces for making wine, beer and other alcoholic beverages on a large scale fell into place. Permanent settlements, based on domesticated plants and animals, led to the emergence of a 'Neolithic cuisine' that included new alcoholic beverages. The invention of pottery (*c.* 10,000 BC in east Asia and *c.* 6000 BC in western Asia) enabled fermented beverages to be kept for extended periods inside well-stoppered vessels. Pottery also absorbed and preserved ancient organic molecules, whose natural sources can now be identified by modern chemical techniques.

The earliest chemical evidence for an alcoholic beverage from anywhere in the world is not a wine or beer *per se*, but a mixed beverage, or 'cocktail'. Based on a chemical investigation of early Neolithic pottery jars dating to *c.* 7000–6600 BC from the village of Jiahu in the Yellow River valley of China, the University of Pennsylvania Museum's Biomolecular Archaeology Laboratory determined in 2004 that the mixed drink was made from rice, fruit (grape and/or hawthorn fruit) and honey.

Specialization takes root

The prehistoric beverage at Jiahu paved the way for unique cereal beverages of the 2nd millennium BC in China, remarkably preserved as liquids inside sealed bronze vessels of the Shang and Western Zhou dynasties (*c.* 1250–1000 BC). The vessels had become hermetically sealed when their tightly fitting lids corroded, preventing evaporation.

Chemical analysis in 2004 revealed that the 3,000-year-old liquids, which still retained a fragrant aroma when first opened, represented filtered rice or millet 'wines'. Tree resins (e.g. China fir), flowers (such as chrysanthemum) and herbs accentuated the aromatic and medicinal qualities of these special brews. The beverages were likely made by mould saccharification, a uniquely Chinese contribution to beverage-making in which an assemblage of mould species are used to break down the carbohydrates of rice and other grains into simple, fermentable sugars.

above left
Molecular investigation of this pottery jar from Jiahu, in China, dating to the 7th millennium BC, revealed that it once contained a mixed fermented beverage of honey, rice and fruit – either grape or hawthorn.

left
A banqueting scene on an impression of a seal from the Royal Cemetery at Ur, of the mid-3rd millennium BC. In the centre of the upper row a male and female drink barley beer from a large jar through tubes; below, dignitaries raise their cups, probably of wine.

Red or white?

At approximately the same time or perhaps somewhat later, beverage-makers had begun to make barley beer and grape wine in western Asia. In 1994 the Pennsylvania Museum laboratory reported that two jars from Hajji Firuz Tepe (Iran), dating to c. 5400–5000 BC, had contained resinated wine.

One of the most exciting recent discoveries using molecular techniques is the study carried out in 2004–05 by researchers at the University of Barcelona. They analyzed amphoras from the famous tomb of the boy-king Tutankhamun in western Thebes (Egypt), dated to around 1322 BC. When Howard Carter and Lord Carnarvon opened the tomb in 1922, among many artifacts related to wine, they found 26 amphoras, which had reddish and yellowish residues on their interior. These vessels, which had been tightly stoppered and sealed, had burst open, possibly under the pressure of secondary fermentation gases that had built up in the hot tomb. The Barcelona researchers showed that a characteristic red pigment of red wine, malvidin, accounted for the reddish colour of the residues inside two of the jars, and that the yellowish residue inside another lacked the pigment, and probably derived from a white wine. The inked labels on the outside of the amphoras provided additional important information. The wines had been made without exception in the Nile Delta region, where the pharaohs had originally established a royal winemaking industry c. 3000 BC.

Fermented beverages became increasingly more specialized in the millennia to follow around the world – so much so that single-product drinks such as grape wine and barley beer were held up as marks of civilization or barbarity depending upon where one lived. Humans were primed by their genetics and environment to discover how to make fermented beverages. Without exception, they readily incorporated these beverages into their social lives, religions, cuisines, pharmacopeias, and economies.

below
Jars filled with imported wine in a chamber in Tomb U-j at Abydos, Egypt, dating to around 3150 BC (see also p. 238).

bottom
A painted scene from the tomb of Nakht, Thebes, Egypt, dating to around 1400 BC, showing grape harvesting and wine-making. Recent research on vessels from Tutankhamun's tomb has shown that they contained both red and white wine.

Medical Science and Archaeology

Charlotte Roberts

Medical science can bring an array of methods to archaeology to help understand both the impact of diseases on past human populations and how they coped with them. Palaeopathology, as this science is known, offers a unique way of exploring the past, using the remains of our ancestors. The most dramatic discoveries over the last 15 years involve instances of interpersonal violence, diseases identified using ancient DNA analysis and studies of specific diseases, as well as revealing novel approaches to treatment of disease and trauma.

Violent injuries caused by interpersonal violence, ranging from head, face and neck injuries to defence wounds to the arms and hands, have been documented on skeletons and mummified bodies ever since people started analyzing human remains from archaeological sites. More unusual are a number of recent sites that have revealed casualties showing wounds that proved fatal, as it is only rarely that mummies or skeletal remains allow us to determine the precise cause of death.

The Battle of Towton in North Yorkshire in AD 1461 killed thousands of people. A University of Bradford excavation in 1996 yielded the remains of about 40 fatally injured men; 27 skulls bore injuries that had not healed by the time of death. The blunt and sharp puncture wounds could be linked to weapons used at the time. These young men had tried unsuccessfully to fend off blows with their forearms. More mysteriously, an early 3rd-century AD Roman burial site at Driffield Terrace in York, excavated by the York Archaeological Trust in 2004, revealed 30 decapitated skeletons from a judicial execution, some of the earliest such victims in England. One suggestion is that the power-hungry Caracalla, son of the recently deceased emperor Septimius Severus, may have ordered their execution.

Archaeologists at Vilnius University excavated a mass grave of soldiers from Napoleon's Great Army in 2002. They recovered the remains of 3,269 young adults, almost all males, victims of the catastrophic retreat from Moscow during the fierce Russian winter. When research is complete, we should know a great deal about their medical condition. DNA analysis of the lice recovered in the grave is eloquent testimony to the presence of louse-borne infectious diseases, such as trench fever.

Facial reconstruction

Methods of facial reconstruction have been applied to skulls from archaeological sites for over 100 years, but only recently to individuals who had chronic disease or disfiguring injuries. A 2005 reconstruction of the face of one of the Towton soldiers showed how the left side of his face was distorted with healed scar tissue, so much so that he would have had difficulty eating and talking. Such reconstructions raise fascinating issues about stigmas associated with disfiguring injuries.

Facial reconstruction is, of course, also known from forensic situations and TV programmes, and can be used to see if famous people's reconstructed faces look like their historical images. The Egyptian pharaoh Tutankhamun's head was scanned using CT (computed tomography – radiographic pictures of thin slices of the body). Three independent teams, in the United States, Egypt and France, used the data to reconstruct his face. Remarkably, they created very similar, if controversial, images of the king.

Infections and environments

Palaeopathology is also making major strides in identifying ancient diseases and chronic medical conditions that afflicted our ancestors. Tuberculosis (TB) is a re-emerging infection that

opposite
Some of the 60 skeletons excavated from Driffield Terrace in York, 30 of which were found to have been decapitated.

right
The skull of one of the decapitated individuals from York was placed next to his feet when he was buried.

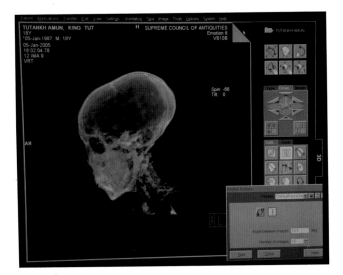

left
A CT (computed tomography)
scan of the skull of the Egyptian
pharaoh Tutankhamun, who died
c. 1322 BC. Around 1,700 digital
'slices', or cross-sectional
radiographic images, of the entire
mummy were taken, revealing
previously unknown features,
including a broken leg.

has its origins in Neolithic Italy. Many scientists theorized that its appearance coincided with the domestication of animals. However, recent DNA research shows that humans caught TB before their animals. Over the past decade, new DNA analyses of the bacteria that cause TB have increased our understanding of its evolution. We know that people from late medieval Wharram Percy, North Yorkshire, England, suffered from the human rather than the animal form, and that people in Africa suffered a specific African form of TB, while the earliest case discovered in England dates to the Iron Age (400–230 BC).

One debate that has raged for generations is whether Christopher Columbus and his crew introduced venereal syphilis into the New World or brought it back to Europe. While it has often been difficult to diagnose venereal syphilis in skeletons, there have been recent successful attempts to make or confirm a diagnosis by looking at microscopic features of the affected bones. Until the early 1990s, few skeletons of Pre-Columbian date with venereal syphilis had been excavated in the Old World, but since then more have been identified from sites in England, Poland, Ireland, France and Israel. It is therefore unlikely that Christopher Columbus and his crew were the culprits who brought venereal syphilis originally from the Americas to Europe.

Researchers are now also looking at the effects of air quality on ancient health, a major issue in modern urban environments. Rural people from late medieval northern England had fewer sinus problems than their urban contemporaries, who lived in polluted environments. And other environmental hazards have also been revealed. Lead levels measured in teeth from sites in England from 5500 BC to the 16th century AD show higher than normal levels in the Roman and late medieval periods, reflecting the use of lead water pipes and cooking vessels by the Romans, and the extensive application of lead glaze by medieval potters. Arsenic levels in skeletons from a copper smelting site in Israel identified people there who had worked in the industry.

Treatment of disease and injury

We know from historical documents that people were quite adept at treating disease and injury, but direct archaeological evidence is still rare. Recent discoveries show that our ancestors did not always leave people to die or suffer, even if treatment methods were basic by modern standards. Trepanation is an operation that has been around for several thousand years and involves 'drilling' a hole in the skull of a person afflicted by injury or disease. Documents tell us that the operation was sometimes undertaken for epilepsy, migraines and headaches. In rare cases, the reason for the surgery is apparent. A skull from an older man from Sedčany in the Czech Republic identified by V. Smrčka and dated to AD 1298–1550 displayed a healed trepanation hole. There was indirect evidence in the skull of a brain tumour called a meningioma, likely the reason for the trepanation.

People in the past suffered from traumatic injuries, just as we do. In many cases, broken bones were left to heal themselves, or set crudely with wooden splints. The 'Amesbury Archer', found in a grave near Stonehenge (p. 42), had suffered a traumatic injury to one knee – it had healed, but he was probably in constant pain. An older man from the late medieval cemetery of St Andrew, Fishergate, York, had suffered a twist-fracture and chronic infection of the knee. The monks had treated him by the application of copper plates (which have antiseptic properties), probably held in place with some binding material such as leather. Egyptian physicians were expert surgeons: a woman from a noble tomb in the necropolis of Western Thebes in Egypt, dated to 1550–1300 BC, had had her right big toe amputated and a false wooden toe fitted on the healed stump. The woman had used the prosthesis for some time: the bottom of the false toe shows wear. Computed tomography revealed secondary effects of the amputation on the neighbouring foot bones.

Palaeopathology offers a unique way of gaining insights into the lives of our ancestors. Recent advances are now allowing us for the first time to answer questions about the history of diseases and ancient medical conditions. We are learning about the treatment of injuries which prolonged peoples' lives, and the terrible brutality of ancient wars. For the first time, too, modern forensic reconstructive techniques are allowing us to gaze on the countenances of ancient people, both famous and obscure.

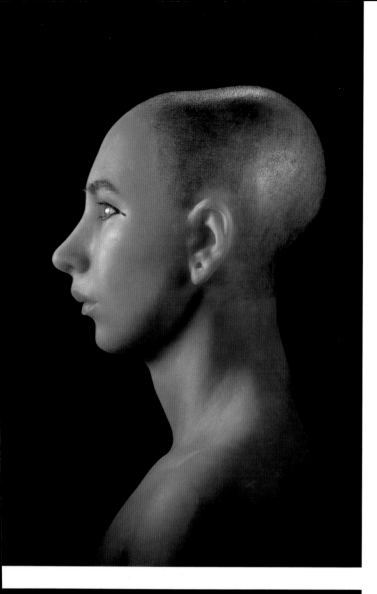

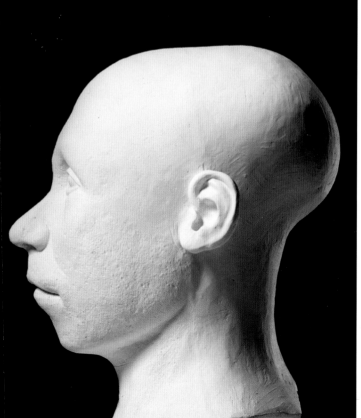

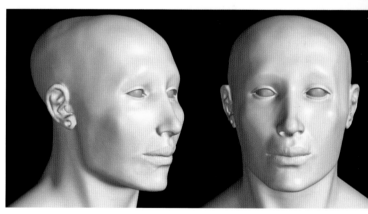

above and left

*Facial reconstructions can be used to establish what people in the past looked like –
both famous and obscure. CT scans of Tutankhamun's skull were given to three
teams to create reconstructions. A French team, headed by forensic sculptor
Elisabeth Daynés, created a lifelike reconstruction (top left and right – with the
pharaoh's famous gold mask in the background) with silicone skin. An American
team (left) were not told who the subject was, but they and an Egyptian team
(above), as well as the French, produced very similar reconstructions.*

Ancient Writing:
Early Hieroglyphs from Abydos, Egypt

Toby Wilkinson

German archaeologists excavating in the cemetery of Umm el-Qa'ab, Abydos, in 1988 uncovered a royal tomb dating to c. 3150 BC. As their work continued, in addition to the ruler's perfectly preserved ivory sceptre and his cellar of imported wine, the burial yielded an even more exciting discovery: the earliest hieroglyphic writing yet found in Egypt.

The written material comprises pots with brief ink inscriptions as well as several hundred bone labels, each measuring 2–3 cm (0.8–1 in) square and inscribed with combinations of 1 to 4 hieroglyphic signs. Each label has a small hole in one corner for attaching it to a box or jar by means of a cord. The labels were thus used to identify the contents, provenance, quantity or ownership of commodities destined for the royal tomb.

Some labels record place-names, such as Bubastis in the Nile Delta, while numerals denote lengths of cloth. Remarkably, the writing on the Abydos labels is not a primitive version of ancient Egyptian script, but already shows its distinctive combination of sound-signs and meaning-signs, with fully formed hieroglyphs.

The discovery has forced Egyptologists to re-evaluate both the date of Egypt's earliest writing and the reasons behind its invention. Previously, the earliest known hieroglyphs were those on the decorated palette of King Narmer (*c.* 3000 BC), where they are used to identify the main protagonists; it was therefore assumed that writing in Egypt was invented to glorify the ruler and immortalize his achievements. The discoveries from Abydos pre-date the reign of Narmer by as much as 150 years, and their purpose is not ceremonial but economic, enabling administrative control over an extensive territory.

The archaeologist who discovered the Abydos inscriptions has argued that they may be the earliest writing from the ancient world, pre-dating the inscribed clay tablets from Uruk, Mesopotamia (modern Iraq), by as much as a century. His claim is based on radiocarbon dates, but the margin of error involved leaves the question unresolved. It seems likely that Egypt and Mesopotamia developed their respective writing systems at about the same time, perhaps stimulated by cultural exchange.

above

Bone labels from the royal tomb U-j at Abydos, inscribed with the earliest known hieroglyphic writing. By means of a cord threaded through the small hole in one corner, each label would have been attached to a box or jar of supplies, to record its contents, provenance or ownership.

Ancient Writing: Biblical Inscriptions

Roberta L. Harris

It is rare that archaeologists find actual evidence of people, places and events mentioned in the Bible. Two inscriptions found recently in Israel are therefore extremely interesting, both for the new light they throw on the biblical texts relating to the reigns of King David and King Hezekiah and for identifying the location of a site not previously known.

The Tel Dan inscription

The ancient city of Dan stands on the headwaters of the River Jordan in northern Israel and has been excavated over many years by Avraham Biran. It was during his 1993 and 1994 seasons that this important inscription was found in several pieces. Originally a victory monument celebrating the conquest of the city of Dan by a foreign king in the 9th century BC, years later it had been smashed up and the pieces used to build a wall alongside the main southern gate of the city. The language of the inscription is Aramaic and the king may well have been Hazael of Damascus, a great Aramean city not far northeast of Dan. The king claims to have defeated and killed Joram son of Ahab, King of Israel, as well as Ahaziah son of Jehoram, 'King of the House of David'.

The latter phrase – very clear in the text – is of the greatest significance because it is the first reference to the dynasty of King David found archaeologically. Since the inscription dates to the 9th century BC, at least a century after the death of David, it is a very contentious piece of evidence for the two 'camps' of scholars who argue for and against the actual existence of David and Solomon and even the Kingdom of Judah itself in the 10th

century BC. The campaign referred to is probably narrated in a different guise in II Kings, chapter 9. Here, Jehu, the usurper of the throne of Israel, claims to have killed both King Joram and all his heirs, as well as Ahaziah of Judah who was visiting the king. The inscription from Tel Dan throws a very different light on the story. It seems it may have been Jehu who assassinated the two kings as the vassal of King Hazael, to whom he owed his throne.

The Ekron inscription

Ekron is recorded in the Hebrew Bible as one of the towns of the Philistine Pentapolis, and two of its kings, Padi and his son, Akish, are also known from inscriptions of the Assyrian King Sennacherib, because Ekron sided with Hezekiah in a revolt against the Assyrians, at the very end of the 8th century BC. Its actual location was unknown, however, until the discovery of this inscription in 1996, dating to the 7th century BC. In five lines of primitive Canaanite script and language it gives the names of a dynasty of Philistine kings of Ekron. This both definitely identifies Ekron as Tel Mikneh, where the inscription was found, and also confirms the existence of one of its kings mentioned in the Assyrian document.

Ancient Writing: China's 'Dead Sea Scrolls'

Wang Tao

One of the most fascinating aspects of archaeology in China today is the great number of early manuscripts that are turning up in ancient tombs. Many of these are written on strips of bamboo, or sometimes wood, which were bound together as documents or books; their immediacy and freshness is incredibly exciting.

As Chinese archaeology has progressed, the last 50 years have witnessed the discovery of a huge number of bamboo slips – especially in the last decade. The ancient documents can be divided into three main categories: first, the bamboo slips of the Chu state, dating from the Warring States period (475–221 BC), mostly found in Hubei, Hunan and southern Henan; secondly, the bamboo slips and wooden tablets of the Qin state, also of the Warring States period and of the subsequent Qin dynasty after the unification of China in 221 BC; and thirdly, the bamboo and wooden documents of the Han dynasty (206 BC– AD 220) and of the Three Kingdoms period (AD 220–80).

In 1993, when robbers looted an ancient tomb at Guodian in Jingmen, Hubei province, archaeologists rushed in and swiftly brought the site under controlled excavation. It was a tomb of the late 4th century BC and belonged to a nobleman of the Chu state. Fortunately, the waterlogged conditions had preserved the organic material, and more than 800 bamboo slips bearing inscriptions in ink were found in the coffin. Among them was a copy of an ancient manuscript of the *Daodejing*, traditionally attributed to the legendary Laozi, and the most important text in Daoism. The *Daodejing* is still considered sacred by the 20 million Daoists who live all over the world.

Also in 1993, a large number of bamboo slips of the Chu state appeared on the Hong Kong antique market. These were purchased by the Shanghai Museum, and their contents proved to be even richer than those from Guodian. They too contained philosophical texts, including the earliest known version of the *Yijing* (*The Book of Changes*), and many other texts by previously unknown writers. These discoveries are of such importance to our understanding of early Chinese philosophical development – on a par with the earliest texts relating to the Bible – that they are sometimes described as China's 'Dead Sea Scrolls'.

left

Archaeologists in Hunan carefully separate bamboo slips excavated from an ancient well at Zoumalou, Changsha, in 2003. They were well preserved in the waterlogged conditions, but their fragility has provided a challenge to archaeologists as well as conservators.

The Qin documents are of a different nature and have been found in more varied contexts. Between 1990 and 1992, the Gansu Institute of Archaeology excavated the Xuanquanzhi, a Han dynasty post-station in northwest China. This station was near the major settlement of Dunhuang and was a key border checkpoint on the 'Silk Route. Almost 20,000 wooden slips were found at the site and many of them recorded communications between central China and the 'Western Regions', the Chinese name for the westernmost part of China and Central Asia.

In the south, in 1993, the archaeological team of the Jingzhou Museum excavated a number of Qin tombs at Wangjiatai in Jiangling, Hubei province. Among the bamboo slips they found a lost copy of the *Guicang* (a divination manual), the *Rishu* (a ritual almanac), the *Xiaolu* and *Zhengshizhichang* (legal texts and guidelines for officials). In the same year, a team from the Shashi City Museum excavated a tomb in Zhoujiatai in Guanzu, also in Hubei province. The bamboo slips found here are similar to those found at Wangjiatai, but also include medical texts and a calendar that covers the period between 213 and 209 BC. These texts give a rich and vivid picture of daily life of society during a transitional period. To this list we can add a cookery book found in a couple's tomb in Yuanling, Hunan province, in 1999 and the most recent discovery, in 2002, at Liye, in western Hunan, where the Hunan Institute of Archaeology found over 30,000 bamboo slips in an ancient well. These are largely administrative documents dated to the beginning and early phase of the Qin unification and are very important for the study of the administration of the Qin empire.

Excavated texts of the Han dynasty and the Three Kingdoms period have also thrown new light on Chinese history and society. In 1993, the Lianyungang Museum excavated six Western Han tombs at Yinwan in Donghai County, Jiangsu province. In one, archaeologists found 133 bamboo slips and 23 wooden tablets, including the private diary of the tomb owner, a list of burial goods, calendars, divination texts, official registries of local population and government employers and properties, and, most surprisingly, a literary text about a 'mythical bird'.

The single largest discovery of ancient texts was made in Changsha, Hunan province, in 1996, when the archaeological team of Changsha City found over 100,000 wooden tablets at Zoumalou, again in ancient wells. The wooden documents date to the 3rd century AD, and belong to the Wu state of the Three Kingdoms period. They are mostly legal or administrative records, and include details of local taxation.

China has a huge quantity of literature and a well-documented dynastic history, but such texts have undoubtedly been repeatedly altered and re-edited through time and are inevitably biased. By contrast, many of the newly discovered documents are previously unknown to historians, and, significantly, they shed new light on aspects of the everyday life and customs of Chinese society in the past.

above
These bamboo slips are mostly legal documents and local government correspondence. The contents and style of calligraphy date them to the 2nd century BC of the Western Han dynasty.

Ancient Writing: New Advances in Maya Decipherment

David Stuart

The hieroglyphic writing system of the ancient Maya of Central America is now deciphered. Today we can confidently say that the inner workings of this most complex of ancient scripts are well understood. The story of the decipherment has its beginnings over a century ago, soon after the initial pioneers of Maya exploration provided accurate published copies of many inscriptions, but the true 'breaking' of the code came far more recently, only in the past few decades – and new discoveries are still providing new challenges.

Maya glyphs are visually complex, even baroque looking, but underneath lies a simple system of two types of elements: a large number of word signs such as *k'ahk'*, 'fire', or *zak*, 'white', and also a number of purely phonetic signs corresponding to basic consonant-vowel syllables (**na**, **no**, **lu**, **ti**, **xa**, and so forth). The syllables could be combined to spell any desired sound combination, and individual words could be written with them as well. For example, there is an established sign for the word *ajaw*, 'lord' or 'king', but scribes could opt to write the word using the syllables **a-ja-wa**, all confined within the standard square or rectangular space known as a glyph block. Many ancient scribes were unusually adept at writing repeated names and phrases in an especially playful manner. Signs could be fused together, inserted into one another, made animate and interactive with one another. Through the systematic comparisons of complex texts at Copán and other sites in the 1980s, I and other epigraphers realized that while the rules of sign combination were rigid, they accommodated a certain amount of scribal whimsy. This balance between rules and artistic flair turns out to be a hallmark of Maya writing, as well as a hindrance to decipherment for many decades.

Maya texts from the Classic period (*c.* AD 250–850) focus mostly on ritual activities and the political exploits of kings and their associates. The newest and most exciting discoveries in Maya decipherment, however, are not so much episodes of royal history or ancient religion, but surprising revelations about the true precision of Maya writing as a logical system for encoding language. Because it is a fully phonetic script, Maya hieroglyphs could record any nuance of spoken language – and indeed did.

New research by me, Stephen Houston and John Robertson suggests that all Classic period Maya inscriptions seem to record one courtly language. This language has its closest descendant in a modern Mayan language called Ch'orti', spoken today by some 30,000 people in the eastern highlands of Guatemala. In ancient times its Classic ancestor was the lingua franca among the elites of the Maya world, and the consistency of the language over time and space has come as a surprise to scholars. Texts carved over several centuries from famous Maya centres such as Copán, Palenque, Tikal and Chichén Itzá are all very much in the same language.

Beyond the recent progress in reading Maya glyphs of the Classic period, the discovery of the earliest known Maya writing suggests that future scholars will face major challenges. In 2005, I was fortunate enough to be visiting the remote ruins of San Bartolo, Guatemala (p. 134), when archaeologists Boris Beltrán and William Saturno unearthed painted glyphs dated to about 300 BC, far earlier than any well-dated examples of writing in the Maya lowlands. Before now, specialists had generally favoured the view that the lowland Maya were latecomers to the adoption of writing in Mesoamerica, with the first firm evidence of Maya glyphs apparently falling several centuries after monumental texts in Oaxaca and even in the Maya highlands. Now we see the lowland Maya as full participants in a wider regional development of script traditions occurring sometime after 500 BC, with the idea of writing being embraced by widespread Mesoamerican cultures speaking very different languages.

The San Bartolo find has forced us to reconsider some of the big questions about the timing of literacy, as well as its role in the development of state-level societies. Significantly, it seems that Maya writing was not used first in monumental displays of royal power, as it was centuries later. Instead, we find at San Bartolo hints of a more intimate usage, based probably on an already established tradition of painted books and calligraphic arts. Much of the future work in Maya decipherment will focus on these earliest texts, attempting to link their obscure forms and structures to the far better understood Classic inscriptions.

opposite left
The carved inscription on Stela 8 at Dos Pilas, Guatemala.

opposite right
The earliest known glyphs from the Maya lowlands (c. 300 BC), discovered in 2005 at San Bartolo.

above
Examples of sign combination and structure in writing the word ajaw, *'lord', 'king': (left) the sign* AJAW *and (right) the combined form* a-ja-wa.

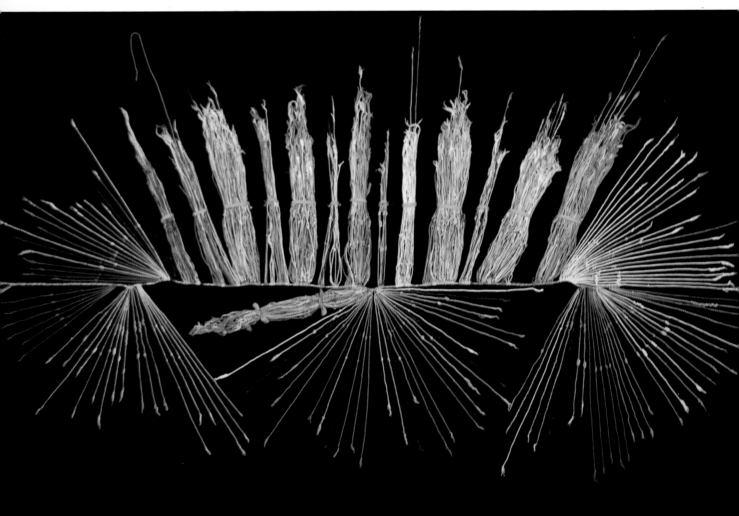

Ancient Writing:
Deciphering the Knotted Strings of the Incas

Research I carried out in 2005 with graduate student Carrie Brezene on the Inca knotted-string records, known as quipus, led to the discovery of the first evidence of both communication between quipus and possibly for an emblem, or insignia, knotted in the cords of quipu samples from the central coast of Peru.

The quipu (or *khipu*, Quechua: 'knot') is the knotted-string device used for record-keeping in the Inca empire. Quipus are composed of a primary cord from which are suspended a variable number of so-called pendant cords. In the majority of examples, knots tied into pendant cords in clusters on different tiers signify numerical values in a base-ten system of registration. Unlike other civilizations in the ancient world – the Mesopotamians, Egyptians and Maya – whose scribes wrote with marks on a variety of two-dimensional surfaces, the knotted-string quipu were the only form of 'writing' known to the Incas. Inca administrators relied on quipus to record the production, collection and redistribution of goods and services within the Inca state. Several examples of pairs of quipus have been identified, containing matching numerical and colour information. Such quipus may have been made as part of a checking system.

The central challenge for researchers has been to explain how the identities of objects were recorded in the quipus, though one idea is that this may have been done using different colours and combinations of colours. It has also been suggested that the numerical values knotted into the strings may have served as identity labels, in much the same way that a social security or telephone number identifies the person to whom it belongs.

Until recently, researchers have had no convincing evidence to support the theory of numbers as labels, nor of sharing of information between samples that was more complicated than matching quipus. However, evidence for number labels and a much more complicated form of the sharing of information was recently discovered in seven quipus found in an urn at the site of Puruchuco, an Inca administrative centre 11.5 km (7 miles) east of the centre of Lima.

What we have referred to as the 'Puruchuco accounting hierarchy' is organized on three levels. Two organizational principles govern this complicated accounting hierarchy: first, samples on the same level match, in what was probably a checks-and-balances feature of these records; and second, the sums of certain groups (as determined by colour patterning) of strings on level I are recorded on strings of the same colour on level II, and the sums of groups of strings on level II are recorded on the two quipus on level III. It is equally possible that the Puruchuco quipu specialists were, in fact, performing the opposite operation

– that is, they may have been dividing the larger values on level III into the smaller values of level II, and then further dividing the values on level II into those on level I. Whichever direction they were interested in, the passing of information between the three levels of quipus in this hierarchy represents the first unambiguous acts of communication between archaeological artifacts known from Pre-Columbian Andean civilizations.

In addition to the relationship of addition and division between the three levels in the seven quipus from Puruchuco, the quipus on levels II and III have a repeating arrangement of three knots of the form called 'figure-eight' (usually used to express the numerical value 'one') on what we term 12-string introductory segments of these samples. These arrangements may represent emblems – signs or labels that perhaps identify the origin of the quipus (Puruchuco), their subject or the identity of the quipu-maker.

Thus, the quipus from Puruchuco contain the first evidence both for the transfer of information between quipus and the possible use of knots as identity labels.

The Cascajal Block:
The New World's Oldest Writing

Michael D. Coe

One of the most spectacular of Mesoamerica's Pre-Columbian cultures is also the oldest: the Olmec civilization of southern Veracruz and neighbouring Tabasco, Mexico, now radiocarbon dated to 1200 to 400 BC, arose among the riverine lowlands of the Gulf Coast. This culture is famous for its enormous basalt sculptures – particularly the colossal portrait heads of their rulers – and exquisitely carved and incised jades. Although Mesoamerican literacy has deep roots (the Maya had a complex writing system from at least 300 BC), until recently, the hard evidence for an Olmec script has been almost non-existent.

In 1999, the Mexican archaeologists Ma. Carmen Rodríguez and Ponciano Ortiz Ceballos inspected and photographed a serpentine block encountered by local road builders at a place called Cascajal, only a few kilometres to the north of the earliest Olmec city, San Lorenzo. Its upper surface had been smoothed and incised with 62 signs that they interpreted as writing, but some of their colleagues (who had never seen the block) doubted its authenticity. To resolve the problem, they and a team consisting of Richard Diehl, Stephen Houston and myself revisited the site in 2006; measured, photographed and redrew the inscription; and inspected the broken pottery which had been found with the block. We are convinced that it dates to about 900 BC, and is thus the oldest writing ever found in the Western Hemisphere.

Most of the glyphs are clearly derived from elements of Olmec iconography, and laid out in more or less horizontal lines that are apparently to be read from left to right, top to bottom. An ant-like sign introduces three of the 'lines', and there are several repetitions of sign groups, perhaps representing phrases. The Cascajal script poses a significant challenge for future decipherers – we have only this one intriguing example of Olmec writing, there is no bilingual text to compare it with and it seems to have spawned no descendants.

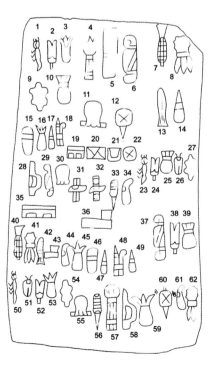

left

The Cascajal block and a drawing of its inscription by Stephen Houston. Signs associated in sequence can be seen in 1–2, 23–24, and 50–53, suggesting that they represent utterances such as words or phrases, and that the text is a true form of writing rather than randomly selected symbols.

Discoveries from the Ice Age

New Evidence from Africa:
Rewriting the Story of Human Origins
Alemseged, Z. & others, 'A juvenile early hominin skeleton from Dikika, Ethiopia', *Nature* 443 (2006), 296–301
Brunet, M. & others, 'A new hominid from the Upper Miocene of Chad, Central Africa', *Nature* 418 (2002), 145–51
Leakey, M. D. & Harris, J. M., *Laetoli, A Pliocene Site in Northern Tanzania* (Oxford, 1987)
Senut, B. & others, 'First hominid from the Miocene (Lukeino Formation, Kenya)', *Comptes Rendus de l'Academie Scientifique* 332 (2001), 137–44
Stringer, C. & Andrews, P. *The Complete World of Human Evolution* (London & New York, 2005)
Ward, C.V., 'Interpreting the posture and locomotion of *Australopithecus afarensis*: where do we stand', *Yearbook of Physical Anthropology* 45 (2002), 185–215
White, T., Suwa, G. & Asfaw, B., '*Australopithecus ramidus*, a new species of early hominid from Aramis, Ethiopia', *Nature* 371 (1994), 306–12

The Mystery of the Skulls from Dmanisi, Georgia
Gabunia, L. & others, 'Dmanisi and dispersal', *Evolutionary Anthropology* 10 (2001), 158–70
Gore, R., 'Dawn of humans: expanding worlds', *National Geographic* (May 1997), 84–109
Rightmire, G. P., Lordkipanidze, D. & Vekua, A., 'Anatomical descriptions, comparative studies and evolutionary significance of the hominin skulls from Dmanisi, Republic of Georgia', *Journal of Human Evolution* 50 (2006), 115–41

The First Europeans and the Pit of the Bones at Atapuerca, Spain
Arsuaga, J. L., Bermúdez de Castro, J. M. & Carbonell, E. (eds), 'The Sima de los Huesos hominid site', *Journal of Human Evolution* 33 (1997), 105–421
Bermúdez de Castro, J. M., Carbonell, E. & Arsuaga, J. L. (eds), 'Gran Dolina Site: TD6 Aurora Stratum (Burgos, Spain)', *Journal of Human Evolution* 37 (1999), 309–700 (special issue)
Bermúdez de Castro, J. M. & others, 'The Atapuerca sites and their contribution to the knowledge of human evolution in Europe', *Evolutionary Anthropology* 13 (2004), 24–41
Gore, R. 'Dawn of humans: The first Europeans', *National Geographic* (July 1997), 96–113
Manzi, G., 'Human evolution at the Matuyama-Brunhes boundary', *Evolutionary Anthropology* 13 (2004), 11–24

Boxgrove: The Oldest Human Fossils in Britain
Pitts, M. & Roberts, M., *Fairweather Eden* (London, 1997; New York, 1998)

Roberts, M. & Parfitt, S. (eds), *Boxgrove: A Middle Pleistocene Hominid Site at Eartham Quarry, Boxgrove, West Sussex*, English Heritage Archaeological Report 17 (London, 1999)
Stringer, C. & others, 'The Middle Pleistocene human tibia from Boxgrove', *Journal of Human Evolution* 34 (1998), 509–47

The 'Hobbit': An Unknown Human Relative?
Brown, P. & others, 'A new small-bodied hominin from the Late Pleistocene of Flores, Indonesia', *Nature* 431 (2004), 1055–61
Falk, D. & others, 'Response to comment on "The brain of LB1, *Homo floresiensis*"', *Science* 312 (2006), 999
Martin, R. D. & others, 'Comment on "The brain of LB1, *Homo floresiensis*"', *Science* 312 (2006), 999
Morwood, M. J. & others, 'Archaeology and age of a new hominin from Flores in eastern Indonesia', *Nature* 431 (2004), 1087–91
Morwood, M. J. & others, 'Further evidence for small-bodied hominins from the Late Pleistocene of Flores, Indonesia', *Nature* 437 (2005), 1012–17

Tombs, Graves and Mummies

The Iceman: A 5,000-Year-Old Murder Victim?
Dickson, J. H., Oeggl, K. & Handley, L. L., 'The Iceman reconsidered', *Scientific American* 288 (2003), 70–79
Gostner, P. & Egarter Vigl, E., 'INSIGHT: Report of radiological-forensic findings on the Iceman', *Journal of Archaeological Science* 29 (2002), 323–26
Müller, W. & others, 'Origin and migration of the Alpine Iceman', *Science* 302 (2003), 862–66
Spindler, K., *The Man in the Ice* (London & New York, 1994)

The Amesbury Archer and the Boscombe Bowmen: Men of Stonehenge
Chippindale, C., *Stonehenge Complete* (London & New York, 3rd ed., 2004)
Darvill, T., *Stonehenge: The Biography of a Landscape* (Stroud, 2006)
Harrison, R., *The Beaker Folk, Copper Age Archaeology in Western Europe* (London, 1980)
Richards, J., *Stonehenge* (London, 2005)

New Revelations from the Pyramids of Giza
Hawass, Z., *Mountains of the Pharaohs: The Untold Story of the Pyramid Builders* (New York & London, 2006)
Hawass, Z. (ed.), *The Treasures of the Pyramids* (Vercelli & Cairo, 2003)
Hawass, Z. & Lehner, M., 'Builders of the Pyramids', *Archaeology* 50/1 (1997), 31–38
Lehner, M., *The Complete Pyramids* (London & New York, 1997)
Verner, M., *The Pyramids: The Mystery, Culture, and Science of Egypt's Great Monuments* (New York, 2001)

The Tomb of Tutankhamun's Mother?
An 18th Dynasty Chamber in the Valley of the Kings
Ertman, E., Wilson, R. & Schaden, O., 'Unraveling the mysteries of KV 63', *KMT. A Modern Journal of Egyptology*, 17.3 (2006), 18–27
Hawass, Z., *Tutankhamun and the Golden Age of the Pharaohs* (Washington, DC, 2005)
Hawass, Z., *The Golden Age of Tutankhamun: Divine Might and Splendor in the New Kingdom* (Cairo, 2004)
James, T. G. H., *Tutankhamun: The Eternal Splendour of the Boy Pharaoh* (London & Cairo, 2000)
Reeves, N., *The Complete Tutankhamun: The King, the Tomb, the Royal Treasure* (London, New York & Cairo, 1995)
Reeves, N. & Wilkinson, R. H., *The Complete Valley of the Kings: Tombs and Treasures of Egypt's Greatest Pharaohs* (London, New York & Cairo, 1996)
Schaden, O., 'KV 63: an update', *KMT. A Modern Journal of Egyptology*, 18.1 (2007), 16–25
Wilson, R., 'KV 63 Update: Clearing the Tomb', *Ancient Egypt, The History, People and Culture of the Nile Valley*, 7.1.37 (2006), 38–44

Pharaoh's Children: The Tomb of the Sons of Ramesses II in the Valley of the Kings
Reeves, N. & Wilkinson, R. H., *The Complete Valley of the Kings: Tombs and Treasures of Egypt's Greatest Pharaohs* (London, New York & Cairo, 1996)
Weeks, K. R., *The Lost Tomb* (New York & London, 2000)
Weeks, K. R., *KV 5: A Preliminary Report on the Excavation of the Tomb of the Sons of Rameses II in the Valley of the Kings* (Cairo, 2nd ed., 2006)
Weeks, K. R. (ed.), *Valley of the Kings: The Tombs and the Funerary Temples of Thebes West* (Vercelli, 2nd ed., 2005)

New Kingdom Tombs at Saqqara
Zivie, A., *Découverte à Saqqarah. Le vizir oublié* (Paris, 1990)
Zivie, A., 'The "Treasury" of 'Aper-El', *Egyptian Archaeology* 1 (1991), 26–28
Zivie, A., 'The tomb of the lady Maïa, wet-nurse of Tutankhamun', *Egyptian Archaeology* 13 (1998), 7–8
Zivie, A., 'La nourrice royale Maïa et ses voisins: cinq tombeaux du Nouvel Empire récemment découverts à Saqqara', *Comptes rendus de l'Académie des Inscriptions et Belles-Lettres* (Jan.–Mar., 1998), 33–54
Zivie, A., 'Une statue rupestre de la déesse Hathor. Fouilles et découvertes dans le tombeau d'un dignitaire de Ramsès II à Saqqara', *Comptes rendus de l'Académie des Inscriptions et Belles-Lettres*, (Jan.–Mar., 2001), 693–710
Zivie, A., 'A Pharaoh's peacemaker', *National Geographic* (Oct. 2002), 26–31
Zivie, A., *Les tombeaux retrouvés de Saqqara* (photographs by Patrick Chapuis) (Paris, 2003)
Zivie, A., 'Mystery of the Sun-god's servant', *National Geographic* (Nov. 2003), 52–59

Zivie, A., Callou, C. & Samzun, A., 'A lion found in the Egyptian tomb of Maïa', *Nature* (15 Jan. 2004), 211–12

Zivie, A., 'La résurrection des "tombes des nobles" de Memphis', in *Archéologies. 20 ans de recherches françaises dans le monde* (Paris, 2005), 367–70

Zivie, A. & Lichtenberg, R., 'The cats of the goddess Bastet', in S. Ikram (ed.), *Divine Creatures. Animal Mummies in Ancient Egypt* (Cairo & New York, 2005), 106–19

Zivie, A., 'A propos de la tombe de Maïa, nourrice de Toutânkhamon', in *Akhénaton et l'époque amarnienne* (Bibliothèque d'Égypte Afrique et Orient) (Avignon & Paris, 2005), 287–309

Zivie, A., 'Le point sur les travaux de la Mission Archéologique Française du Bubasteion', *Bulletin de la Société Française d'Egyptologie* 162 (Mar. 2005), 28–45

Zivie, A., 'Le messager royal égyptien Pirikhnawa', in *British Museum Studies in Ancient Egypt and Sudan*, 6, 2006, 68–78, papers from a conference held at British Museum, July 2005 'Egypt and the Hittites: contacts, conflict and diplomacy in the Late Bronze Age' (www.thebritishmuseum.ac.uk/bmsaes/)

Where the Living Feasted with the Dead: The Royal Tombs of Qatna, Syria

Al-Maqdissi, M., Luciani, M., Morandi Bonacossi, D., Novák, M. & Pfälzner, P., *Excavating Qatna*, Vol. 1, *Preliminary Report on the 1999 and 2000 Campaigns of the Joint Syrian-Italian-German Archaeological Research Project at Tell Mishrife* (Damascus, 2002)

Al-Maqdissi, M., Dohmann-Pfälzner, H., Pfälzner, P., & Suleiman, A., 'Das königliche Hypogäum von Qatna', *Mitteilungen Deutschen Orient-Gesellschaft* 135 (2003), 189–218

Novák, M. & Pfälzner, P., 'Ausgrabungen im bronzezeitlichen Palast von Tall Mishrife – Qatna 2002', *Mitteilungen Deutschen Orient-Gesellschaft* 135 (2003), 131–66

Novák, M. & Pfälzner, P., 'Ausgrabungen in Tell Mishrife/Qatna 2003. Vorbericht der deutschen Komponente des internationalen Kooperationsprojektes', *Mitteilungen Deutschen Orient-Gesellschaft* 137 (2005), 57–78

Pfälzner, P., 'The world of the living and the world of the dead', *German Research* 2–3 (2004), 16–20

Pfälzner, P., 'Syrien: Qatna. Ahnenkult im 2. Jahrtausend v. Chr.', *Welt und Umwelt der Bibel* 2 (2005), 56–59

Pfälzner, P., 'Syria's royal tombs uncovered', *Current World Archaeology* 15 (2006), 2–13

The Royal Tombs of Nimrud, Iraq: The Treasures of Assyrian Queens

Damerji, M. S., 'Gräber Assyrischer Königinnen aus Nimrud', *Jahrbuch des Römisch-Germanischen Zentralmuseums* 45 1998 (1999), 19–84

Hussein, M. M. & Suleiman, A., *Nimrud, a City of Golden Treasures* (Baghdad, 2000)

Layard, A. H., *Nineveh and its Remains* (London, 1849)

Mallowan, M. E. L., *Nimrud and its Remains* (London, 1966)

Oates, J. & Oates, D., *Nimrud, an Assyrian Imperial City Revealed*, British School of Archaeology in Iraq (London, 2002)

The Great Ryzhanovka Barrow: An Intact Burial of a Scythian Nobleman

Chochorowski, J. & Skory, S., 'Prince of the Great Kurgan', *Archaeology* (Sept./Oct., 1997), 32–39

Chochorowski, J. & Skory, S., 'The "collateral" (female) burial at the Great Ryzhanovka Barrow', *Studies in Ancient Art and Civilization* 8 (1997), 71–92

The Valley of the Golden Mummies, Egypt

Fakhry, A., *Bahria Oasis. The Egyptian Deserts* (Cairo, 1942)

Forbes, D. C., *Tombs. Treasures. Mummies: Seven Great Discoveries of Egyptian Archaeology* (Sebastopol & Santa Fe, 1998)

Hawass, Z., *Secrets from the Sand: My Search for Egypt's Past* (Cairo, London & New York, 2003)

Hawass, Z., *Valley of the Golden Mummies* (Cairo, London & New York, 2000)

Riggs, C., *The Beautiful Burial in Roman Egypt: Art, Identity, and Funerary Religion* (Oxford & New York, 2005)

Bodies from the Bog: New Insights into Life and Death in Pagan Celtic Ireland

Bermingham, N. & Delaney, M., *The Bog Body from Tumbeagh* (Bray, 2006)

Glob, P. V., *The Bog People* (London, 1969)

Ó Floinn, R., 'Irish bog bodies', *Archaeology Ireland*, (2) No. 3 (1988), 94–97

Stead, I. M., Bourke, J. B. & Brothwell, D., *Lindow Man: The Body in the Bog* (London, 1986)

Turner, R. C. & Scaife, R. G. (eds), *Bog Bodies. New Discoveries and New Perspectives* (London, 1995)

Warriors, Musicians and Acrobats at the Tomb of the First Emperor of China

Hessler, P. & Mazzatenta, O. L., 'Rising to life, treasures of ancient China', *National Geographic* (Oct. 2001), 48–67

Meng Jianming, Zhang Lin, *Awakened Qin's Terracotta Army* (Shaanxi, 2001)

Shaanxi Archaeology Institute, *Museum of Terracotta Warriors and Horses of Emperor Qin Shihuang, Excavation of the Precinct of Qin Shihuang's Mausoleum in 1999* (Shaanxi, 2000)

The Spitalfields Lady: The Finest Roman Grave Ever Found in London

Milne, G., *English Heritage Book of Roman London* (London, 1995)

Thomas, C., 'Laid to rest on a pillow of bay leaves, *British Archaeology* 50 (Dec. 1999)

Thomas, C., *Life and Death in London's East End: 2000 Years at Spitalfields* (London, 2004)

Moche Tombs at Dos Cabezas, Peru

Donnan, C. B., *Moche Art of Peru: Pre Columbian Symbolic Communication* (Los Angeles, 1978)

Donnan, C. B., 'Masterworks of art reveal a remarkable pre-Inca world', *National Geographic* (June 1990), 17–33

Donnan, C. B., 'Moche funerary practice', in T. Dillehay (ed.), *Graves for the Living* (Dumbarton Oaks, 1995)

Donnan, C. B., 'Moche burials uncovered', *National Geographic* (March 2001), 58–73

Power and Prestige: Middle Sicán Elite Tombs of North Coastal Peru

Shimada, I. & Griffin, J. A., 'Precious metal objects of the Middle Sicán', in *Mysteries of the Ancient Ones*, special edition of *Scientific American* 15(1) (2005), 80–89

Shimada, I. & others, 'An integrated analysis of Pre-Hispanic mortuary practices: a Middle Sicán case study', *Current Anthropology* 45(3) (2004), 369–402

Shimada, I., 'Late Prehispanic coastal states' in L. Laurencich Minelli (ed.), *The Inca World: The Development of Pre-Columbian Peru, A.D. 1000–1534* (Norman, 2000), 49–110

Shimada, I., Gordus, A. & Griffin, J. A., 'Technology, iconography, and significance of metals: a multidimensional analysis of Middle Sicán objects' in C. McEwan (ed.), *Pre-Columbian Gold: Technology, Iconography, and Style* (London, 2000), 28–61

Shimada, I., *Cultura Sicán: Dios, Riqueza y Poder en la Costa Norte del Peru* (Lima, 1995)

The Red Queen and Other New Maya Tombs

González Cruz, A., 'Noble exhumado en Palenque', *Arqueología Mexicana*, vol. 2, no. 9 (Aug.–Sept. 1994), 39–45, 66–68

González Cruz, A., 'El Templo de la Reina Roja, Palenque, Chiapas', *Arqueología Mexicana*, vol. 5, no. 30 (Mar.–Apr. 1998), 61

Ruz Lhuillier, A., *El Templo de las Inscripciones, Palenque* (Mexico City, 1973)

Skidmore, J., 'Tomb finds at El Peru', Mesoweb Reports & Notes. Reported on the Mesoweb internet site: www.mesoweb.com/reports/waka2.html (2005)

Tarpy, C., 'Place of the standing stones: unearthing a king from the dawn of the Maya', *National Geographic* (May 2004), 66–79

Chachapoya: Mummies in the Cloud Forest of Peru

Church, W. B. & Hagen, A. von, 'Chachapoyas: cultural development at an Andean cloud forest crossroads', in H. Silverman & W. H. Isbell (eds), *Handbook of South American Archaeology* (forthcoming)

Hagen, A. von & Guillén, S., 'Tombs with a view', *Archaeology* 51(2) (1998), 48–54

Muscutt, K., *Warriors of the Clouds: A Lost Civilization in the Upper Amazon of Peru* (Albuquerque, 1998)

Schjellerup, I., *Incas and Spaniards in the Conquest of Chachapoyas. Archaeological and Ethnohistorical Research in the North-eastern Andes of Peru*, Gothenburg Archaeological Theses, 7 (Gothenburg, 1997)

Inca Mummies: Child Sacrifice on Andean Peaks

Aufderheide, A., *The Scientific Study of Mummies* (Cambridge, 2003)

Chamberlain, A. & Parker Pearson, M., *Earthly Remains: The History and Science of Preserved Human Bodies* (Oxford & New York, 2001)

Parker Pearson, M., *The Archaeology of Death and Burial* (Stroud & College Station, 1999)

Reinhard, J., *The Ice Maiden: Inca Mummies, Mountain Gods, and Sacred Sites in the Andes* (Washington, DC, 2005)

Reinhard, J. & Ceruti, C., *The Inca Ceremonial Center*

on Mount Llullaillaco: A Study of the World's
Highest Archaeological Site (Los Angeles, 2007)

The Prittlewell Prince:
An Anglo-Saxon Royal Burial
Blair, I., 'The Anglo-Saxon prince', Archaeology
(Sept./Oct. 2005), 24–28
Carver, M. O. H., Sutton Hoo: A Seventh-Century
Princely Burial Ground and its Context
(London, 2005)
Lucy, S., The Anglo-Saxon Way of Death
(Stroud, 2000)
MoLAS, The Prittlewell Prince: The Discovery of a
Rich Anglo-Saxon Burial in Essex (London, 2004)
Welch, M. G., Anglo-Saxon England (London, 1992)

Treasures of Ancient Art

At the Origins of Art:
New Discoveries of Decorated Caves
Aujoulat, N. & others, 'The decorated cave of
Cussac', International Newsletter on Rock Art 30
(2001), 3–9
Broglio, A. & Dalmeri, G. (eds), Pitture Paleolitiche
nelle Prealpi Venete. Grotta di Fumane e Riparo
Dalmeri (Verona, 2005)
Chauvet, J.-M., Brunel Deschamps, E. & Hillaire, C.,
Chauvet Cave. The Discovery of the World's Oldest
Paintings (London & New York, 1996)
Clottes, J. (ed.), Return to Chauvet Cave
(London & New York, 2003)
Clottes, J., Courtin, J. & Vanrell, L., Cosquer
Redécouvert (Paris, 2005)
Martinho Baptista, A., No Tempo sem Tempo. A Arte
dos Caçadores paleolíticos do Vale do Côa (Côa,
Centro Nacional de Arte rupestre, 1999)
Ripoll, S., Muñoz, F., Pettitt, P. & Bahn, P.,
'New discoveries of cave art in Church Hole
(Creswell Crags, England)', International
Newsletter on Rock Art 40 (2004), 1–6

Black Pharaohs: A Cachette of Statues
from Kerma, Sudan
Bonnet, C. & Valbelle, D., The Nubian Pharaohs:
Black Kings on the Nile (Cairo, 2006)
Clayton, P., Chronicle of the Pharaohs. The Reign-by-
Reign Record of the Rulers and Dynasties of Ancient
Egypt (London & New York, 1994)

A Celtic Warrior Prince from Glauberg, Germany
Baitinger, H. & Pinsker, B. (eds), Das Rätsel der
Kelten vom Glauberg (Stuttgart, 2002)
Bosinski, M. & Herrmann, F.-R., 'Zu den
frühkeltischen Statuen vom Glauberg', Berichte
der Kommission für Archäologische
Landesforschung in Hessen 5, 1998/99 (2000)
41–48
Frey, O.-H. & Herrmann, F.-R., 'Ein frühkeltischer
Fürstengrabhügel am Glauberg im Wetteraukreis,
Hessen. Bericht über die Forschungen
1994–1996', Germania 75 (1997), 459–550
Herrmann, F.-R., 'Die Statuen vom Glauberg in
ihrem Fundzusammenhang', Madrider
Mitteilungen 44 (2003), 215–22

Artistic Splendours from the Greek
and Roman World
Gawlikowski, M., 'Palmyra', Current World
Archaeology 1.12 (2006), 26–37

Jones, D., 'Hellenistic dancing satyr fished up
off Sicily' Minerva 14.4 (2003), 4–5
Mattusch, C. C., 'A note on the Apoxyomenos
of Vele Orjule', Minerva 13.6 (2002), 49–50
Merrony, M. W., 'Sensational mosaic from the Wadi
Lebda Roman villa, Libya', Minerva 16.4 (2005), 4
Salviati, F., 'Conservation of the bronze satyr from
Mazzara del Vallo', Minerva 12.3 (2001), 6
Sténuit, M.-E., 'The Apoxyomenos of Vele Orjule',
Minerva 13.5 (2002), 41–44
Wendowski, M. & Ziegert, H., 'The Wadi Lebda
Roman villa, Libya', Minerva 16.6 (2005), 33–34

Turkey's Pompeii:
The Magnificent Mosaics of Zeugma
Besgelen, N., Zeugma from the Air (Istanbul, 2000)
Dunbabin, K., Mosaics of the Greek and Roman World
(Cambridge, 2001)
Early, R. & others, Zeugma: interim reports: rescue
excavations (Packard Humanities Institute) …
house and mosaic of the Synaristôsai, and recent
work on the Roman army at Zeugma, Journal of
Roman Archaeology, Supplementary Series, 51
(2003)

The Maize God and the Mythology of Kings:
Maya Paintings at San Bartolo, Guatemala
Saturno, W. A., Stuart, D. & Beltrán, B.,
'Early Maya Writing at San Bartolo, Guatemala',
Science 311 (2006), 1281–83
Saturno, W., Taube, K. A. & Stuart, D., The Murals
of San Bartolo, El Petén, Guatemala, Part 1:
The North Wall, Ancient America, Number 7.
Center for Ancient American Studies
(Barnardsville, NC, 2005)
Taube, K. A., The Major Gods of Ancient Yucatan.
Studies in Pre-Columbian Art and Archaeology
32 (Dumbarton Oaks, Washington DC, 1992)
Taube, K. A., 'Flower Mountain: concepts of life
beauty and paradise among the Classic Maya',
Res: Anthropology and Aesthetics 45 (2004), 69–98

Torcs, Coins and Gold Cups:
Ancient Hoards from Britain
Hill, J. D., Spence, A. J., La Niece, S. & Worrell, S.,
'The Winchester Hoard: a find of unique Iron Age
gold jewellery from southern England',
Antiquaries Journal 84 (2004), 1–22
Needham, S., Parfitt, K. & Varndell, G., The
Ringlemere Cup: Precious Cups and the Beginning
of the Channel Bronze Age (London, 2006)
Priest, V., Clay, P. & Hill, J. D., 'Iron Age gold
from Leicestershire', Current Archaeology 188
(2003), 358–62
Rainbird Clarke, R., 'The Early Iron Age treasure
from Snettisham, Norfolk', Proceedings of the
Prehistoric Society, 20 (1954)
Stead, I. M., 'The Snettisham Treasure: excavations
in 1990', Antiquity, 65 (1991), 447–65

The Hoxne Treasure: A Late Roman Hoard
Bland, R. & Johns, C., The Hoxne Treasure;
an Illustrated Introduction (London, 1992)
Guest, P. S. W., The Late Roman Gold and Silver Coins
from the Hoxne Treasure (London, 2005)
Hobbs, R., Treasure: Finding our Past
(London, 2003), 78–87
Johns, C., Catalogue of the Hoxne Hoard, Vol.2:
Jewellery, Silverware and Other Objects
(forthcoming)

Spillings:
The World's Biggest Viking Silver Hoard
Korpås, O., Widerström, P. & Ström, J., 'The recently
found hoards from Spillings farm on Gotland,
Sweden', Viking Heritage Magazine no. 4 (2000)
Merrony, M., 'Treasure Island: a remarkable silver
hoard from Gotland, Sweden', in The Vikings:
Conquerors, Traders and Pirates. Vol 5:
Encyclopaedia of Underwater Archaeology
(London, 2004)
Widerström, P. & Ström, J., 'Fenster Europa:
Schweden. Schatzkammer in der Ostsee',
Archäologie in Deutschland no. 6 (2002)
Widerström, P. & Östergren, M., 'The Spillings
Hoard, Sweden: a Viking sensation',
Minerva 14.1 (2003)

Portraits in Pottery:
Ceramic Vessels from Lake Titicaca
Kolata, A. L., The Tiwanaku: Portrait of an Ancient
Civilization (Cambridge, MA & Oxford, 1993)
Korpisaari, A. & Pärssinen, M. (eds), Pariti: isla,
misterio y poder. El tesoro cerámico de la cultura
Tiwanaku (La Paz, 2005)
Stanish, C., Ancient Titicaca. The Evolution of
Complex Society in Southern Peru and Northern
Bolivia (Berkeley, Los Angeles & London, 2003)
Stone-Miller, R., Art of the Andes from Chavín
to Inca (London & New York. 1995)
Young-Sanchéz, Margaret (ed.),
Tiwanaku: Ancestors of the Inca
(Denver, Lincoln & London, 2004)

Statues of the Buddha from Qingzhou, China
Return of the Buddha: The Qingzhou Discoveries
(Washington, DC & London, 2002)
Sun Xinsheng, 'Time and cause for the destruction
of the Buddhist statues from the site of the
Longxing Monastery,' Arts of Asia, vol. 31, no. 1
(2001), 41–53
Wang Ruixa & Zhou Linlin, 'Typological analysis of
Northern Qi Buddhist statues unearthed from the
site of Longxing Monastery', Arts of Asia, vol. 31,
no. 1, (2001), 41–53

Lost Cities

Caral: The Oldest Civilization in Peru
and the Americas
Feldman, R., 'Aspero, Peru: Architecture,
Subsistence Economy and other Artifacts of a
Preceramic Maritime Chiefdom', Ph.D.
dissertation, Department of Anthropology,
Harvard University (1980)
Williams, C. & Merino, F., Inventario, Catastro y
Delimitación del Patrimonio Arqueológico del Valle
de Supe (Lima, 1979)
Zechenter, E., 'Subsistence Strategies in the Supe
Valley of the Peruvian Central Coast during the
Complex Preceramic and Initial Periods', Ph.D.
dissertation, Department of Anthropology,
University of California, Los Angeles (1988)

Pyramid City, Giza
Lehner, M., The Complete Pyramids
(London & New York, 1997)
Lehner, M., 'The Pyramid Age settlement of the
Southern Mount at Giza', Journal of the American
Research Center in Egypt 39 (2002), 27–74

Lehner, M. & Wetterstrom, W. (eds), *Giza Reports I: Project History, Survey, Ceramics and Main Street and Gallery III.4 Operations* (Boston, 2007) http://www.aeraweb.org

Jinsha: Changing the Map of Ancient China

Bagley, R. (ed.), *Ancient Sichuan: Treasures from a Lost Civilization* (Seattle, 2001)

Zhu, Zhangyi, Zhang Qing & Wang Fang, 'The Jinsha site: an introduction', *Journal of East Asian Archaeology*, Vol. 5, nos 1–4 (2003), 247–76

Towards a New Jerusalem

Mazar, E., 'Did I find King David's Palace?', *Biblical Archaeology Review* 32.1 (2006), 16–27, 70

Mazar, E., *The Complete Guide to the Temple Mount Excavations* (Jerusalem, 2002)

Shanks, H., 'The Siloam Pool where Jesus cured the blind man', *Biblical Archaeology Review* 31.5 (2005), 16–23

Saxon London, Concealed Beneath City Streets

Blackmore, L., Bowsher, D., Cowie, R. & Malcolm, G., 'Royal Opera House', *Current Archaeology* 14, 2 (1998), 60–63

Cowie, R., & Blackmore, L., *Lundenwic: Excavations in Middle Saxon London 1987–2000*, MoLAS Monograph Series (forthcoming)

Malcolm, G. & Bowsher, D., with Cowie, R., *Middle Saxon London: Excavations at the Royal Opera House 1989–1999*, MoLAS Monograph Series 15 (London, 2003)

Vince, A., *Saxon London: An Archaeological Investigation* (London, 1990)

Jamestown: The Fort that was the Birthplace of the United States of America

Horn, J., *A Land as God Made It* (New York, 2005)

Hume, I. N., *The Virginia Adventure* (New York, 1994)

Kelso, W., *The Buried Truth* (Charlottesville & London, 2006)

Enigmas of Ritual and Religion

Carved Creatures from the Dawn of Agriculture: Göbekli Tepe, Turkey

Cauvin, J., *The Birth of the Gods and the Origins of Agriculture* (Cambridge, 2000)

Lewis-Williams, D. & Pearce, D., *Inside the Neolithic Mind. Consciousness, Cosmos and the Realm of the Gods* (London & New York, 2005)

Özdogan, M. & Basgelen, N. (eds), *Neolithic in Turkey. The Cradle of Civilization. New Discoveries* (Istanbul, 1999)

Schmidt, K., *Sie bauten die ersten Tempel. Das rätselhafte Heiligtum der Steinzeitjäger. Die archäologische Entdeckung am Göbekli Tepe* (Munich, 2006)

Secrets Revealed at Britain's Henges

Cleal, R. M. J., Walker, K. E. & Montague, R., *Stonehenge in its Landscape: Twentieth-Century Excavations* (London, 1995)

David, A. & others, 'A hidden Stonehenge: geophysical survey at Stanton Drew, England', *Antiquity* 78 (2004), 153–69

Pitts, M., *Hengeworld* (London 2001)

Pollard, J. & Reynolds, A., *Avebury: The Biography of a Landscape* (Stroud 2002)

Watson, C., *Seahenge: An Archaeological Conundrum* (London 2005)

The Nebra Sky Disc:
The Oldest Representation of the Heavens

Hansen, R., 'Die Himmelsscheibe von Nebra – neu interpretiert: Sonne oder Mond? Wie der Mensch der Bronzezeit mit Hilfe der Himmelsscheibe Sonnen-und Mondkalender ausgleichen konnte', *Archäologie in Sachsen-Anhalt* 4 (2007)

Meller, H., 'Die Himmelsscheibe von Nebra – ein frühbronzezeitlicher Fund von außergewöhnlicher Bedeutung', *Archäologie in Sachsen-Anhalt* 1 (2002), 7–20

Meller, H. (ed.), *Der geschmiedete Himmel. Die weite Welt im Herzen Europas vor 3600 Jahren* (Stuttgart, 2004)

Meller, H., 'Star Search', *National Geographic* (Jan. 2004), 77–87

Meller, H. & Bertemes, F. (eds), *Der Griff nach den Sternen – Die Himmelsscheibe von Nebra* (Halle, 2007)

Schlosser, W., 'Zur astronomischen Deutung der Himmelsscheibe von Nebra', *Archäologie in Sachsen-Anhalt* 1 (2002), 21–23

Helmets and War-Trumpets:
A Ritual Hoard from Tintignac, France

Hunter, F., 'The carnyx in Iron Age Europe', *The Antiquaries Journal*, 81 (2001), 77–108

Lalande, P., 'Ruines romaines de Tintignac (Corrèze)', *Bulletin de la Société Scientifique, Historique et Archéologique de la Corrèze* VII (1885), 632–713

Le Carnyx et la lyre – Archéologie musicale en Gaule celtique et romaine, (Besançon, Orléans & Evreux, 1993–94)

Maniquet, C., *Le sanctuaire antique des Arènes de Tintignac* (Limoges, 2004)

Maniquet, C., 'Découverte d'un formidable dépôt gaulois. Les carnyx de Tintignac', *Archéologia*, 419 (2005), 16–23

Maniquet, C., 'The Tintignac celtic warrior hoard', *Minerva*, 16. 4 (2005), 29–31

Symbols of Religion and Power:
The Pyramid of the Moon, Teotihuacán

Sugiyama, S., 'Governance and polity at Classic Teotihuacan', in J. Hendon and R. Joyce (eds), *Mesoamerican Archaeology: Theory and Practice* (Oxford, 2003), 97–123

Sugiyama, S., *Human Sacrifice, Militarism, and Rulership: Materialization of State Ideology at the Feathered Serpent Pyramid, Teotihuacan* (Cambridge & New York, 2005)

Sugiyama, S. & López Luján, L. (eds), *Sacrificios de Consagración en la Pirámide de la Luna* (Teotihuacán Museo de Templo Mayor, National Institute of Anthropology & History and Arizona State University, Mexico City, 2006)

Sugiyama, S. & Cabrera, R., 'The Moon Pyramid Project and the Teotihuacan state polity: a brief summary of the 1998–2004 excavations', *Ancient Mesoamerica*, 18 (2007)

Sugiyama, S. & López Luján, L., 'Dedicatory burial/offering complexes at the Moon Pyramid, Teotihuacan: a preliminary report of 1998–2004 explorations', *Ancient Mesoamerica* 18 (2007)

Moche Ritual Sacrifice at Huaca de la Luna, Peru

Benson, E. P. & Cook, A. G. (eds), *Ritual Sacrifice in Ancient Peru* (Austin, 2001)

Bourget, S., *Sex, Death and Sacrifice in Moche Religion and Visual Culture* (Austin, 2006)

Donnan, C. B., *Moche Portraits from Ancient Peru* (Austin, 2004)

Donnan, C. B. & McClelland, D., *Moche Fineline Painting: Its Evolution and Its Artists* (Los Angeles, 1999)

Pillsbury, J. (ed.), *Moche Art and Archaeology in Ancient Peru* (Washington, DC, 2001)

Discoveries from the Deep

The World's Oldest Boats, from Abydos, Egypt

Adams, M. D. & O'Connor, D., 'The royal mortuary enclosures of Abydos and Hierakonpolis', in Z. Hawass (ed.), *Treasures of the Pyramids*, (Cairo, 2003), 78–85

Galvin, J., 'Abydos: life and death at the dawn of the Egyptian civilization', *National Geographic*, (April 2005), 106–21

Ward, C., 'Sewn planked boats from Early Dynastic Abydos, Egypt', in C. Beltrame (ed.), *Boats, Ships and Shipyards: Proceedings of the Ninth International Symposium on Boat and Ship Archaeology, Venice 2000* (Oxford, 2003), 19–23

Alexandria Underwater:
Greek Cities Beneath the Sea in Egypt

Goddio, F. & Bernand, A., *L'Égypte engloutie, Alexandrie* (London, 2002)

Goddio, F. & Fabre, D. (eds), *Egypt's Sunken Treasures* (London, 2006); *Trésors Engloutis d'Égypte* (Paris, 2007)

Goddio, F. & others, *Alexandrie, Les quartiers royaux submergés* (London, 1998)

Yoyotte, J., 'Le second affichage du décret de l'an 2 de Nekhtnebef et la découverte de Thônis-Héracleion', *Égypte, Afrique & Orient* 24 (2001), 24–34

Yoyotte, J., 'Les trouvailles épigraphiques de l'Institut européen d'archéologie sous-marine dans la baie d'Abû Qîr', *Bulletin Société Française d'Égyptologie* 159 (2004), 29ff.

The Ancient Port and Ships of Pisa

Bruni, S., 'Pisa, la città delle navi. Il porto urbano di Pisa etrusca e romana dallo scavo al museo: prospettive e problemi', in A. Zampieri (ed.), *Pisa. Memorie di una città*, vol. I (Pisa 2002), 11–65

Bruni, S. (ed.), *Il porto urbano di Pisa antica. I. La fase etrusca. 1: Il contesto e il relitto ellenistico* (Milan, 2003)

Bruni, S. (ed.), *Il porto urbano di Pisa antica. I. La fase etrusca. 2: I materiali* (Milan, forthcoming)

Slayman, A. L., 'A cache of vintage ships', *Archaeology* 52.4 (Jul./Aug. 1999), 36–39

Various authors, *Le navi antiche di Pisa. Guida archeologica* (Milan, 2005)

Various authors, *Pisa. Un viaggio nel mare dell'antichità* (Milan, 2006)

HMS *Pandora*: The Ship Sent to Find the *Bounty* Mutineers

Campbell, J. & Gesner, P., 'Illustrated catalogue of artefacts from the HMS *Pandora* wrecksite excavations 1977–1995', *Memoirs of the*

Queensland Museum Cultural Heritage Series, 2 (1) (2000), 53–159

Gesner, P., 'The *Pandora* project: reviewing genesis and rationale', *Bulletin of the Australian Institute for Maritime Archaeology,* 12 (1) (1988), 27–36

Gesner, P., Pandora: *An Archaeological Perspective* (Brisbane, 1991)

Gesner, P., *George Hamilton's Account of HMS* Pandora, *Last Voyage, Discovery and Significance* (Australian Maritime Series, No 4; Sydney, 1998)

Gesner, P., 'HMS *Pandora* Project – A report on stage 1: five seasons of excavation', *Memoirs of the Queensland Museum, Cultural Heritage Series,* 2 (1) (2000), 1–52

Henderson, G., 'Finds from the wreck of HMS *Pandora*', *International Journal of Nautical Archaeology,* 9 (3) (1980), 237–43

Submarine and Ironclad:
American Civil War Wrecks

Bourne, J. Jr., 'Iron vs. Oak: the day the wooden navy died' *National Geographic* (March 2006), 136–47

Hicks, B. & Kropf, S., *Raising the* Hunley: *The Remarkable History and Recovery of the Lost Confederate Submarine* (New York, 2003)

Mindell, D. A., *War, Technology, and Experience Aboard the USS* Monitor (Baltimore, 2002)

Oeland, G., 'The H.L. *Hunley*: secret weapon of the Confederacy', *National Geographic* (July 2002) 82–101

Ragan, M. K., *The* Hunley: *Submarines, Sacrifice, and Success in the Civil War* (Charleston, 1999)

Sheridan, R. E., *Iron from the Deep: The Discovery and Recovery of the USS* Monitor (Annapolis, 2003)

Walker, S. M., *Secrets of a Civil War Submarine: Solving the Mysteries of the H.L.* Hunley (Minneapolis, 2005)

Scientific Discoveries

DNA and Archaeology

Cavalli-Sforza, L. L. & Cavalli-Sforza, F., *The Great Human Diasporas* (Reading, MA, 1995)

Renfrew, C. (ed.), *America Past, America Present: Genes and Languages in the Americas and Beyond* (Cambridge, 2000)

Smith, B. D., *The Emergence of Agriculture* (New York, 1998)

Stringer, C. B. & McKie, R., *African Exodus* (New York, 1996)

Wells, S., *The Journey of Man: A Genetic Odyssey* (Princeton, 2003)

Ice Ages, Floods and Droughts:
The Impact of Climate Change in the Past

Alley, R., *The Two-Mile Time Machine; Ice Cores, Abrupt Climate Change, and Our Future* (Princeton, 2000)

Fagan, B., *Floods, Famines, and Emperors: El Niño and the Fate of Civilizations* (New York, 1999)

Fagan, B., *The Long Summer: How Climate Changed Civilization* (New York, 2004)

Fagan, B., *Chaco Canyon: Archaeologists Explore the Lives of an Ancient Society* (New York, 2005)

Philander, G., *Our Affair with El Niño: How We Transformed an Enchanting Peruvian Current into a Global Climate Hazard* (Princeton, 2006)

Ancient Wine and Beer

Gallagher, L., 'Stone Age beer', *Discover* 26.11 (2005), 54–59

Guasch-Jané, M. R., Cristina, A.-L., Jáuregui, O. & Lamuela-Raventós, R. M., 'First evidence of white wine in ancient Egypt from Tutankhamun's tomb', *Journal of Archaeological Science* (in press)

Guasch-Jané, M. R. & others, 'Liquid chromatography with mass spectrometry in tandem mode applied for the identification of wine markers in residues from ancient Egyptian vessels', *Analytical Chemistry* 76 (2004), 1672–77

McGovern, P. E., *Ancient Wine: The Search for the Origins of Viniculture* (Princeton, 2006)

McGovern, P. E. & others, 'Fermented beverages of Pre- and Proto-Historic China', *Proceedings of the National Academy of Sciences* USA 101.51 (2004) 17593–98 (on-line at www.pnas.org; 10.1073/pnas.0407921102)

Nelson, M., *The Barbarian's Beverage: A History of Beer in Ancient Europe* (London, 2005)

Medical Science and Archaeology

Arnott, R. G., Finger, S. & Smith, C. U. M., *Trepanation. History – Discovery – Method* (Lisse, 2003)

Fiorato, V., Boylston, A. & Knusel, K., *Blood Red Roses: The Archaeology of a Mass Grave from the Battle of Towton AD 1461* (Oxford, 2001)

Prag, J. & Neave, R., *Making Faces. Using Forensic and Archaeological Evidence* (London, 1997)

Roberts, C. A. & Manchester, K., *The Archaeology of Disease* (Stroud, 2005)

Roberts, C. A. & Buikstra, J. E., *The Bioarchaeology of Tuberculosis. A Global Perspective on a Declining Disease* (Gainesville, 2003)

Ancient Writing: Early Hieroglyphs
from Abydos, Egypt

Davies, V. & Friedman, R., *Egypt* (London, 1998), 35–38

Dreyer, G., *Umm el-Qaab I. Das prädynastichen Königsgrab U-j und seine frühen Schriftzeugnisse* (Mainz, 1998)

Wilkinson, T., 'Did the Egyptians invent writing?' in B. Manley (ed.), *The Seventy Great Mysteries of Ancient Egypt* (London & New York, 2003), 24–27

Ancient Writing: Biblical Inscriptions

Athas, G., *The Tel Dan Inscription: A Reappraisal and a New Interpretation,* JSOT Supp. 360; CIS 12 (Sheffield, 2003)

Biran, A. & Naveh, J., 'An Aramaic stele fragment from Tel Dan', *Israel Exploration Journal* 43 (1993), 81–98

Biran, A. & Naveh, J, 'The Tel Dan inscription: a new fragment', *Israel Exploration Journal* 45 (1995) 1–18

Gitin, S., Dothan, T. & Naveh, J., 'A royal dedicatory inscription from Ekron', *Israel Exploration Journal* 48 (1997) 1–18

Demsky, A., 'Discovering a goddess: a new look at the Ekron inscription identifies mysterious deity', *Biblical Archaeology Review* 24.5 (1998), 53–58

Gitin, S., Dothan, T. & Naveh, J., 'Ekron identity confirmed', *Archaeology* 51.1 (1998), 30–31

Schniedewind, W. M., 'Tel Dan Stela: new light on Aramaic and Jehu's revolt', *Bulletin of the American School of Oriental Research* 302 (1996), 75–90

Ancient Writing: China's 'Dead Sea Scrolls'

Lewis, M. E., *Writing and Authority in Early China* (Albany, 1999)

Ling Li, 'Formulaic structure of Chu divinatory bamboo slips', *Early China* 15 (1990), 71–86

Shaughnessy, E. L. (ed.), *New Sources of Early Chinese History: An Introduction to the Reading of Inscriptions and Manuscripts* (Berkeley, 1997)

Tsuen-hsuin Tsien, *Written on Bamboo and Silk: The Beginning of Chinese Books and Inscriptions* (Chicago & London, 2nd ed., 2004)

Ancient Writing:
New Advances in Maya Decipherment

Coe, M. D. & van Stone, M., 2001 *Reading the Maya Glyphs* (London & New York, 2001)

Robertson, J., Houston, S. & Stuart, D., 'Tense and aspect in Maya hieroglyphic script', in S. Wichmann (ed.), *The Linguistics of Maya Writing* (Salt Lake City, 2004), 259–89

Saturno, W. A., Stuart, D. & Beltrán, B., 'Early Maya writing at San Bartolo, Guatemala', *Science* 311 (2006), 1281–83

Houston, S., Robertson, J. & Stuart, D., 'More on the language of Classic Maya inscriptions', *Current Anthropology,* 42 (2001), 558–59

Ancient Writing:
Deciphering the Knotted Strings of the Incas

Ascher, M. & Ascher, R., *Mathematics of the Incas: Code of the Quipus* (New York, 1997)

Quilter, J. & Urton, G. (eds), *Narrative Threads: Accounting and Recounting in Andean Khipu* (Austin, 2002)

Urton, G., *Signs of the Inka Khipu: Binary Coding in the Andean Knotted-String Records* (Austin, 2003)

Urton, G. & Brezine, C. J., 'Khipu accounting in ancient Peru' *Science* 309 (2005), 1065–67

The Cascajal Block:
The New World's Oldest Writing

Diehl, R. A., *The Olmecs: America's First Civilization* (London & New York, 2004)

Rodríguez Martínez, M. del Carmen & others, 'Oldest writing in the New World', *Science* 313:5793 (2006) 1610–44

Sources of Illustrations

a = above, c = centre, b = below, l = left, r = right

1 William Saturno; 2–3 Sandro Vannini/Zahi Hawass collection; 5a Javier Trueba/Madrid Scientific Films; 5b Xia Juxian, Guo Yan; 6a Christopher B. Donnan; 6c U. Seitz-Gray (Frankfurt/Main); 6b The Trustees of the British Museum; 7a Photo Juraj Liptak. Landesamt für Denkmalpflege und Archäologie Sachsen-Anhalt (LDA); 7ac Franck Goddio/Hilti Foundation, photo Christoph Gerigk; 7bc Zahi Hawass collection; 7b Z.Radovan/ BibleLandPictures.com; 10–11 Mountain High Maps copyright 1993 Digital Wisdom Inc./Drazen Tomic; 12 Kenneth Garrett; 13 Johan Reinhard; 14l Heather Alexander/Amenmesse Project; 14r Steve Bourget; 15 French Ministry of Culture and Communication, Regional Direction for Cultural Affairs – Rhône Alpes Region – Regional Department of Archaeology; 16–17 Handout/Reuters/Corbis; 18a Reuters/Corbis; 18b Handout/Reuters/Corbis; 19, 20 © John Sibbick; 21 John Reader/Science Photo Library; 22 Michel Brunet; 23l Reprinted with permission from Clarke and Tobias, SCIENCE 269:521–24 (1995) © 2007 AAAS; 23r National Museums of Kenya, Nairobi; 24 Gurum Tsibakhashvili; 25, 26 Kenneth Garrett; 27 Gurum Tsibakhashvili; 28–29, 30a Javier Trueba/Madrid Scientific Films; 30b Giorgio Manzi; 31l&r Javier Trueba/ Madrid Scientific Films; 32 Mike Pitts; 33 Mark Roberts, Boxgrove Projects; 34l Beawiharta/Reuters/Corbis; 34r Reproduced with permission of artist Peter Schouten and the National Geographic Society; 35l&r Kenneth Garrett; 36–37 Sandro Vannini/Zahi Hawass collection; 38a Qatna-Project of the Altorientalisches Seminar of Tübingen University/photo K. Wita; 38c Aladin Abdel Naby/Reuters/Corbis; 38b Karen Nichols, Wessex Archaeology; 40 Kenneth Garrett; 41a Regional Hospital of Bolzano/photo Dr Paul Gostner; 41bl&br Kenneth Garrett; 42 Dave Norcott, Wessex Archaeology; 43l Elaine Wakefield, Wessex Archaeology; 43al Dave Webb, Wessex Archaeology; 43ar&r Elaine Wakefield, Wessex Archaeology; 44 Tom Goskar, Wessex Archaeology; 45a Dave Norcott, Wessex Archaeology; 45b Elaine Wakefield, Wessex Archaeology; 46, 47, 48l&r, 49a&bl Zahi Hawass collection; 49br Kenneth Garrett; 50 Sandro Vannini/Zahi Hawass collection; 51 Heather Alexander/Amenmesse Project; 52–53 George B. Johnson; 54 Sandro Vannini/Zahi Hawass collection; 55 Zahi Hawass collection; 56, 57a, bl&br Francis Dzikowski © Theban Mapping Project. All Rights Reserved; 58, 59, 60l&r, 61 Photo P. Chapuis/MAFB © Hypogées; 62 Qatna-Project of the Altorientalisches Seminar of Tübingen University/photo K. Wita; 64l Manoocher; 64r Qatna-Project of the Altorientalisches Seminar o f Tübingen University/photo K. Wita; 64c Manoocher; 65 Qatna-Project of the Altorientalisches Seminar of Tübingen University/ photo K. Wita; 66, 67a&b, 68a, bl&br © Bill Lyons; 69 Courtesy British School of Archaeology in Iraq;

70, 71a&b Jan Chochorowski; 72, 73, 74al, ar&b, 73 Zahi Hawass collection; 75a Ron Watts/Corbis; 75b Tarek el-Awady/Zahi Hawass collection; 76a&b Kenneth Garrett; 77 Zahi Hawass collection; 78a, bl&br, 79 By kind permission of the National Museum of Ireland, Dublin; 80, 81a&b, 82l&r, 83l,r&b Xia Juxian, Guo Yan; 84 & 85l&br Andy Chopping/Museum of London Archaeology Service; 85ar Torla Evans Museum of London Archaeology Service; 86, 87a&b Kenneth Garrett; 88–89 Christopher B. Donnan; 90 Photo Y. Yoshii/PAS; 91 Painting by C. Samillán and I. Shimada; 92l Photo I. Shimada; 92r Photo Y. Yoshii/PAS; 93a Drawing by S. Mueller and I. Shimada; 93b Photo I. Shimada; 94–95, 95, 96, 97tl&tr Kenneth Garrett; 97bl&br Reuters/Daniel Leclair; 98, 99t&b Adriana von Hagen; 100, 101, 102, 103, 104–05 Johan Reinhard; 106l&r Maggie Cox/Museum of London Archaeology Service; 107a&b Andy Chopping/Museum of London Archaeology Service; 108al, ar&b, 109 Museum of London Archaeology Service; 110–11 Stéphane Compoint; 112a © Mission de l'Université de Genève à Kèrma; 112c Kenneth Garrett; 112b Stéphane Jasinski – Nothingtosea; 114–15 French Ministry of Culture and Communication, Regional Direction for Cultural Affairs – Rhône Alpes Region – Regional Department of Archaeology; 116l MCC.
A. Chéné – CNRS; 116r Jean Clottes; 117a&b French Ministry of Culture and Communication, Regional Direction for Cultural Department of Archaeology; 118,119a&b CNP/Min. Culture/Corbis Sygma; 120, 121a&b © Mission de l'Université de Genève à Kèrma; 122l DAI, Athens, Emile 493; 122r DAI, Athens, Hege 1100; 123l&r U. Seitz-Gray (Frankfurt/Main); 124 Filippo Monteforte/ epa/ Corbis; 125 Regionale Siciliana – CRICD – Servizio Documentazione – Fototeca – Satiro danzante – Museo del Satiro Ex Chiesa di S. Egidio – Mazara del Vallo (Trapani) fotografo S. Plano (CRICD); 126l Photo Stéphane Jasinski – Nothingtosea; 126r © Stanislav Kowalski; 127 Fototeka Hrvatskoga restauratorskog zavoda and Robert Sténuit; 128 Marlies Wendowski; 129 Michal Gawlikowski; 130, 131, 132, 133 Bruce Sampson; 134, 135, 136–37 Kenneth Garrett; 138–39 William Saturno; 138b Kenneth Garrett; 140, 141, 142l&r The Trustees of the British Museum; 143a Empics; 143b, 144a, bl&br, 145a&b The Trustees of the British Museum; 146a Kenneth Jonsson; 146b Göran Ström; 147 Dan Carlsson; 148al, ar, bl&br, 149a&b Antti Korpisaari; 150, 151, 152, 153l,c&r Qingzhou Museum; 154–55, 156a Kenneth Garrett; 156c Museum of London Archaeology Service; 156b Courtesy of APVA Preservation Virginia/Historic Jamestowne; 159a Proyecto Especial Arqueológico Caral-Supe; 159b Peruvian National Institute /epa/Corbis; 160–61 Kenneth Garrett; 162 Mark Lehner; 163a Kenneth Garrett; 163b Mark Lehner; 164a&b, 165, 166, 167

Chengdu Museum; 168l&r courtesy of the Shalem Center © Dr Eilat Mazar; 169 www.HolyLandPhotos.org; 170a Faith Vardy/ Museum of London Archaeology Service; 170b Maggie Cox/Museum of London Archaeology Service; 171 The Trustees of the British Museum; 172,173, 174, 175 Courtesy of APVA Preservation Virginia/Historic Jamestowne; 176–77 Kenneth Garrett; 178a photo K. Schmidt, © DAI, Berlin; 178c Mike Pitts; 178b Steve Bourget; 180 I. Wagner, © DAI, Berlin; 181 D. Johannes, © DAI, Berlin; 182 Ch. Gerber, © DAI, Berlin; 183 D. Johannes, © DAI, Berlin; 184 © English Heritage; 185 Mike Pitts; 186–87 Wendy George, 1999; 187 Mike Pitts; 188 Drawing Klaus Pockrandt. Landesamt für Denkmalpflege und Archäologie Sachsen-Anhalt (LDA); 189 Photo Juraj Liptak. Landesamt für Denkmalpflege und Archäologie, Sachsen-Anhalt (LDA); 190, 191l, 191r Photo Patrick Ernaux/Inrap; 192 Kenneth Garrett; 193, 194 Saburo Sugiyama; 195a Jesus Lopez; 195b Saburo Sugiyama; 196–97, 198a&b, 199 Steve Bourget; 200–01 Franck Goddio/Hilti Foundation, photo Christoph Gerigk; 202a Kenneth Garrett; 202c Reuters/Corbis; 202b Monitor Collection, NOAA; 204–05 Institute of Fine Arts, New York University; 206a Kenneth Garrett; 206b Institute of Fine Arts, New York University/ American Research; 207 Richard Schlect/National Geographic Image Collection; 208, 209, 210l&r, 211 Franck Goddio/Hilti Foundation, photo Christoph Gerigk; 212–13 Giovanni Lattanzi; 213, 214 Stefano Bruni; 215al Giovanni Lattanzi; 215ar Stefano Bruni; 215b Giovanni Lattanzi; 216, 217a&b, 218, 219al, cl, ar & br Queensland Museum; 220 USN Photo; 221 Library of Congress, Washington, DC; 222a Friends of Hunley; 222b Ira Block/National Geographic Image Collection; 223l&r Friends of Hunley; 224–25 Kenneth Garrett; 226a Ira Block/National Geographic Image Collection; 226c York Archaeological Trust; 226b Kenneth Garrett; 228a M. Ponce de León and Ch. Zollikofer, University of Zurich, Switzerland; 228bl&br Eurelios; 229 M. Ponce de León and Ch. Zollikofer, University of Zurich, Switzerland; 230 British Antarctic Survey/Science Photo Library; 231 Ira Block/ National Geographic Image Collection; 232a Courtesy Juzhong Zhang and the Institute of Archaeology, Zhengzhou; 232b The Trustees of the British Museum; 233a DAI, Cairo; 233b From *The Tomb of Nakht at Thebes*, by Norman de Garis Davis, 1917; 234, 235 York Archaeological Trust; 236 Kenneth Garrett; 237al Elisabeth Daynès/ National Geographic Image Collection; 237ar Kenneth Garrett/National Geographic Image Collection; 237bl&br Zahi Hawass collection; 238 DAI, Cairo; 239l&r Z.Radovan/ BibleLandPictures.com; 240, 241 Cultural Relics Publishing House, Beijing; 242l&r, 243 David Stuart; 244a&b Gary Urton; 245 akg-images, London; 246l Michael D. Coe; 246r Stephen Houston